The Quest of Ajneya:
A Christian Theological Appraisal of the Search for Meaning in his Three Hindi Novels

The Quest of Ajneya

A Christian Theological Appraisal of the Search for Meaning in his Three Hindi Novels

ROGER HARDHAM HOOKER

Foreword

HARISH TRIVEDI

MOTILAL BANARSIDASS PUBLISHERS
PRIVATE LIMITED • DELHI

First Edition: Delhi, 1998

ISBN: 81-208-1570-x

MOTILAL BANARSIDASS
41 U.A. Bungalow Road, Jawahar Nagar, Delhi 110 007
8 Mahalaxmi Chamber, Warden Road, Mumbai 400 026
120 Royapettah High Road, Mylapore, Chennai 600 004
Sanas Plaza, Subhash Nagar, Pune 411 002
16 St. Mark's Road, Bangalore 560 001
8 Camac Street, Calcutta 700 017
Ashok Rajpath, Patna 800 004
Chowk, Varanasi 221 001

PRINTED IN INDIA

BY JAINENDRA PRAKASH JAIN AT SHRI JAINENDRA PRESS,
A-45 NARAINA, PHASE I, NEW DELHI 110 028
AND PUBLISHED BY NARENDRA PRAKASH JAIN FOR
MOTILAL BANARSIDASS PUBLISHERS PRIVATE LIMITED,
BUNGALOW ROAD, DELHI 110 007

CONTENTS

ACKNOWLEDGEMENTS

This book owes much to many people: Dr Paul Joyce read the whole text at various stages of its gestation and made many helpful suggestions. A memorable conversation with Dr Nicholas Sagovsky during a sabbatical leave in Cambridge alerted me to the importance of the subject of 'authorial intention'. Professor Harish Trivedi has offered continual encouragement as well as some important comments on an early version of Chapter Five. Dr Satyendra Srivastava has given me continual support and much practical help with difficulties in translation. I owe a debt of gratitude to Professor David Ford who has shared his wisdom and insight about the frontier between Christian theology and literature and about many other areas which are relevant to the book, while Dr Julius Lipner's formidable knowledge of Hinduism has saved me from many errors of judgement and stimulated many new insights. Without the continued support, criticism, and encouragement of these two scholars the book could not have been written. Finally, I record a wholly inadequate word of appreciation for my wife, without whose support I would have given up long before I reached the end.

A NOTE ON TRANSLATIONS AND DIACRITICAL MARKS

All translations from Hindi sources are my own unless otherwise stated. For Sanskrit material I have normally used published translations. I have transliterated key words from both languages, using italics and putting the words in square brackets. This leads to inevitable problems with diacritical marks: although Hindi and Sanskrit have the same alphabet, each language has some letters which are not in the other. In the case of Hindi these are mostly found in words taken over from Urdu of which there are many in the three novels studied in this book.

However, the major problem concerns the inherent 'a'. In Sanskrit this is always pronounced after a consonant whereas in Hindi it is normally suppressed when it comes at the end of a word (eg Sanskrit *Rāma* becomes Hindi *Rām*) and in some medial positions, but within Hindi this rule is not consistently applied. Thus, the name which I have transliterated as *Tulsi Das* can also be found spelt as *Tulasi Dasa* or *Tulsi Dasa*. Given this variety it is not possible to use a system of diacriticals marks which can satisfy both Sanskrit and Hindi norms at the same time, but I have as far as possible used the normal Sanskrit diacritical system for words used in a clearly Sanskrit context, while for Hindi I have for the most part followed the system used in R S McGregor's admirable Oxford Hindi–English Dictionary. This still leaves the problem of the inherent 'a' unresolved, and so I have opted for a hybrid system which will satisfy neither Sanskrit nor Hindi purists, but which at least has the merit of being internally consistent throughout the book.

For proper names which occur more than once or twice -- such as the names of the main characters of the novels -- I have normally used Anglicised forms in order to minimise the disruption to the flow of the text, but I have put the transliterated forms in square brackets after their first appearance in order to indicate how they are normally pronounced, for example, Chandramadhava [*Candramadhava*]. For the authors of modern books, and for words which are so well known in English as to have become Anglicisėd when they are used in that language — for example Sanskrit, Delhi, Lucknow, and most other place names -- I have kept to the familiar English forms.

R. H. HOOKER

FOREWORD

The subject of this book is the Hindi author Sachchidanand Hiranand Vatsyayan 'Ajneya' (1911-87), one of the chief makers of Indian literature in the twentieth century though yet little known in the West or even among anglophone Indians. Ajneya began writing in the 1930s during the hey-day of romanticism in Hindi literature, but he soon asserted his own original bent and inclination by emerging as the first important modernist poet as well as the first modernist novelist in Hindi. He was the founding father of *prayogavād* (literally experimentalism but broadly modernism) in Hindi poetry at a time when it was yet to divide into the divergent streams of modernism and progressivism (*pragativād*). Having published two volumes of his own poetry in 1933 and 1942. Ajneya made a decisive intervention in the development of Hindi poetry by editing an anthology of seven young poets including himself, *Tār Saptak* (1943; The Seven Notes); this proved to be probably the single most influential volume of verse published in Hindi this century. In the years which followed, Ajneya not only confirmed his own status as the foremost modernist poet in Hindi through publishing three further *Saptaks* or anthologies of seven newer poets each in 1951, 1959 and 1978, and by editing for many years the journals *Pratīk* and *Nayā Pratīk* (Symbol and New Symbol). He was thus, so to say, not only the T.S. Eliot of Hindi but also its Ezra Pound—and perhaps its Harriet Monroe and its Harriet Shaw Weaver besides! He was not only the prime modernist writer in Hindi himself but he was also the cause of modernity in numerous others.

Similarly, in fiction, Ajneya's first and greatest novel! *Shekhar: Ek Jīvanī* (2 Vols., 1941 & 1944; Shekhar: A Life), though published only a very few years after Premchand's classic *Godān* (1936), inaugurated a whole new mode of writing fiction, again unmistakably modernist in its intense psychologizing of character, its play with chronology, its ellipses and episodic fragmentariness, its lyrical prose and, above all, the centrality it accorded to subjectivity and interiority. In this poetry as well as his fiction, Ajneya engaged dialogically and creatively with some major contemporary writers of the West, notably T.S. Eliot and D. H. Lawrence. With him, Hindi literature caught up with English literature, it came abreast of it to stand right beside it, and henceforth, it was to be in part swayed and shaped by the same winds and currents and movements as shaped the literature of the West.

It is only appropriate, then, that Ajneya should prove to be a suitable subject of study not only for Indian scholars but also for scholars from the West. The author of the present book, which is the first full-length study of Ajneya to be published in English, happens to be exceptionally well qualified for the project. The Reverend Dr. Roger Hooker belongs to a vocation, that of Christian priesthood, which has through the last two hundred years —ever since William Carey of the Serampore Mission and the Fort William College and right through J.N. Farquhar, C.F. Andrews and Edward Thompson, among others—made a singular contribution to a systematic exploration and mapping of the various Indian languages, literatures and culture. Dr. Hooker himself came to India early in his career, in 1965. He spent seven years in Bareilly and Allahabad learning Hindi and then another six years learning Sanskrit in Benares. Such formidable learning, exceptional even for a modern Indian, shows in this work in various ways. On the one hand, Dr. Hooker can cite not only the Brihadaranyaka or the Chhandogya or the Taittiriya upanishads but also the relatively less known Maitri and Mahanarayana; on the other hand, in explaining common Hindi words such as *āsthā* and *snigdha* and *uddeshya* and *swastha* (44, 89, 125, 166), his erudite procedure often is to cite first the etymological Sanskrit meaning (frequently from that classic authority, the dictionary of Sir Monier Monier-Williams) and only then to go on to the common Hindi usage which is sometimes widely variant.

Back in England, Dr. Hooker has chosen to live and work in a multi-ethnic parish in Smethwick in the West Midlands, near Birmingham, where a substantial proportion of the population is of South Asian origin; in fact, the very next-door neighbour of Dr. Hooker in his 'semi-detached' house is a South Asian. Alongside his clerical work—and he is now Adviser on Inter-faith

Relations to the Bishop of Birmingham—Dr. Hooker has also cultivated an extensive acquaintance with works of modern Hindi literature. (His personal library of Hindi books must be among the more impressive in England; I recall borrowing from him some works of Yashpal during my own sojourn at the University of Birmingham a decade ago.)

Dr. Hooker has already published a book which was the first fruit of his rich and varied background and interests, *Themes in Hinduism and Christianity: A Comparative Study* (Frankfurt am Main: Verlag Peter Lang, 1989). In this work, he took up successively the seven concepts of myth, time, evil purity, images/idols, renunciation, and woman as they are to be found expressed in both Hinduism and Christianity, and compared them with a degree of erudition which readers in both traditions will find truly impressive. But the outstanding feature of the book was the scrupulous even-handedness with which he treated both Hinduism and Christianity. Both religions were to him equal, except that at some points he seemed to be bending over backwards to be fair to Hinduism, so that in the event Hinduism ended up as somewhat more equal than Christianity. His whole attitude was summed up (perhaps unwittingly and therefore perhaps even more authentically) in a statement in his 'Introduction' where he said that he had 'tried to be as fair and objective about Christianity as I have about Hinduism'—not, we may note, as fair about Hinduism as about Christianity but in fact the other way round!

In the same 'Introduction' Dr. Hooker also incidentally mentioned 'my own fascination with language', which goes to explain his constant interest in literature. From discussing theological issues in his first book, it has been a natural step for him to move on to discuss literary texts from a theological point of view. The textuality of the Bible, which is of course the Book, has always been a vital aspect of the Christian faith, and especially in English because of the stylistic beauty of the Authorized Version. Correspondingly, many of the early classics of Hindi literature, such as the works of Kabir, Sur Das, Tulsi Das and Meera, are nothing if not (semi-)scriptural at the same time. An apprehension of religion through literature, and an understanding of literature through religion, have thus been familiar practices in both Hinduism and Christianity though what is here new, and perhaps startlingly so, is the move by Dr. Hooker to adopt a religious and theological approach to a writer so avowedly modern and modernist as Ajneya. His present work may be one of the first Ph.D. theses written in the United Kingdom on any individual Hindi writer; it almost certainly is the first thesis on a modern Hindi writer undertaken in a British Faculty of Theology.

II

Dr. Hooker has chosen to study here not all the multifarious works of Ajneya in many genres but rather his three novels: *Shekhar, Nadī ke Dvīp* (1952: *Islands in the Stream*) and *Apne Apne Ajnabī* (1961: *To Each His Own Stranger). Fiction* has traditionally proved far more amenable than any other form of literature to studies from other disciplines such as history, sociology, anthropology and ethics or philosophy, for the reason that on the whole, it represents human life and society in a more realistic or discursive form than any other genre of literature. In the present case, such suitability is further enhanced by the circumstance that Ajneya's fictional magnum opus, *Shekhar*, is candidly and even self-reflexively a closely autobiographical work. In the social and ethical issues raised in this work, the author would seem to be implicated hardly any less than the hero.

Shekhar is the story above all of rebellion, of headstrong individualist rebellion initially against one's parents, then against schools and colleges and teachers, against systems of social oppression and discrimination such as those affecting the untouchables, and against conventional norms governing interpersonal and sexual morality. It is also a story of armed 'terrorist' rebellion against British rule but this part of the story somehow remains embedded within the narrative frame rather than emerge as the chronological climax of the novel.

Of these many rebellions, Dr. Hooker has chosen to focus his attention almost exclusively on Shekhar's rebellion against what he terms as the Brahminical Hindu tradition which Shekhar is born into and inherits. In Dr. Hooker's central formulation, though Shekhar/Ajneya (and this author/character distinction is for the purpose of his discussion often elided) may have rebelled against his Hindu tradition, he still owed an abiding if subliminal allegiance to it. Dr. Hooker finds that, notwithstanding all the rebellion, Ajneya 'still felt a Brahmin's traditional responsibility for society' (27). Though he may have offered 'a radical reinterpretation of some of the key themes of Brahminical Hinduism' (137), the paradox remained that what seemed in Ajneya's writings 'new and indeed revolutionary' was deep within 'very traditional' (149). Indeed, in the context of Ajneya's crucial quest for 'freedom', it is the conclusion of Dr. Hooker that his 'roots were to be found within the very Brahminical Hinduism which in other ways he so totally rejected,' though he himself may not have known it at 'the level of conscious reflection' (182).

Some Hindi readers may here wonder whether any Indian (let alone Ajneya) has in recent times felt 'a Brahmin's traditional responsibility for society,' even if he knew quite what it was. If there persisted a vestigial Hindu subconsciousness in Ajneya despite his conscious project of critiquing and even rejecting many aspects of traditional Hinduism, it is to be discerned not so much in his novels, the third and last of which was published in 1961, but in several of his non-fictional pronouncements of later years, such as his discourse on the Indian understanding of time in a series of lectures published as *Saṃvatsara* (1978; in English, *A Sense of Time*), or in his pointed critique of T. S. Eliot's essentially Christian concept of time as being contradictory and inadequate when compared with the Indian (i.e., Hindu) conceptualization of time, in *Aal Vāl* (1971) and *Antarā* (1975). (These are discussed by Dr. Hooker below.) It was also during this later phase of his life, following extended foreign travel and a long sojourn at the University of California at Berkeley in the 1960s, that Ajneya seemed to have gone back to his 'roots,' on the rebound as it were, in a pattern familiar enough from numerous other examples. Had Ajneya written a fourth novel at this time it would, one surmises, have been quite to Dr. Hooker's purpose.

Dr. Hooker suggests two corollaries of Ajneya's at least ostensible rejection of traditional Hinduism which are of special interest. Firstly, he argues that together with Ajneya's rejection of his Hindu inheritance and his 'fiercely critical' attitude to it, there went a 'willingness' on his part 'to use Christian themes' (181), and to '[draw] on Christianity' (218). He cites in particular the episode in *Shekhar* where the originary Biblical story of Genesis is retold and substantially reinterpreted (118); a passage in which the baptism of Jesus in the river Jordan by John is evoked (92-93); and another incident in the same novel which 'it is possible' that Ajneya may have 'modelled on the parable of the Good Samaritan' (88). Ajneya was, of course, well familiar with the Bible, not only through his early private education by an American padre and later by American and English Christian teachers in both the Madras Christian College and the Forman Christian College, Lahore; he had also won gold medals, as Vidya Nivas Mishra informs us, 'for his knowledge of English literature, the Bible, and Rabindranath Tagore.'

It seems likely, however, that as for many other educated Indians, a knowledge of the Bible remained on the same literary-secular level for Ajneya as was his knowledge of English literature and Tagore. Indeed, as Hindi readers of the novel may recall it is in this wider cultural context that Shekhar himself is given the soubriquet 'John the Baptist' affectionately and with some 'dry goodwill' by a female character, Manika, who is in her belief and conduct not only most unChristian but for that matter equally unHindu (*Shekhar* II: 11)! Again, in a reference which is more a literary metaphor than a religious allusion, Shekhar reflect: 'Is each person the Jesus Christ of another, carrying his cross for him?' (*Shekhar* II: 75)

In a famous poem of Ajneya's titled 'Āzādī ke Bees Baras', published in his own translation as 'Countdown (Twenty Years of Independence),' the metaphoric allusion to the Messiah (*masīha* in Hindi) and his cross is even more casually unChristian and in fact debunking:

Oh, my messiah!
Alas, my messiah!
Twenty years of Independence have gone by
And brought you nothing,
Not even an at least recognizable
Rotten old cross—...

(*Signs and Silence*: 98-99)

Even in *Shekhar*, there are at least two references to Christianity which are quite negative. At a public meeting on social reform which Shekhar addresses, someone interjects to blame Western education and Christian teachers for spreading irreverence towards the Hindu religion (*Shekhar* II: 148). And in another quite outrageous instance, Shekhar's father tells him of an episode from his youth when an idealistic young comrade of his, who went about spreading among the people an anti-British patriotic message, was poisoned to death by some Christian missionaries who were riled by him (*Shekhar* II: 136)!

III

In any case, it is to Dr. Hooker's credit that even as he highlights some passages in *Shekhar* and in the other two novels which have an explicit or implicit Christian content, he does not at all suggest or imply that they are proof of any inclination on the part of Ajneya towards Christianity. He does not conscript or co-opt Ajneya or even Shekhar for the Christian faith, he does not even read the texts 'against the grain' as critics of various ideological persuasions are only too apt to do these days, and he has no hidden agenda. For someone who is himself firmly committed to the faith, who has adopted in this study a specifically Christian theological approach, and whose implied reader here is a fellow-Christian if not indeed a fellow-Christian theologian Dr. Hooker is commendably open and liberal in his stance towards non-Christians. Referring to the episode when Ajneya spent a month in a French monastery in 1955, reflecting on and interrogating some of the basic tenets of Christianity, Dr. Hooker acknowledges that Ajneya here was 'struggling with a set of ideas which he (found) strange and uncongenial' (195).

The second related formulation that Dr. Hooker puts forward in his discussion of Ajneya's persistent allegiance to his Brahminic Hindu inheritance is perhaps of even greater interest to his lay literary readers. As he puts it at one point in his study: 'Ajneya the Brahmin is. . . in some sense a guardian of tradition, but Ajneya the novelist is its critic and re-interpreter' (57). The dichotomy here posed between the Brahmin and the Novelist, between what one is born as and what one may choose to become, between (to invoke a phrase from T.S. Eliot which Ajneya uses as virtually an epigraph to *Shekhar*) the man who suffers and the artist who creates, is worth pondering. It perhaps equally implies a separation between the author as a person and the author as a person or a narrator, a distinction often blurred in the minds of common readers of novels known to be broadly autobiographical. And it certainly does underline the difference between an empirical, individual view of religion or tradition, and a more meditative literary or creative one, and demonstrates how the one may exist quite independently of the other, or even in opposition to it.

As already pointed out, Ajneya's many references to Brahminic-Sanskritic sources or indeed to Christian-Western sources may seem to many of his Hindi readers as of rather more literary-cultural than religious import. *Shekhar*, in any case, is one of the most widely allusive intercultural, interliterary, intertextual, polyphonic novels that one may ever hope or wish to read, containing as it does numerous quotations in the original (and in the roman script) from many English poets, besides quotations from Sanskrit, Bengali, Panjabi and Urdu verse, while it also takes the hero to some predominantly Tamil- and Malayalam-speaking areas. Indeed, so wide and various is the web of literary allusions in *Shekhar* that (as I recall Ajneya once telling me with that serenely radiant and wry smile of his) when the novel was given a literary prize shortly after publication (the Mangla Prasad Paritoshik, was it?), the citation singled out for praise, among other things, the '*pāṇḍitya*' of the novelist, i.e., his learning or erudition!

Hindi readers of Ajneya will therefore be pleased to find that though Dr. Hooker's ostensible object of attention is theological, he displays nevertheless a literary sensitivity to Ajneya's work which is truly illuminating. The word-count he offers of the frequency of use in the various novels of some key terms in Ajneya's quest for freedom, such as *mukti*, *moksha*, *svatantratā*, *svādhīnatā* and *svachchanda* (149-50) are a proof of his attention to stylistic detail, while his analysis of the four main groups of images into which he divides Ajneya's depiction of freedom—'height, flight, experiences connected with water, and absorption into a larger whole' (153 ff.)—is an example of close reading of the New Criticism school somewhat reminiscent of Caroline Spurgeon's study of Shakespeare's imagery. Even a simple-sounding formulation such as that, while in English one speaks of petting through something Hindus will speak instead of getting across something (the ocean of life, etc.) arises out of Dr. Hooker's long and intimate acquaintance with the very idiom of Hindu thought. (One wonders, however, which of these collocations would be used by that rapidly multiplying breed, the English-speaking 'Hindu'!)

Finally, even the inter-faith dialogue between Hinduism and Christianity, which Dr. Hooker makes the precise and narrow focus of his study, will probably be seen by many of his secular readers in a considerably larger context. Dr. Hooker claims at the beginning of this book that its originality lies in seeing Ajneya against his 'Hindu background,' something which his Hindi critics haven't attempted to do, busy as they have been with tracing the various European influences on him! (2, 53) (Actually, there's an instructive contraflow parallel here: in the case of T.S. Eliot many Indian critics have shown exceptional, even undue, alacrity in trying to establish the influence on him of Hindu or Buddhist sources.) Initially, Dr. Hooker's terms of discourse may seem so original to an Indian reader as to sound even a little strange; it certainly is odd, for example, to find the atheist Ajneya as well as some of his critics routinely described as 'Hindu' (177). And if no Hindi critic has so far treated Ajneya primarily as a brahmin writer, it is probably for the reason that for Hindi (rather than 'Hindu') critics, Ajneya's so-called Brahminism is not much of an issue in his writings. (Nor for that matter is R. K. Narayan's for his Indian readers, yet the English critic William Walsh opens his book on Narayan by similarly asserting in the very first sentence that Narayan is an Indian of 'the purest brahmin stock'.) And if the Brahminism of Ajneya is such a crucial factor for Dr. Hooker, it is probably as much because of his own contemporary context in Britain, in which, as he puts it, immigrants of other faiths are for the first time posing 'theological challenges' (7) to Christianity.

The wish to initiate a multi-faith 'dialogue' with other religions is an acutely felt need of the Church in Britain today, and that seems to be a major reason for Dr. Hooker adopting the approach that he does in this study. The early colonial Christian compulsion to *convert* seems now to have historically evolved into a post-colonial Christian compulsion to *converse*, to hold the other faiths in a mutually interrogative dialogue of a kind for which the other faiths have perhaps not shown an equal and corresponding inclination. (Could it be a case of 'poor little talkative Christianity,' in E.M. Forster's withering phrase, trying to be sociable to other rather more self-contained religions, in some of which self-reflexive silence is more of a cardinal virtue than dialogue—as incidentally, and notoriously, it was for Ajneya in his personal life?) Once again, it is a measure of the exceptional sensitivity and sympathy with which Dr. Hooker approaches his subject that he recognizes that while he himself may wish to become Ajneya's 'dialogue partner' now through this study, he is anyhow 'the privileged listener to a dialogue which is already happening within the novels' (182), on Ajneya's own terms and within his own cultural parameters, without the presence or stimulus of any external interlocutor.

In any case, for Dr. Hooker's non-Christian non-British readers, this book will have a wider appeal and attraction which will lie not so much in his theoretical frame as in the textual picture, not so much in his chosen perspective as in the actual content, not so much in a Christian view of Ajneya the Brahmin as in a British view of Ajneya the Novelist. Whatever its explicit orientation, this book remains at the same time a finely focused and highly discriminating study of Ajneya the novelist, from which all students of Ajneya and Hindi literature will benefit.

Department of English HARISH TRIVEDI
University of Delhi
November 1996

INTRODUCTION

This book is about three novels written in the Hindi [*Hindī*] language of North India by *Saccidānanda Hirānanda Vatsyāyan 'Ajñeya'* (pronounced 'Agyeya') (1) who lived from 1911 to 1987. Ajneya was a Hindu but this is a word which will require elucidation. 'Hinduism' is an umbrella term which is commonly used to describe the vast range of rituals, stories, philosophy and theology, together with popular practice and belief which have flourished in the Indian sub-continent (2) for close on four millenia. To say that Ajneya was a Hindu, without further qualification, is rather like saying that someone is a European. We shall therefore have to locate him as precisely as possible within the Hindu tradition. Similarly, it is not enough to say that he wrote three novels. We shall have to ask what kind of novels they were, and how they relate to others of the same *genre*.

Next, from his dates it is obvious that he lived through a period of rapid political and social change and this fact is naturally reflected in his novels. His paternal grandfather was a traditional Brahmin [*Brāhmaṇ*] priest (3) in the Punjab (4), and his father was employed in the Archaeological Department of the Government of British India, a job which took him to many parts of India, including among other places, Bihar, Kashmir, and the Nilgiri Hills of the South. As a young man Ajneya was involved in revolutionary violence against British rule and spent several years in jail. These events assume large importance in his first novel, Shekhar: A Life. [*Śekhar: Ek Jīvanī*] (In future referred to as SL)(5) During the Second World War he joined the Indian Army in order to fight against Japan as did the leading character of his second novel, Islands in the Stream. [*Nadī ke Dvīpa*] (IS)(6) After the war he earned his living as a journalist and writer. He visited Europe, and his final novel -- To Each His Stranger [*Apne Apne Ajnabī*] (TEHS)(7) -- is set in Scandanavia. He also taught at Berkeley California and visited Japan. This dramatic extension of the horizons of experience across three generations of the same family is striking, but not of course untypical of many in India and elsewhere who lived during the same period. Moreover, like many of his Indian contemporaries Ajneya learnt English and this opened up to him the world of English literature, and through translations, of European literature as well.

In addition to the three novels which are our theme, Ajneya published fourteen volumes of poetry, seven collections of short stories, twenty-seven books of essays on a wide variety of subjects, three diaries of reflections which he called 'inner journals' [*antaḥ prakriyāeṁ*], a drama, and two books in which he described his travels in India and in Europe.(8) He wrote many articles for a wide variety of journals, and as a journalist and editor of newspapers was constantly involved in producing material of a more ephemeral kind. He also dominated the Hindi language literary scene for over forty years and his creative writing has already spawned a flood of critical response which shows no sign of abating.(9) To describe this material in detail would take us beyond the parameters of our book. We refer to it at this point in order to demonstrate by contrast the originality of our own approach. Hindi critics have looked at the literary style and merits of the novels in the context of the developing Hindi literary tradition. They have also considered the influence upon them of English and other European literature. No-one has so far set the novels against the background of the Hindu tradition and examined how Ajneya re-interprets important aspects of this, and no-one has looked at them from the perspective of Christian theology. This is what we shall be doing and in both these respects we shall claim that this book breaks new ground.

In the Appendix we set out the contents of the novels in summary form. We do this for the convenience of the reader since outside a few Indological libraries they are not readily available in England. Also a degree of familiarity with the contents of the books will be necessary for ease of reference in subsequent chapters.

But do these novels deserve the study of Christian theologians? If they do, then what theological method should we adopt in order to engage with them? To begin our answer to the first of these questions we invoke the aid of Ajneya himself. In a long passage in one of his 'inner journals', Antarā, he sets out his personal agenda more fully than he does anywhere else. This agenda is powerfully elaborated in the novels. He begins by saying:

> [W]ithout being myself a theologian or a law-giver, I am deeply involved in the problem of ethics [?] I live in times when scriptural texts do not suffice. Query marks hang over all the answers they offer; they neither satisfy the conscience nor are relevant or expedient. In the changed context, then, the first and fundamental question is: what is the sanction behind any code of ethics? On what touchstone to test what still holds true and what is false? In a religious, God-centred, believing society the criterion was clear: the imperatives were categorical and compelling and they were accepted with complete trust. But how can one place one's trust in book sanctions when the very existence of God is questioned?(Ajneya [1984] p. 14)(10)

In Ajneya's first novel we shall see that his main character, a young man called Shekhar [*Śekhar* -- pronounced 'Shaker'], is in total and passionate revolt against the Brahminical Hindu tradition in which he is being nurtured, and in particular against the oppression of women and of outcaste groups, an oppression for which certain traditional texts provided the sanction. More than this, he explicitly rejects belief in God, a God whom he sees as doing little more than providing support for these sanctions. With rejection of belief in God goes rejection of belief in the next world which is seen as the place of reward for keeping, or of punishment for breaking the rules of this unjust social order.(11) In other words Shekhar rejects an unjust and imposed notion of the sacred. In a Christian context such an imposed sacredness could be described as 'heteronomy', a term first used by Paul Tillich.(Tillich [1953] p. 93)(12) Yet Ajneya is no mere root and branch iconoclast, for he sees that what is replacing traditional society is just as bad if not worse:

> The progress of science shook the foundations of a transcendental ethic; then biology, by establishing the theory of evolution, joined man (13) and beast in a new common context. Science, depriving us of the spiritual or transcendental basis of ethics, could have established us on the humanistic grounds of reason, but scientificism (*sic*), in its first flush, also to some extent led us astray...Whether or not there is a God is a question which falls outside the realm of science. Science cannot pronounce on questions of faith, just as faith cannot provide answers to questions in the

> realm of science, but if we deny the Oversoul (14) no basis remains for believing in the soul: and conscience, the inner voice, or whatever name we give it, becomes merely a relative term. Relative to what? We may ask but there is no answer. Consequently the gross distortion of humanism produced an extreme materialism and personal survival became the highest value. "Whatever helps one to survive is ethical." This, made respectable under the name of 'secularism' is the ruling principle today. To call this doctrine of pure survivalism 'humanism' is a clear travesty of man: it would be more honest to call it animalism, for survival is the basic instinct of all creatures. It isn't that man doesn't or shouldn't have the urge to survive, but for him survival has to have a different context. Instead of being a blind biological instinct it becomes a deliberate purposive, social act of choice. For man, "I wish to live" is to be translated "I wish to remain free". Not free from society, but free in society; for society too is an effective device created and perfected for the pursuit of freedom. (Ajneya [1984] pp. 16-7)

So Ajneya rejects an attitude of mere animal 'survivalism', an attitude which we shall see embodied in the characters of Chandramadhava [*Candramādhava*] and Hemendra [*Hemendra*] in IS and in Rameshvar [*Rāmeśvar*] in SL. Thus our author is waging a war on two fronts, against the social injustice produced by certain aspects of the tradition in which he was brought up and against a self-sufficiency which while rejecting heteronomy offers nothing in its place. Such self-sufficiency we can describe as 'autonomy'.(Tillich [1953] pp. 93-4)(15). Ajneya claims that this attitude reduces humanity to the level of the animals.

What does he want to put in the place of these two unacceptable alternatives? We see the germ of his positive view of what society might be in the last few lines of the above quotation: we have the capacity to choose and in this lies our freedom, a freedom which is properly exercised in society, for society exists to make its pursuit possible. He expands on this vision later in our passage:

> Humanism breaks aways from animalism the moment we recognise that, on the evolutionary scale, man is the first animal for whom life is not merely survival but the creation of values. Survival is for *all* creatures; man conceives of and postulates a higher value than man. A human value greater than man -- this paradox is the first problem of a humanist ethics and also the resolution of the problem. Human values greater than man, life values greater than

> life. Man is the first animal to find something for which even life may be sacrificed, and that 'something' is itself a creation of Man. Not the creation of an isolated individual, but of the entire human community: that is to say, this value is not founded on human intuition, but is based on some principle recognisable by and accepted by mankind in general. Only such a sense of values can be the source or foundation of a humanist ethics. Otherwise we remain nothing more than wild beasts at large in a dense jungle.(Ajneya [1984] p. 17)

In these words we see Ajneya struggling for something akin to what Tillich called 'theonomy' (Tillich [1953] pp. 94 and 164-5). Bonhoeffer struggled for something similar which could be described as 'this worldly transcendence'(16), that is to say, a sense of God perceived as somehow present within and not imposed from outside the human struggle. Ajneya would not have used such explicitly Christian terminology, but if something which in Hindu terms is at least comparable to theonomy and 'this worldly transcendence' forms the ground base of these novels then we can already claim that Ajneya's vision has brought him close, in this respect at least, to some contemporary understandings of Christianity. This degree of consensus enables us to identify the differences. The most important of these is that in the above three quotations from his 'inner journal' Ajneya actually appears to rule out the possibility of God. This is reflected in the novels where we find that in SL Shekhar becomes an atheist, while in IS two of the four main characters Bhuvan [*Bhuvan*] and Rekha [*Rekhā* -- pronounced 'Raykha'] are agnostic if not atheist while a third (Chandramadhava) becomes a Communist in the course of the story. Yet the fourth character, Gaura [*Gaurā*], is open to a transcendent dimension of life. That possibility is much more confidently and explicitly embodied in the character of Selma [*Selmā*] in TEHS.(17) Thus there is a significant shift across the three novels. We shall have to ask whether the paradox to which Ajneya referred in the above quotation -- 'a human value greater than man' -- can ultimately be sustained without some kind of transcendent foundation, a foundation for which the word 'God' might be the most appropriate reference. Indeed Ajneya himself seems to move in that direction even though he does not explicitly come to that conclusion. He also wrote, as we saw above, that 'Man is the first animal to find something for which even life may be sacrificed'. Sacrifice for the sake of 'a human value greater than man' implies choice, the costly choice of a higher good instead of the easy option of a lesser one. Ajneya develops the notion of freedom of choice in the final part of our passage:

> We can now also sharply delineate another human value: the value of voluntary choice, freedom of choice. Of the human values greater than man that man has created, this is primary. Because man has created something greater than himself, therefore, he is free to choose it. This then becomes the ethical criterion for judging his actions: how far does he freely and consciously *choose* (Ajneya's italics) his values? Because these values are greater than man, therefore, every exercise of choice by an individual is made on behalf of all mankind and acts upon it. This constitutes moral responsibility.(Ajneya [1984] pp. 18-9)

We are reminded here of Peter Berger who in his book The Heretical Imperative points out that choice is part of the modern human condition, a point which separates us from our forebears most of whom lived in unitary societies where such a range of moral options was not available.(Berger [1980] pp. 1-31) This is another important area where we find ourselves standing side by side with our author and not over against him. In SL and IS freedom of choice takes on a large significance when two of the female characters are faced with the prospect of arranged marriages which they do not want to undertake. In each case the men to whom they turn for advice urge them to make their own independent choices. In TEHS we find Ajneya disagreeing with Jean-Paul Sartre about the nature and possibility of freedom. Indeed, the theme of freedom is of great importance to our novels, to Ajneya's writing as a whole and to his view of what human life is about.(18) Its significance is already apparent in the quotations we have made from his 'inner journal'.

This then is the agenda which makes the study of these novels such a worthwhile enterprise for a Christian theologian. In them we can, so to speak, overhear a modern Hindu writer questioning his own tradition. We shall argue that although on the surface he rejects much in that tradition, at a deeper level he is offering a creative re-interpretation of it. This means that he is not simply a maverick, a solitary rebel talking to other rebels. Indeed it is precisely his rootedness in his own tradition which makes possible his revolt against it. That rootedness also means that our study of the novels has a significance beyond its immediate context. Although we are studying the work of only one writer, that study is part of the wider dialogue of Christians with Hindus. We also listen to him engaging in dialogue with western culture, a dialogue which at certain explicit points includes Christianity. We watch him searching for new values to undergird human authenticity in the modern world -- a world which in so many of its aspects seems to us as well as to him to erode human significance. Our encounter with his thought will thus have several layers or facets, and while this will make our study complex, it will, we trust, give it a richness of texture and argument which could break new ground for Christian theologians in their encounter with other religions. This is something which a study of purely religious texts could not have afforded.

We turn now to the second question which we raised above, which concerns method: how do we engage theologically with these three novels? We need a method which has its roots in Christian theology but which neither rejects what Ajneya says because it is pre-judged to be wrong or inadequate by our own Christian criteria, nor which claims him as a crypto-Christian by obliterating the very real differences between his perspective and our own. We need to be able to take him seriously as someone who can challenge our own Christian view, which must therefore be deliberately put at risk and so made open to such challenge. How can this be done? In order to discuss this question we must first set it in the larger context of contemporary inter-religious encounter.

In recent years Christians in Britain and indeed across the world have become increasingly aware of the theological challenges posed by the existence and content of other religions. Since the early seventies an increasing number of books addressed to the subject has been published.(19) This debate is important for it is concerned both with the intellectual credibility of Christian believing and with the nature of continuing Christian identity. It is properly more concerned with the fact that other religions actually exist than it is with the particularities of their content. This is of vital importance: when Christianity is the only known religion, then theology can operate within its traditional parameters, but once Christians realise that there are other religions which offer their own interpretations of the mystery of human life and destiny, and that these interpretations have satisfied millions of people for many centuries, then the nature of the theological enterprise is permanently changed. It now has to take account of plurality, a plurality which once it is acknowledged appears to make all religious claims relative. Theology now has to ask how -- and if -- the absolute and universal claims which Christianity has traditionally made can be sustained in a world where others make their own distinctive, and sometimes rival, claims. It also has to ask what value it can within its own terms give to these other claims. These issues go to the heart of Christian identity and believing, but the debate needs to be supplemented by studies such as the present one which concentrate in depth on a narrow but important area of actual content. Without this kind of locating in the particularities of another tradition the debate runs the risk of descending into unreality, for other religions are too easily reduced to the role of counters in a theological 'game' which Christians play with one another.

One fruitful way of studying religions is to see them as cultural-linguistic systems. What this entails has been spelled out by George Lindbeck: he describes religions as

> comprehensive interpretive schemes, usually embodied in myths or narratives and heavily ritualised, which structure human experience and understanding of self and world.
> ... a religion can be viewed as a kind of cultural and/or linguistic framework or medium that shapes the entirety of life and thought... It is not primarily an array of beliefs about the true and the good (though it may involve these), or a symbolism expressive of basic attitudes, feelings, or sentiments (though these will be generated). Rather it is similar to an idiom that makes possible the description of realities, the formulation of beliefs, and the experiencing of inner attitudes, feelings and sentiments. Like a culture or language it is a communal phenomenon that shapes the subjectivities of individuals rather than being primarily a manifestation of those subjectivities. It comprises a vocabulary of discursive and nondiscursive symbols together with a distinctive logic or grammar in terms of which this vocabulary can be meaningfully deployed. (Lindbeck [1984] pp. 32-33)

The value of Lindbeck's approach lies in the fact that it allows for a rich and many-layered description of religions, a kind of analysis which is fundamental to our book. Its weakness is that it can make the boundaries of a religion appear to be impenetrable. Yet we have already seen that in his own life and experience Ajneya, like many of his contemporaries, stepped outside the traditional boundaries of Hinduism. Throughout the book we shall be demonstrating that it is equally possible -- and necessary -- to cross these boundaries in the opposite direction: a sympathetic observer can so to speak step inside the Hindu world and describe what (s)he sees. At this point Lindbeck can indeed be an invaluable guide, for he teaches us that to explore another religion means exploring the nature of its symbols and their inter-relationship, observing how these actually function in the life of the community.

Fundamental to this model is a certain understanding of the relationship between symbols and language on the one hand and experience on the other: religious people do not first have experiences and then attempt to find appropriate words and symbols in which to express them. They first become familiar with the symbols and learn the language, and it is this which makes it possible for them to have the experiences, (and difficult if not impossible to have other experiences which are available to those who live in other cultural-linguistic systems). Therefore much of what may be said within the framework of a particular religious tradition makes immediate sense within it but not outside -- hence the need to interpret other traditions by sympathetic study and observation from within their boundaries. It thus becomes difficult to argue that all people have a similar experience which is then clothed in the different cultural-linguistic forms of particular religions, for the culture and language remain primary and formative.

The Jesuit scholar Michael Barnes, drawing on the work of Lindbeck, Geertz and Wittgenstein (20), makes the point that such frameworks are built on the assumption that life has order and therefore meaning. Disorder and absurdity are disarmed because they can always be interpreted within that wider framework:

> Religion begins with the acknowledgement of order in the universe and develops as people try to accept the manifestations of disorder. One of the most obvious threats to the cohesion, perhaps even to the very existence of a society, is the suspicion that maybe there is no such thing as order, that all is a mirage. Hence the need to

> formulate through a symbol-system an image of the world as ordered and of disorder as explicable and temporary.(Barnes [1989] p. 98)

Barnes finds Lindbeck's thesis inadequate in one important respect. It accounts for continuity within religious traditions but does not allow sufficiently for change.(Barnes [1989] p. 100)(21) Jesus Christ, Prince Siddhartha who became the Buddha, Muhammad and Guru Nanak can all be understood only within their respective cultural-linguistic frameworks, but each in important respects subverted the framework of his day.(22) Eventually indeed they were seen as founders of new systems. Within all traditions this process of challenge and renewal continues, though normally in less radical ways. Prophets challenge certain aspects of their religious inheritance, but their insights are later incorporated into an amended and more profound interpretation of it. Sometimes the challenge is so radical that it is rejected altogether. This may lead to schism and so within all religions there are to be found rival and sometimes literally warring schools of interpretation.(23) Our three novels can be set within this tradition of prophetic challenge.

This model for the interpretation of religion is very similar to John Bowker's proposal that religions can be usefully interpreted as information systems.(Doctrine Commission [1981] pp. 159-89) Just as in Lindbeck's analysis religious systems have clear boundaries, so too, according to Bowker do information systems. Information, if it is important, is never allowed to be uncontrolled or freely available: 'organised systems are *necessary* for the continuity and transmission of information.'(p.160) And so 'It is channelled, protected and organised, in ways which require systems for those purposes.'(p.161) Further, it is kept in the hands of stewards who ensure that it is properly used in this generation and then passed on to the next. Those who are to join the stewards are carefully selected and then trained so that their attitude towards the information with which they are now entrusted becomes identical with that of those who were stewards before them. Only on those terms are they allowed to have access to the information and given authority both to act as its guardians and to pass it on to others.

This model is useful because it enables us to compare religions with many other bodies which are also concerned with the appropriate transmission of vital information. The medical and legal professions, a university and a business company are obvious examples. As far as the control and handing on of information is concerned these all function in broadly similar ways.(p.167)

Precisely because information is so important most institutions which guard and transmit it, including religions, are inherently conservative. By setting the conservatism of religions in this wider context Bowker enables us to understand it sympathetically. This is important for an imaginative understanding of Ajneya's novels. As we have seen above, he believed that the dominant information system or cultural-linguistic framework of his day had broken down: 'I live in times when scriptural texts do not suffice. Query marks hang over all the answers they offer.' Yet he can only be understood in terms of what he rejects. His novels can only make very limited sense outside the Hindu framework of meaning. To understand that framework with imaginative sympathy is an important prerequisite for understanding Ajneya's criticisms and reshaping of it.

So far all we have claimed for the cultural-linguistic thesis is that it provides a framework within which Ajneya's novels can be placed and understood. Can we now use it as a model for Christianity and ask whether it can provide a theology on the basis of which dialogue is possible for Christians? At the heart of the model is the claim that symbols, language and culture make us what we are. They enable us to be religious in a particular way. Language addressed to us by others is the way in which we are incorporated into a community. We do not have private religious feelings which happen deep inside us and which we then put into words, rather do the words which are addressed to us enable us to have the feelings. Faith comes by hearing. It follows that to be human is to be persons in relationship and not isolated Cartesiǎn monads.(24) Much western theology has functioned on the Cartesian model, indeed Lindbeck includes it in another model which he calls the experiential-expressive -- and which he then rejects as inadequate.(Lindbeck [1984] pp. 15-25)

Philosophical support for the cultural-linguistic model is provided by the later Wittgenstein as interpreted by Fergus Kerr:

> Why do we retreat from our world, why do we withdraw from

> the body in the hope that more direct illumination about our minds and about the gods is to be found by gaining access to something other than what we say and do? That is the hidden theological agenda of the later Wittgenstein.(Kerr [1986] p. 147)

In more positive terms:

> The locus of meaning is not the epistemological solitude of the individual consciousness but the practical exchanges that constitute the public world which we inhabit together.(Kerr [1986] p. 58)

This view therefore puts a high premium on belonging to a community which lives in the context of a shared tradition, for this is at least a part of what is meant by 'the public world'. Some of the implications for a Christian anthropology which this argument suggests are worked out by A I McFadyen.(McFadyen [1987])(25) Fundamental to his thesis is the claim that 'persons are social beings whose essence is communication and therefore not discrete and essentially private'.(p.i) This means that 'Human Being is not a static, pre-social substance but a response to external address'.(p.3) He sees the Trinity as determinative for this understanding of human nature:

> The Father, Son and Spirit are neither simply modes of relations nor absolutely discrete and independent individuals, but Persons in relation and Persons only through relation. Persons exist only as they exist for others, not merely as they exist in and for themselves.(p.12)

Therefore 'The structural openness of human being for another is a social refraction of the openness of God'.(p.20) In the Christian context personality is constituted by the call of Christ who in the Gospel narratives calls fishermen and tax-collectors out of their original context and into a new one in which they become disciples.(p.48) Their old world is transformed by giving it a new meaning. This relationship to Christ gives persons a transcendent dimension to their being so that they are not to be reduced to mere cyphers in a collective whole, or to discrete atomistic individuals. This new relationship corresponds on the human level to the pattern of life of the Trinity. Human persons as well as the Persons within the Trinity 'exist only as they exist for others, not merely as they exist in and for themselves'.

We could hardly expect Ajneya to accept such an explicitly Christian account of human nature. While he might have accepted the priority of language and community (26) he could hardly have agreed to set this within the context of the Trinity. But we are not asking him to do this, we are simply asking whether it is possible to start from such a position ourselves and on its basis to have a conversation with Ajneya in which we can actually listen to and be questioned by what he says. We claim that this is possible, for McFadyen insists that I need the other in order to be myself, because 'A person becomes an ordered whole only in the process of public communication and self-transcendent relatedness'.(p.162) He claims that in dialogue we acknowledge the other as a 'positive mystery'(p.137), and he writes of a 'communicative pause in which the other is let be' and of 'a readiness to be silent before the mystery of the other'.(p.138) This accords happily with and indeed makes possible our own insistence above that we must ensure that our theology does not force Ajneya's novels into a Christian mould. There are wider implications here for inter-religious dialogue in general. Historically religions, and indeed different 'denominations' within the same religion, have usually related to one another by means of mutual repulsion. Thus Norman Daniel has shown how Christians in the Middle Ages denigrated Islam as a means of coping with its threatening presence.(Daniel [1966] *passim*) Within Christianity it is arguable that the open Bible of the Protestant Reformation provoked the closed one of traditional Roman Catholicism, while Catholic veneration of Mary provoked Protestant neglect of her. Such re-actions always impoverish those who make them, they lead to a stereotyping of the 'other' and this makes meeting impossible. But if I need the other truly to be myself, and if that need is derived from the nature of the Trinity itself as the model of humanity, then the ground is cut from beneath these traditional re-actions.

How far whole religious communities can be open to one another in the way we have suggested is necessarily doubtful, but this path is certainly open to individuals, and only as they take it can they have the hope of persuading at least some members of their own communities to follow them. This fact encourages us to read the novels of Ajneya and to do so with attention, the kind of attention to the other which in the terms of McFadyen's argument I must offer in order to be a fully human being, and which on Christian terms is a reflection of the life of the Trinity. It is at this point and in this way that dialogue happens: as I expose myself to 'the other' -- in this case the three novels of our author -- so my own horizons of awareness are extended. I am not just acquiring new information but entering another world. I have constantly to return to my own world and ask how far my new discoveries can be included within it. In so far as I can include them, the boundaries of my own cultural-linguistic world, and therefore of my own self, are extended.

It follows that genuine dialogue necessarily involves risk, the risk of having one's convictions and one's identity put in question, but unless one is something and stands for something in the first place, unless in other words one is committed, one neither has nor is anything which is worth risking. Recognising the necessity of commitment and of risk is important for both sides of our proposed conversation. It forms the conclusion of our Christian case for dialogue, but we can also apply it from the other side, that is to Ajneya himself. In writing his novels and publishing them he too was inviting a dialogue in which he put his convictions and his identity at risk. To justify and elaborate this statement we turn to an important essay by Paul Ricoeur, 'The Hermeneutics of Testimony'. Ricoeur writes:

> The term testimony should be applied to words, works, actions, and to lives which attest to an intention, an inspiration, an idea at the heart of experience and history which nonetheless transcend experience and history.(Ricoeur [1981] pp. 119-20)

Each of Ajneya's novels 'testifies' in that sense, though the testimony of each of them is different from the other two. Such testimony carries with it an implicit invitation to dialogue, to agree or to disagree with what is said. To quote Ricoeur again:

> Testimony is a dual relation: there is the one who testifies and the one who hears the testimony. The witness has seen, but the one who receives his testimony has not seen but hears. It is only by hearing the testimony that he can believe or not believe in the reality of the facts that the witness reports. Testimony as story is thus found in an intermediary position between a statement made by a person and a belief assumed by another on the faith of the testimony of the first.(p.123)

Ajneya's novels can be understood as occupying this intermediary position of 'testimony as story' for we shall see that each of them in its different way states a case on which the reader is implicitly invited to pass judgement, if not actually accept as true. If this be so then to enter into a critical conversation with them in the way we have proposed can be seen as a response to an invitation which Ajneya himself makes, an invitation to which his many other critics have made their own responses.

Such then is the theological basis for our conversation with these novels, but it is an argument which depends on the large assumption, which we made in our opening paragraph, that in order to understand what the novels say we must first set them in their original context. That context, we went on to suggest, includes not only that part of the Hindu tradition within which Ajneya was nurtured, but also his life-story, his other writings, and, within the novels themselves, the purpose and intention of their author. This proposal runs into formidable objections not from theologians, nor we think from Hindus such as Ajneya, but from certain contemporary western literary critics. They would say that we have fallen for 'the intentional fallacy', which is the belief that the study of a literary work can or should lead us to the mind of its author.(27) Such critics, notably of the structuralist school, claim that the intention of an author is not only irrelevant to the interpretation of a text but actually prevents us from getting at its meaning. All we have is the text itself and it is this alone which we must interpret, regardless of its author or original context. In part these theories are a healthy and necessary reaction against some earlier and in particular Romantic views which suggested that a text was indeed a direct expression of the mind of its author. Here we agree with John Barton who suggests that without reverting to that extreme position it is possible and indeed necessary to hold a modified view of the importance of authorial intention:

> New Critics, structuralists and proponents of 'canon criticism' all agree that the essential flaw in asking about the intentions of an author, rather than about the inherent meaning of a text, is that to do so is to abandon literary criticism for psychology. A question about intention is a question about the state of someone's mind. Now 'intention' is an enormous issue in philosophy, which we cannot go into in detail here. But it does seem reasonable to ask whether the matter is really as simple as New Criticism makes it. Surely questions about intention need not be so crudely

> psychological as to lead automatically to speculations about the author's 'inner life'...it is not clear why anti-intentionalism should be applied as an absolute dogma. What we can know about the author from sources other than the text itself is not a *criterion* of the text's meaning, certainly; but it can still provide useful hints as to what the text is *likely* to mean.(Barton [1984] pp. 168-9)

That describes our own position: the subject of the book is the texts of the novels, and we are not trying to use these texts in order to gain access to the mind of their author. Yet at the same time in the context of the book we want to push Barton's argument further than he does himself. We hold that at certain points the life and thoughts of our author can not only 'provide useful hints' about what the texts might mean, but are actually important for their interpretation. We can argue this point differently without any reference to Ajneya or his novels: knowledge of the wider context of any text is essential for the simple reason that the same words in one context may mean something completely different in another. In other words context plays an important role in the determination of meaning.(28) At some points in the book we shall certainly want to exclude all thought of the author and his intentions and use structuralist modes of interpretation, but this does not mean that we are required to accept structuralism as a total and comprehensive literary theory. We refuse to let it become an idol. Instead we reduce it to the more modest and we would claim appropriate role of a tool, a tool which has its uses along with other tools.

This attitude to structuralism has larger implications. George Steiner has argued powerfully that all literary works presuppose for their understanding a transcendent reference which he calls a presence of God, a presence which structuralism and its successor critical theories deny. For them

> The word *rose* has neither stem nor leaf nor thorn. It exudes no odour. It is, *per se*, a wholly arbitrary phonetic marker, an empty sign. Nothing whatever in its (minimal) sonority, in its graphic appearance, in its phonemic components, etymological history or grammatical functions, has any correspondence whatever to what we believe or imagine to be the object of its purely conventional reference.(Steiner [1989] p. 95)

In other words individual words now no longer refer directly to anything in the outer world, their meaning can only be understood in relation to other words in the same text, which now functions as a self-contained world with its own rules. Steiner calls this the 'repudiation of the covenant of reference' (*sc* 'of words to the outside world') a covenant which he claims lies at the heart of western culture. Further if 'non-reference constitutes the true genius and purity of language' then this entails 'a central supposition of "real absence"'.(p.96)

On Steiner's terms then, to accept our modified version of authorial intention as legitimate, and to reject structuralism as a total literary explanation and to use it, as we have suggested, merely as a convenient tool which 'works' in some contexts and not in others is by implication necessarily to stake a claim for a 'real presence' in literary texts. For

> A semantics, a poetics of correspondence, of decipherability and truth-values arrived at across time and consensus, are strictly inseparable from the postulate of theological-metaphysical transcendence. Thus the origin of the axiom of meaning and of the God-concept is a shared one.(p.119)

> This issue is, quite simply, that of the meaning of meaning, as it is re-insured by the postulate of the existence of God. "In the beginning was the Word." There was no such beginning, says deconstruction; only the play of sounds and markers amid the mutations of time.(p.120)

That 'axiom of meaning' is implicit in our approach to Ajneya, and we would claim, implicit in the testimony (in Paul Ricoeur's sense) which he makes through his novels to his readers. But here we must be careful, we are not claiming that Ajneya is a crypto-theist, simply that his testimony necessarily implies some kind of transcendent reference, however that may be understood. The question of how if at all that reference can be equated with Christian understandings of God is one with which we shall in different ways be grappling throughout this book.

We end this Introduction with a synopsis of the argument which we shall be setting out in the chapters which follow.

In our first two chapters we set our three novels in their original context. This context has several over-lapping dimensions. In Chapter One we give a brief sketch of certain key elements of the Hindu tradition in order to be able to locate Ajneya within it. We then move on to the political and social events through which he lived and in which he was caught up, in so far as these are reflected in the novels. In Chapter Two we place the novels in the the context both of the contemporary Hindi language novel and of its European step-parent. In our third chapter we begin to establish in detail the consensus to which we referred on page 5. We shall argue that our author is concerned to demonstrate that human life lived in this present world of time, space and matter, has an ultimate significance. It is not simply a preparation for a putative next world. In order to make such a claim Ajneya has to reshape not only the transcendental but also the social boundaries of traditional Hinduism, and in particular to reject the notion of ritual purity and the social inequalities which went with it. This third chapter will thus both begin our conversation with the novels and provide the foundation for continuing it in subsequent chapters.

Our fourth chapter takes the consensus further and is devoted to the central theme of the purification of vision through suffering. This is important for Ajneya and is closely connected with his vision of 'a human value greater than man'. For if suffering can indeed purify vision then it can also lift human beings above 'mere survivalism'. Here too Ajneya re-interprets his own tradition for we shall see that the purification of vision is a central theme in Hindu philosophy and practice. In Chapter Five we consider another key theme: freedom. We have already noted that this is of central importance in our author's thought. Not surprisingly it assumes large importance in the novels and we shall see how he reshapes some of the traditional Hindu imagery which was used to describe it. In this chapter we find that the freedom to which Ajneya's characters aspire takes them into solitude and away from human society and culture. Within all five of these chapters there are implicit some large questions about the nature of time. Besides being an important subject of debate within the Hindu philosophical tradition this is a major pre-occupation of Ajneya himself in some of his writings outside the novels. The question of time is interwoven with the significance of narrative as the context in which human identity is shaped and discovered, for none of the novels is a straightforward chronological story. We shall devote the sixth chapter to a study of these issues and this will serve to sharpen the debate which we open up in Chapter Five. The final chapter will pull the threads of the argument together and attempt to bring it to a conclusion.

These then are the themes of subsequent chapters. They are not only central to the subject matter of the novels, they are key themes for Christian theology or indeed for any attempt to make sense of the mystery of human life. Indeed they can all be interpreted as variations on a single theme: the search for a meaning to life in an age where traditional accounts of its significance have broken down. In this Introduction we have set out a theological argument which will, we trust, enable us to engage with these novels and attend to their message and their struggle. We believe that in this process our own horizon of awareness will be extended and the cause of Hindu-Christian dialogue advanced in a new direction and in a new manner.

NOTES

1. Since this is the first appearance of our author's name we print it in full. Subsequently we refer to him simply by his pen name 'Ajñeya', for the origin of which see below, p. 39.
2. 'The Indian sub-continent' is the phrase commonly used to describe the area which now (1994) comprises India, Pakistan and Bangladesh. Until 1947 this area was one country, India. Pakistan came into existence in 1947 as two separate geographical entitites but one political unit, East and West Pakistan. In 1972 East Pakistan became a separate independent country as Bangladesh. Subsequently the term 'West' was dropped from the title of the other unit which thus simply became Pakistan. Ajneya's ancestral roots were in the Punjab which is divided between what are now India and Pakistan. Much of his first novel, the second volume of which was published in 1944, is set within it and assumes a pre-Partition (1947) situation. Throughout the book we shall refer indifferently to 'India' or to 'the Indian sub-continent', taking this historical background for granted.
3. For the meaning of the phrase 'traditionãl Brahmin priest', see below, pp. 24-25.
4. This and subsequent statements in this paragraph about Ajneya's background and life are expanded and references given in Chapter One, pp. 28-47.
5. This was published in Delhi in two separate volumes in 1941 and 1944. It has not yet been translated into English. We use what is called on the fly leaf the 'current edition' [*vartmāna saṃskaraṇa*] 1975, but this is no different from the original. Indeed the Hindi word *saṃskaraṇa* translates both 'edition' and 'impression'. This means that without a detailed study of the texts concerned it is impossible to tell which is meant.

   The Hindi language has no capital letters, but for ease of reference we use them throughout the book to transliterate the first letter of words whose English equivalents would normally begin with a capital.

6. This was published in Delhi in 1951. We use the third edition (? impression), 1976. This is no different from the second which only differs from the first in two insignificant respects: the author tidies up certain infelicities of language, and where he uses other languages in the text provides Hindi translations. An English translation by Ajneya himself was published in New Delhi in 1980. For details of this see the Bibliography.
7. This was first published in Delhi in 1961. We use the third impression (? edition) of 1970 which does not differ from its two predecessors. An English translation by Ajneya himself and G C Roadarmel was published in Delhi in 1967. For details of this see the Bibliography.
8. This list is taken from Macve [1991] pp. 97-100.
9. Macve lists thirty-five volumes.(Macve [1991] pp. 101-4)
10. This work, entitled Preparing the Ground, is a translation, by Ajneya and Manas Mukul Das of Ajneya's second 'inner journal' *Antarā* (Delhi [1975]) which is no longer in print in India and is not in any Indological library in Britain .
11. See below pp. 76-7.
12. It is not necessary to subscribe to Tillich's total system in order to accept and use a small part of his analysis.
13. Here and elsewhere in the English translations of his own works Ajneya uses language which we would now describe as sexist. We have at no point amended these translations, but we recognise that given his own protest at the oppression of women, particularly in SL, he would, had he been writing today, certainly have used inclusive language.
14. For the reasons given in note 10 it has been impossible for the author to find a copy of the original Hindi version of this book, but the word translated 'Oversoul' is almost certainly *paramātmā* -- the Supreme Spirit of which human spirits or souls are often believed to be parts as sparks are parts of the fire, or droplets of the ocean. This is common Hindu belief at the popular level, and it is this view which is reflected in this passage. The philosopher-theologians would express matters with much more subtlety than this. See also Monier-Williams [1899] p. 588.
15. Tillich [1953] pp. 93-4. The parallel is not exact here, but the point is that for Tillich autonomy means 'autonomous reason' and Ajneya sees that this is an insufficient basis for human living.
16. Bonhoeffer's somewhat inchoate thoughts on this subject are to be found in the 'Outline for a Book' at the end of Letters and Papers from Prison,

    > Our relationship to God is not a religious relationship to a supreme Being, absolute in power and goodness, which is a spurious conception of goodness, but a new life for others, through participation in the Being of God. The transcendence consists not in tasks beyond our scope and power, but in the nearest thing to hand.(Bethge (ed) [1953] p. 179)
17. Later in the book we elaborate and provide evidence for all these assertions.
18. Again, we elaborate on these statements and provide supporting references at a later point in the book.
19. Some important contributions to this debate are: Hick [1973] and (ed) [1974]; Hick and Knitter (eds) [1987]; Griffiths [1978] and [1982]; Smith [1978] and [1980]; D'Costa [1986] and (ed) [1990]; Knitter [1985].

20. The key essay by Geertz is 'Religion as a Cultural System' which can be found in Banton (ed) [1965]. The importance of Wittgenstein for the subject is expounded by Kerr [1988].
21. Another weakness of Lindbeck's thesis is that he gives primary importance to language and neglects the significance of the visual element of human experience. An important corrective to this imbalance is to be found in Chidester [1992]. This is not a reason for rejecting Lindbeck, but for using him with caution.
22. The Buddha rejected the continuity of the *ātman* through successive rebirths, the inequalities of the caste system, and Vedic sacrifice. Muhammad preached against the polytheism practised in Mecca, while Guru Nanak rejected most of the externals of contemporary Hindu practice, including the use of images in worship and the practice of pilgrimage.
23. In the history of Christianity this is so obvious as to need no further reference. The main division in Judaism is that between Orthodox and Reformed schools, with Conservative as a third option in the USA, while the main division in Islam is between Sunnis and Shias.
24. Descartes attempted to build his philosophy on the basis of his own self-awareness -- *cogito ergo sum* -- and from there moved on to the ideas of his own mind. Whatever, as in mathematics, belonged to a logical and coherent whole was to be accepted as true. Descartes' method has had great influence. However,

    > Descartes radically misdescribes his own crisis and thus has proved a highly misleading guide to the nature of epistemological crises in general. The agent who is plunged into an epistemological crisi knows something very important: that a schema of interpretation which he has trusted so far has broken down irremediably in certain highly specific ways.

    (MacIntyre, 'Epistemological Crises, Dramatic Narrative, and the Philosophy of Science' in Hauerwas and Jones (eds) [1989] p. 143.) MacIntyre rejects Descartes' position on the grounds that all our experience is based on the narrative history of which our lives form a part: it follows that Descartes was not the isolated individual he supposed himself to be, but actually drew his insights from the past. Lindbeck rejects the Cartesian thesis on different grounds, but in fact he and MacIntyre are interdependent. Both imply that we all formulate our ideas as members of communities which are, whether or not their members actually realise it, heirs to traditions.
25. McFadyen's thesis has been revised and published as a book: McFadyen [1990].
26. In 1976 Ajneya wrote an essay in which he recognised the significance of language in a way comparable to Lindbeck and Wittgenstein. The essay is the introduction to an anthology of some of his poems which he translated into English with the help of L Nathan. He writes:

    > To use *language* to assert one's freedom from traditions -- what irony ! Language is our oldest, most rigorous, inescapable cultural tradition; to draw upon it to make our assertion -- and it is necessary to draw upon language to make any assertion -- makes the claim meaningless.(*Agyeya [1976] p. 15)

    He does not press his argument to include the community which uses the language, but we can claim that this is implicit in what he writes.

27. See Eagleton [1983] p. 19. The whole book is a valuable introduction to current literary theory.
28. Barton himself illustrates this by quoting from a short piece by the Argentinian writer J L Borges in which a character rewrites Cervantes Don Quixote 'using identically the same words as the original. Borges shows amusingly how this changes the meaning of every word of the text.' (Barton [1984] p. 173)

* Ajneya's name is occasionally anglicised in this fashion.

1

THE RELIGIOUS, SOCIAL AND POLITICAL CONTEXT OF AJNEYA'S NOVELS

We begin this chapter by elaborating what it means to describe Ajneya as a Hindu. This means locating him within that tradition and discovering what he knew of it through his up-bringing, education, and experience. This will then lead us into considering his early years in the context of the political and social movements in which he was caught up. This is important not simply as background to the novels, but even more so because the story of Shekhar, the leading character of SL, closely follows Ajneya's own early life. In the Introduction to SL Ajneya admits the links but explicitly claims that in spite of what the critics may say, the book is not an autobiography (SL Vol. 1 pp. 9-10). There are also traces of some events of his mature years in the career of Bhuvan, the main character of IS, though the links are significantly fewer than in SL. There are no such personal links with the content of TEHS, though in some of his other writings Ajneya has much to say about its background and genesis.

First then, what does it mean to say that Ajneya was a Hindu? It can be argued that Hinduism really consists of a number of inter-related regional traditions which have all changed during the course of their long history. Nonetheless, within the vastness and variety which make up these traditions there are a number of common threads which serve both to bind them all together into a kind of unity, and to make them recognisably different from other religious and cultural systems, with which in other ways they have much in common.(1) Three of these threads are important in beginning to describe the context within which Ajneya lived and wrote.

First is the fact that for most Hindus right practice or *dharma* (2) has normally been considered of greater importance than right belief. There is a common phrase in Hindi *'roṭī aur beṭī'*—'bread and daughter'—which is often used to express one important aspect of this. Social acceptability is defined by whom one is prepared to eat with and to whom one will marry one's daughters. To step outside the customary boundaries in these two areas of life, as many of Ajneya's characters do, is to lose one's status in society and therefore one's traditionally defined identity. By contrast one can be a monotheist, polytheist or atheist and still stay within these social limits. In other words identity is more a matter of right belonging than of right believing. It is also corporate rather than individual: 'I belong therefore I am'. It is therefore not surprising that although the question of whether or not God exists was important for some of Ajneya's characters, it was not the central question which pre-occupied them. In SL and IS they are more concerned with discovering a viable form of *dharma* because they believed that the traditional system was so oppressive and corrupt that it should be destroyed (in SL); or else as westernised characters they lived most of their lives outside it and so needed to find an alternative (in IS). TEHS stands apart from its two predecessors in that it is set in Europe, its two main characters are European, and they are deliberately placed in a context which cuts them off from society.

Second, the Hindu social order is based on the caste system.(3) This consists of a hierarchical structure of institutionalised inequality which has traditionally been held to be divinely sanctioned.(4) Again, there are regional variations.(5) Further, some scholars maintain that caste is to be understood as peculiar to the Indian sub-continent, and that it is therefore *sui generis,* while in the view of others it is a local variant of a much more widespread phenomenon, namely class structure.(6) Ajneya was born into a Brahmin or priestly family, and this fact conveniently limits the scope of this part of our enquiry. The Brahmins across India are by no means homogeneous in customs and life-style, but in all parts of the country they form the apex of the caste system. Traditionally they have always been privileged people, enjoying a high social status, but this has not always meant commensurate wealth and economic power. This, as we shall see below, was true of Ajneya's own grandfather. This high status carried with it important responsibilities. In particular the Brahmins are the guardians of the tradition of Sanskrit learning (7) which it is their duty to hand on to the next generation.(8) We shall see below how such learning formed an important part of Ajneya's early education.

The caste system has often been criticised by westerners for the inequalities which it creates, but it has always provided a tightly-knit structure of inter-dependence within which individuals have found both security and support, and a clear if relatively unchanging role which is defined by tradition. It is true that those at the bottom of the system have often been terribly oppressed and exploited by those above them, but the treatment of Jews and black people in western societies means that western Christians are hardly in a position to claim moral superiority over this sort of issue. Further, the worst excesses of caste have been challenged by movements which have arisen within Hinduism itself.(9) Hindi-language novelists have been among the fiercest critics of the dark side of caste, and in SL criticism both of caste and of the oppression of women is one of Shekhar's major pre-occupations.

The third thread which unites most parts of the Hindu tradition is belief in rebirth. As with the caste system here too a simple theoretical scheme is belied by a much more complex situation in reality. The key term is *karma* which means an action, and in particular religious action such as a sacrifice which is performed in the hope of some sort of gain. By extension from this ritual background the theory of *karma* maintains that every act has a consequence and that a person's lot in this life is determined by their good and bad actions in previous lives. *Dharma* provides the moral framework in whose terms the meaning of good and bad is discerned. The way in which *karma* is actually understood to function varies in different parts of the scriptures as it also does in society (Fuller [1992] 245-52]). The details of this need not concern us here for the point we are concerned to establish is that in Hindu belief we are not ultimately confined within the boundaries of our present human existence. We have all lived on this earth many times before and will return many times again.(10) What continues through successive lives—or 'births [*janma*]', to use the normal Hindu word—is the *ātman* or soul. A famous verse in the *Bhagavadgītā* says:

> As a man casts off his worn-out clothes And takes on other new ones [in their place], So does the embodied soul cast off his worn-out bodies And enters others new. (*Bhagavadgītā* 2.22, translated in Zaehner ed [1978] p. 256)

The *ātman* may be reborn not only in human but in animal or even insect form as well. Because life is thus perceived as being spread across a succession of earthly appearances instead of being limited to just one, history and historical events need not have the urgency and finality which they normally have for Christians, nor is there the same pressure for the individual to get everything right in this life. At the same time it is human existence alone which is recognised as the field of moral endeavour.(11) The differences between Hindu and Christian perceptions at this point should therefore not be exaggerated. Nevertheless they are real. From the Hindu side one could argue that it is the insistence on the necessity of getting everything right now, since this life is the only one we have, which has produced the dark and bloody history of Christianity. Burning people at the stake for supposedly deviant beliefs has never been Hindu custom.(12)

Of our three novels SL is the one in which traditional Hindu themes receive the most explicit treatment, but even here rebirth is hardly mentioned, though at one point Shekhar implicitly repudiates it in the light of evolutionary theory.(SL Vol. 1 p. 37). For him it appears that heaven and hell—which are also part of much traditional Hindu belief—are more important than rebirth. When he is living with a group of orthodox Brahmins in a student hostel in Madras he is appalled at the way in which outcaste students are prevented from coming anywhere near their mess. To allow them to do so would be to jeopardise the status of the Brahmins in the next world (SL Vol. 1 p. 207). Shekhar implicitly rejects such belief in the next world for reasons we investigate in Chapter Three. At this point we simply note that rebirth is often reconciled with heaven and hell by making the latter into temporary abodes between births.(13)

We have already seen that Ajneya was acutely conscious of the fact that he lived in 'times where scriptural texts do not suffice'.(14) This meant that as a Brahmin he could not fulfil his traditional role as guardian and teacher of the scriptures, yet as we saw in our quotations from *Antarā* in the Introduction he still felt a Brahmin's traditional responsibility for society. But what kind of Brahmin was he and how did he understand his new role in a rapidly changing world?

Before attempting an answer to that question we must say a word about our sources for his life. Two of these are primary: first, there are scattered references to his life in a volume of his essays entitled *Ātmanepad*.(15)(Ajneya [1960]) These references are supplemented by the transcript of an extended radio interview. This took place in 1984 and was published in 1993.(16) There is a considerable distance in time between both of these sources, especially of course the second, and many of the events to which they refer. Our secondary sources for Ajneya's life are works by other authors. There is a biography which we shall not use (17), but in addition several critical writers on Ajneya open their works with a biographical sketch. Few of these writers supply us with critical apparatus or footnotes and so we remain unsure of the sources of their information. However since the ones to whom we shall refer all knew Ajneya personally, and since when they cover the same ground they do not significantly disagree either with one another or with what Ajneya tells us himself in our two primary sources, we can be reasonably confident of their accuracy. We shall make use of three of them in this chapter.

First, in his biographical sketch Dr Gopal Ray (Ray [1975]) conveniently sets our author's life in the framework of contemporary political events, which at that time were almost exclusively those of India's struggle for independence from British rule. We shall use Ray's account when describing the young Ajneya's part in these events, but we shall need to give flesh to his framework from more extended and strictly historical accounts of the period. Second, we shall make use of Vidyanivas Mishra (Mishra [1990])(18), who is important because he does supplement what we learn from our author's own works. The following quotation captures the mood of his approach:

> As long as I have known him I have done so as a brother [*bhāī ke rūpa meṁ*], but as one who never claimed a brother's natural authority [*adhikār*]. What is it in his loving personality [*ātmīya*

> *vyaktitva*]...which at once touches one without being overwhelming, and without making any demands becomes diffident [*saṅkucit*]?(Mishra [1990] p. 3)

Those words suggest that Mishra is very much emotionally involved with his subject and that he is unlikely to maintain a critical distance from him. This calls for a degree of caution in our use of him. Thirdly, we shall make occasional use of a book by Prabhakar Macve (pronounced 'Marchway') (Macve [1991]), who unlike Ray and Mishra supplements his factual account of Ajneya's life with some shrewd critical comments on their subject.

We can now return to our question: what kind of Brahmin was Ajneya and how did he understand his new role in a rapidly changing world? He was of a '*Bhaṇot Sāraswat* Brahmin family from Kartarpur in Jalandhar', a district of the Punjab.(Mishra [1990] p. 5) 'Bhaṇot' refers to his *jāti* (19), while '*Sāraswat*' refers to the area where this *jāti* had its ancestral roots. His forebears were domestic priests [*purohit*]. He describes his immediate family background in these words:

> ...by the time my father retired he occupied a high post, but he got his elementary education in a Sanskrit school, where he lived with his *guru* (20), carried his wooden sandals and washed his garment. Having come first in his Matric. (*sic*) examination he won a scholarship through which he was able to complete his university course. He was appointed a Lecturer. In the university too he came first in all his examinations. From Lecturer he was made Research Fellow in the Archaeology Department and eventually Head, and this set his life in a new framework. [My] grandfather was a scholar [*vidvān*] of Sanskrit but he did not know the name of wealth. Although he lived in a condition of great poverty [*vipannāvasthā*] he was respected in society because of his knowledge [*vidyā*].(Vatsyayan [1983] p. 171)

Here we get a glimpse of the extraordinarily rapid expansion of horizons which took place in this family in the short space of three generations. The brief description of Ajneya's father's education is entirely in accord with tradition. Brahmin boys would often live with their teacher or *guru* who would not only teach them Sanskrit but would also expect them to perform menial tasks such as those described above. This gives us a valuable picture of Ajneya's traditional roots. When he describes his own education, which was very different from his father's, we shall see how some of that tradition was handed down to him. It will be important for our purposes to discover just what he studied in order at later stages in the book to see how he re-interpreted his inheritance. It will also be important to discern some of the western literary influences to which he was exposed and to learn what we can about his social and political attitudes. All these are points where knowledge of the author's background is important for understanding the text of the novels. A further point is that to understand the background of Ajneya is also to understand the background of Shekhar and thus better to understand the nature of his rebellion against it.

Having located our author within the context of Brahminical Hinduism we now turn to his life. Where this is directly reflected in parallel incidents in the novels we give the relevant page numbers in brackets.

Ajneya was born in 1911 at an archaeological site at Kasiya near Patna, where his father was working.(SL Vol. 1 p. 47) His first four years were spent in Lucknow (SL Vol. 1 pp. 67-9), where like most Brahmin boys he was taught the rudiments of Sanskrit from a very early age. He tells us himself that he learnt to repeat the *Aṣṭādhyāyī* by heart and remembered the 'loving rebukes' of his *paṇḍit*, or teacher. *Aṣṭādhyāyī* literally means 'The Eight Chapters'. These were attributed to the grammarian *Pāṇini*.(21) A child starting to learn Sanskrit in the traditional way would, like Ajneya, begin by learning these chapters by heart. From 1915-19 the family lived in Srinagar, in Kashmir.(SL Vol. 1 pp. 79 and 102) There he was taught the *Raghuvaṅśa*, the *Bāla Rāmāyaṇa* and the *Bāla Mahābhārata* by another Sanskrit *paṇḍit*.(Mishra [1990] p. 6) The *Raghuvaṅśa* is a long poem by Kalidasa [Kālidāsa], the most famous of Sanskrit poets, and describes the legendary history of a line of famous kings, one of whom was Rama [*Rāma*], whose adventures were originally described in the Epic that bears his name, the *Rāmāyaṇa*. The *Mahābhārata*, one of the longest books in the world, is a vast compendium of myth, law and philosophy. The word *Bāla* before the titles of these two Epics means 'children's'. The young Ajneya's first acquaintance with these two works was thus through (presumably) shortened children's editions.

Ajneya himself supplements Mishra's account of his early education in his extended radio interview. He says that there were often arguments in the family home based on the *Rāmāyaṇa* and the *Mahābhārata*. He says that he read the *Vālmīki Rāmāyaṇa* (22) in the original in spite of the fact that he did not know Sanskrit—by which he presumably means that he did not know it well enough to read fluently.(Lele [1993] pp. 22-3). This evidence for familiarity with the *Rāmāyaṇa* will be important in Chapter Three where we shall argue that at an important point in his second novel he may be deliberately re-interpreting a passage from this Epic.

He also makes another point in the interview in reply to the question why he had never written a long epic poem as most poets before him had done:

> In the tradition of those who were writers before me, up until Gupta-ji (23) no-one could be called a great poet until he had not only written a long poem [*mahākāvya*], but one based on a famous story [*prasiddha kathā*] taken from the *Mahābhārata* and *Rāmāyaṇa*...I do not think that a modern epic can be written in that kind of metrical verse [*bandhe hue chanda*]. The modern 'epic' is the novel.(Lele [1993] p. 162)

Ajneya here is in one sense cut off from his inheritance in that he finds a traditional literary form unusable, yet at the same time he is still engaged with it as he shows by comparing the functions of the traditional epic and the modern novel. Thus he almost if not quite claims that novels in general—and so *a fortiori* his own—re-interpret tradition in form if not in content.

His upbringing was not of course confined to literature, and Mishra tells us that at home the family practised the rituals of *Smārta* Brahmins who accept a wider group of authoritative texts than other Brahmins (Mishra [1990] p. 6), but during his lifetime our author hung very lightly to the ritual aspects of his tradition.(24) His education included other things besides Sanskrit learning. He was taught *Śekh Sādī* by a Muslim *maulvī*. This is a book used to teach Urdu [*Urdū*] to children. Urdu was the language of culture and administration under the Moghul Empire and was commonly learnt by educated and cultured Hindus as well as Muslims. He was also taught English by an American padre (25), though this man built on foundations laid by Ajneya's father:

> I could speak 200-250 English words before I knew the letters of the alphabet, and began to speak the language.(Vatsyayan [1983] p. 21)

We note that as a boy Ajneya learnt three languages, (though none of them was the one in which he was to win his literary reputation). This is not uncommon for Indian children and reflects the linguistic complexity of the country. Like other writers of the period he used both Urdu and English words in his novels where he felt that these were appropriate.

His early education took place at home because his father had no faith in modern school education, nor did he send his son to the kind of traditional Sanskrit school which he had attended himself.(SL Vol. 1 pp. 55 and 161) In 1919 he went with his father to Nalanda, (where presumably the latter's work as an archaeologist took him). His father began to make him write Hindi. He favoured a simple and pure form of the language and was totally opposed to Hindustani.(26) The family then moved to Patna and here 'the seed of Saccidananda's revolt against English sprang into life'.(27) Tantalisingly, Mishra, who includes this comment in his account of this period, gives no further details.(Mishra [1990] p. 7)(SL Vol. 1 pp. 108-40) In 1921 Ajneya's father was transferred to Ootacamund, a hill station in the Nilgiri Hills of South India.(SL Vol. 1 pp. 159-63) The family were now removed from the storm centre of politics in the North—of which we shall have more to say in a moment. Here Ajneya began to develop a love for nature, study, and writing. He also learnt to appreciate solitude:

> I was a natural lover of solitude [*ekāntapriya*] and circumstances kept me alone, but living in a bungalow...three miles from Ootacamund I became as it were immersed [*ḍūb hī gayā*] in solitude—though a solitude that was full of the pulsating life of nature. We were not worried by the fact that outside the family no-one could understand a word we spoke, and that we could not understand a single word of anybody else !(Vatsyayan [1983] p. 22)(SL Vol. 1 pp. 159-63)

Ajneya expands on this passage elsewhere:

> It is perhaps correct to say that our affections [*sneha-bhāva*] were not displayed, but to say they were not there is a mistake. You won't find in our family the confident expression [of affection]

> that you find in other families. Most of our childhood was spent in country or mountain areas, all of us aquired a free [*svatantra*] or independent nature [*ātma-nirbhar svabhāva*], and almost all of us to some extent became introverted.(Vatsyayan [1983] p. 174)(34)

Yet there was a dark side to his family life: we learn from Mishra that he was very close to and learnt much from his elder sister (SL Vol. 1 pp. 78-80, 88-9, 132-3 and 143-4) but in 1975 he wrote: 'He (sc my father) and the whole family have for years broken all relations with me—I have been considered as dead.'(Ajneya [1984] p. 88)(28). Mishra refers to his tense and strained relationships with his family (Mishra [1990] p. 8) and this forms a powerful and important theme in SL.(SL Vol. 1 pp. 25 and 179) Macve adds that his participation in the revolutionary movement and his experience in jail formed a cocoon around him which others could not penetrate. He revealed himself to no-one and lived up to his pen-name (29), he never committed himself to others in his life and embodied Sartre's principle, 'the other is hell [*dūsarā narak hai*]'.(Macve [1991] pp. 6-9) (30) Ajneya's own brief account of these years is further supplemented by Mishra who tells us of his continuing education in Sanskrit in the South: he was taught Sanskrit through the medium of Tamil for six months. (This hardly squares with Ajneya's own comment that the family were cut off from their neighbours because they could not speak the language. Perhaps he picked up some elementary Tamil.) He also read the *Bhagavadgītā* for the first time.

This completes our picture of the extent of Ajneya's early education in Sanskrit. What is not mentioned is as significant as what is. We note in particular that there is no mention of philosophy. In his later years he made no secret of his ignorance of this subject, claiming that he was a writer, not a philosopher.(31) In both IS and TEHS we find the characters indulging in philosophical discussion, but none of them lay claim to any profound technical grasp of the subject. This fact imposes certain limits on the possibilities of our conversation with the novels. What Ajneya does is re-interpret the symbolic framework rather than the intellectual content of that part of Brahminical Hinduism within which he was nurtured.

Ajneya's social attitudes are also important for our purposes. His father rejected discrimination on the grounds of caste but hoped his sons would always adhere to those qualities which he regarded as being at the heart of the Brahmin ideal—'renunciation, fearlessness, and truth [*tyāga, abhaya aur satya*]'.(Mishra [1990] p. 8) Ajneya took this further in his radio interview. He says it is wrong to think that the form of *dharma* is permanently fixed at any one time. By its very nature it is constantly changing. In particular he agrees with his interviewer that 'the caste system, many kinds of rituals, [social distinctions between] high and low, discrimination on the grounds of caste, and untouchability' must all be re-interpreted according to modern needs.(Lele [1993] p. 53) He adds:

> I regard untouchability as wholly unacceptable [*agrāhya*]. I have never given it any place in my own life. I regard the caste system too as an enormous social injustice [*sāmājik anyāya*]. All these things should be broken down, and they very easily can be too, beginning with oneself.(Lele [1993] p. 54)

We find these attitudes powerfully reflected in SL (eg Vol. 1 pp. 215-33), indeed, as we pointed out in the Introduction, we shall argue in Chapter Three that in this first novel Ajneya is attempting to reshape the traditional internal boundaries of Hindu society in the interests of social justice. This means that caste discrimination and the oppression of women are especial targets of his criticism.

At his father's insistence he read the Scriptures of other religions, and we shall refer to his use of the Bible in subsequent chapters. He also made good use of his father's well-furnished library, reading, so Mishra tells us, the poetry of Wordsworth, Shelley, Tennyson, Longfellow and Whitman; the plays of Shakespeare, Marlowe and Webster; and the novels of Lytton, George Eliot, Thackeray, Goldsmith, Tolstoy, Turgenev, Gogol, Victor Hugo and Melville. Even for a precociously intelligent boy in his early teens this list is hard to credit.(SL Vol. 1 p. 153) We can legitimately assume that Mishra is projecting back into these early years reading which was actually done later.(Mishra [1990] p. 7) Ajneya put this and his later reading to good use for there are many quotations from English authors in IS. More profoundly, as we observed in the Introduction, Indian critics have shown how deeply influenced his novels were by western literary models.(32)

In 1925 the family left the South and returned to Lahore, in the Punjab (SL Vol. 2 p. 9), to a tense and violent political situation. This we must briefly describe.(33) Contemporary historians stress the continuities in the emergence of modern India: neither the establishment of British rule nor its demise fractured these continuities. At the time when Ajneya was growing up political activity and awareness were spread unevenly across the country and in different segments of society. We pick up the story during the First World War: Britain and her allies claimed to be fighting the war on the basis of high moral principles, such as the 'rights of nations'. Not surprisingly Indian politicians began to argue that these same principles should be applied in their own country.(Brown [1985] p. 190) The British rulers of India responded to these demands with 'a carefully balanced combination of reform and repression'.(Brown [1985] p. 194) In 1919 the Rowlatt Act was passed in the Indian Legislative Council in order to strengthen the hand of the government in its struggle against political violence. The Punjab was identified as a province particularly prone to this.(Brown [1985] p. 196)

Although the Act quickly lapsed and its main provisions were never actually put into effect, its enactment led to Gandhi's appearance on the stage of all-India politics. In protest against the Rowlatt Act he asked his followers to abandon their normal occupations on a particular day and spend the time in fasting and prayer instead. Violence broke out in the Punjab and martial law was proclaimed in Amritsar, the state capital. It was in a walled enclosure in this city that troops under the orders of General Dyer shot and killed over three hundred unarmed civilian protesters. This was the notorious Jallianwalla Bagh massacre. It was one of the main factors which led Gandhi to proclaim a movement of non-violent non-co-operation with the government in 1920. The movement

> marked a major change in the depth and dimensions of concerted political hostility to the *raj*. Never before had the British faced a continental campaign against their rule, master-minded by Congress, drawing support from deep within the provinces.(Brown [1985] p. 217)

The campaign lasted until 1922 when Gandhi abruptly suspended it because, according to Ray, of an outbreak of violence in the United Provinces. This left a political vacuum which was to some extent filled by a number of underground revolutionary movements.(Gopal Ray [1975] p. 24)

By the time the family returned to the Punjab in 1925 Ajneya was fourteen, and already he was being drawn into a rudimentary political awareness. He remembered an incident on a train, when an Englishman had returned half-naked from the bathroom into his compartment in which Indian women were present. He laughed when Ajneya's father rebuked him for his bad manners, and so his father turned the man off the train.(34) Ajneya also studied in a school with English boys for two or three months, an experience which he did not enjoy. He was involved in a playground fight with some of them and this led the head teacher to give him a card complaining of his conduct, to show to his father, but Ajneya simply threw the card away.(Mishra [1990] p. 8)(SL Vol. 1 p. 54) He took his Matriculation privately and returned to the South for two years (1925-27). During this period he was a student at Madras Christian College, where his subjects were maths, physics, chemistry and Sanskrit. It was at this time that he became aware of the appalling way in which South Indian Brahmins treated the outcastes.(35)(SL Vol. 1 pp. 207-10)

Mishra tells us that Ajneya returned to the North in 1927 and enrolled for his B.Sc. in Forman Christian College, Lahore.(SL Vol. 2 pp. 9-11) He was much influenced by two College teachers at this time: one of these was J M Banade, a physics teacher who urged him to make a comparative study of the different religions. We learn more of his influence from a collection of essays Ajneya later wrote about his travels in India during the Second World War:

> Professor B (*sic*) was my physics teacher. Besides physics, because of being connected to a mission institution he had to take some classes in Christian religious instruction. I was in one of his classes but I do not remember him saying anything to any of us about Christian religious doctrine [*Īsāī dharma ke siddhāntoṁ kī bāt*] in a way that was separate from our own religions. On the contrary, it was only in his 'Bible class' that we made an extensive and detailed study of Radhakrishnan's Hindu View of Life, and it was there that we were introduced to the thought of Confucius and Lao-Tse, Buddha and *Śaṅkara*, Pascal and Spinoza. He often used to say that 'To follow one's own religion with full discrimination [*vivekapūrṇa*] is true Christianity'. Sometimes he also used to say, 'It is expected of me that I will make more and

> more Christians. At present I do not know which of you is a Christian and which is not, but if ever anyone comes to me having changed his religion I will know this much, that he at least is no true Christian'...When he explained Christian belief he spoke only of the doctrine of substitutionary atonement [*pratinidhik śodha*], which he held to be a great truth of human life: in his view it was the foundation of the doctrine of non-violence [*ahiṃsā*].(Vatsayayan [1953] pp. 85-6)

Banade was evidently a man of wide sympathies who rejected the over-simplicities of the traditional missionary approach to Hindus. This picture of him demonstrates that concern about the relationship between Christian faith and other faiths is not a new issue. The reference to the doctrine of substitutionary atonement is also important. Ajneya explains its significance in a footnote for the benefit of his Indian readers:

> The doctrine of the Christian religion that a person's sin [*ek ke pāp*] can be purified [*kī śuddhi*] by the penance [*tapasyā*] or suffering [*kaṣṭa-sahan*] of another—of which the shining example is Jesus' choosing of the cross for the forgiveness [*pāp-mocan*] of the sins of the human race [*mānavatā*]. (Vatsyayan [1953] p. 85)

He makes important use of this theme towards the end of SL.(Vol. 2 p. 80)

Banade's was by no means the only influence to which the young Ajneya was exposed at this time. With some companions he organised his own secret political cell. Though while he was at College he was not actively involved in revolutionary activity he was to be so later. In 1929 he was, like Shekhar in SL, a volunteer officer for the Congress session which met under the leadership of Motilal Nehru, father of independent India's first Prime Minister.(SL Vol. 2 pp. 33-45) He passed his B.Sc. and then entered for the M.A. course in English. His own revolutionary cell joined the Hindustan Socialist Republican Association about which we shall have more to say below. His career as a revolutionary lasted from 1929 until 1936. He distributed tracts and collected weapons, and then he and his companions planned to secure the release from jail of Bhagat Singh, a leading anti-British revolutionary of the time.(36) However, the plan was cancelled because one of their number was 'martyred through an accident [*ek durghaṭnā se śahīd hue*]'.(Mishra [1990] p. 9; Lele [1993] pp. 120-1)(SL Vol. 1 p. 34)(37)

Ajneya was involved in establishing a bomb-making factory in Delhi (SL Vol. 2 p. 213)—under the cover of a workshop called The Himalayan Toilets Factory(!).(SL Vol. 2 pp. 215-6) Here he was 'scientific adviser'.(38) He then took part in establishing a weapon repair shop in Amritsar. It was here that he was arrested with two companions in November 1930. He was released from one charge under the Arms Act, but arrested in Delhi on a new charge of conspiracy in 1931, and the case against him went on until 1933. During this period he was held in solitary confinement in Delhi jail where he made good use of his time. He devoted himself to study and wrote extensively.(Mishra [1990] pp. 9-10) His experience in prison had a profound effect on him. In SL Shekhar is arrested at a Congress camp and spends ten months in jail.(Vol. 2 pp. 49-99). At the end of Volume Two he is still free but the whole novel is a description of Shekhar's life written in jail while he is under sentence of death. The arrest and trial which led to the death sentence were presumably to be part of the projected third volume which was never published.

Ajneya's—and so Shekhar's—involvement in revolutionary activity needs to be more precisely located in its contemporary context in the Punjab. The Congress Party in the state had been founded in 1890. Its aim throughout India was to be a comprehensive party including both Hindus and Muslims in its membership, but its support in the Punjab was to remain limited because of mutual suspicion between Hindus who formed 31% of the population and Muslims who formed 55%. (11% were Sikhs and the remaining 3% consisted of various minority groups). As we have seen, in 1920-1921 the first Non-Co-operation Movement achieved considerable public support, but this was to prove ephemeral. Even by the mid-thirties the Party was still largely confined to urban areas and had failed to mobilise significant rural support, largely because the Hindus suspected it of being too conciliatory towards the Muslims. (Heeger [1972] p. 40) Hence the political vacuum to which reference was made above. (Ray is too simplistic in explaining this vacuum simply in terms of Gandhi's abrupt suspension of the Non-co-operation Movement). Into it there moved various revolutionary groups. Whereas in Bengal and Maharashtra such groups used the symbols of Hinduism to attract support, their contemporaries in the Punjab were secular.(Mohan [1985] pp. 7-8) They shared with Congress the goal of independence for India but disagreed about the means to achieve it. In their view Congress was too bourgeois in its membership and too timid in its methods.(Mohan [1985] pp. 210-1) Even though the revolutionaries were not actually Marxist they looked for inspiration to the still recent Russian revolution of 1917. Prominent among the organisations which were active during these years was the Hindustan Socialist Republican Association which deliberately set about attracting students to its cause and to which reference was made above.(Mohan [1985] pp. 7-8 and 209). The mood of this movement is caught in the following quotation from its manifesto which was issued in 1929:

> Upheavals have always been a terror to holders of powers and privileges. But Revolution is a phenomenon which nature loves and without which there can be no progress either in nature or human affairs...Revolution may be anti-God but it is certainly not anti-man. It is a vital living force which is indicative of eternal conflict between the Old and the New, between Life and Living Death, between Light and Darkness. There is no concord, no symphony, no rhythm without revolution.(Mohan [1985] p. 201)

In SL we find Shekhar indulging in a similar kind of heady rhetoric:

> Come all you revolutionaries [*vidrohiyo*]; first destroy this fraud! Know, understand, proclaim that we are not the enemies [*virodhī*] of this or that piece of bad organisation...we want to change everything. The driving passion of our revolt [*vidrohī preraṇā*] is against religion, society, political power, economic power, and in the end against our own personality [*apne vyaktitva*]!(SL Vol. 1 p. 28)

The fact that Ajneya joined the revolutionary movement was therefore not strange, for many of his contemporaries did so as well, and the fact that in the Punjab that movement was secular in its inspiration naturally helped to move his thinking in a secular direction. Had he lived at this period of his life in Bengal or Maharashtra he would have been a very different kind of novelist. Yet he wrote later that he did not remain a convinced member of the revolutionary party.(Vatsyayan [1983] p. 56)(39) This too is reflected in SL for we shall see in later chapters that while Shekhar's social thinking and writing was revolutionary, membership of a revolutionary party was secondary and of much less significance.(SL Vol. 2 pp. 232-6)

Ajneya spent four years in jail and for a further two years after his release was under police supervision (1931-36). We learn from Ray that while he was in prison he saw no newspapers and had no contact with the outside world apart from such news as he could glean from newly arrived prisoners. He was allowed to write one letter a month to his family. Yet it was during this time that he wrote a volume of poetry (40), his first collection of short stories (41), and an early draft of SL (Mishra [1990] p. 9) These he managed to smuggle out of the prison with the aid of Jainendra Kumar [*Jainendra Kumār*], another Hindi writer and revolutionary. Kumar shewed them to Prem Chand [*Prem Cand*], who was a leading Hindi novelist and editor of a literary journal. Prem Chand wanted to publish the stories and asked for the name of the author. Kumar replied that it was *ajñeya*—'unknowable'—by which he meant: 'It is not safe to tell you.' Prem Chand published the stories under this pseudonym which our author continued to use.(Lele [1993] p. 115)(42) The use of such pen names is so common as to be almost normal among Hindi authors. This period of Ajneya's life was, in the words of Mishra, 'a time of great spiritual turmoil, physical suffering, and the pain of shattered dreams'.(Mishra [1990] pp. 9-10) All of this we find powerfully reflected in SL.

In addition to all these influences, we must now ask how far his life in the next few years can shed light on the text of his second novel, IS, which was published in 1951. The story is set against the background of the Second World War. Ajneya's most significant public act during this period of his life was to join the army in order to fight against the Japanese—on the face of it an astonishing *volte face* for someone who had so recently been in jail for taking part in revolutionary violence against British rule. In March 1943 he wrote a long letter in which he justified this decision:

> I am among those whose belief [*viśvāsa*] is that this war must be fought—and that to take part in it is our duty. It is my belief that on the outcome of this war depends the well-being [*hitoṁ kā*] of the world-wide international community. Therefore I also believe this, in this war national [*rāṣṭrīya*]—a single country's—interests [*hit*] are of secondary importance...The argument that India will achieve independence if the Fascist side wins is so empty and crude that to answer it is unnecessary. (Vatsyayan [1983] p. 300-1)

Bhuvan, the leading male character of IS, also joins the army and justifies his decision in very similar terms.(IS pp. 281-2 and 312) Further, Mishra tells us that in the years between his release from police supervision and the outbreak of war (1936-39) Ajneya's political views had changed. He could now respect Gandhi and Nehru in a way he had not found possible before.(Mishra [1990] p. 11)

Ajneya makes another point in this letter:

> I have an experience—albeit indistinct [*aspaṣṭa anubhava*] — that there is a larger life than this one—for which I cannot offer [*utsarga*] myself fully—I am standing on the edge of madness but stop myself from going completely mad...but that greater [dimension] [*viśāltar*] is so private [*nijī*], as private as one's faith [*āsthā*] which is personal to an individual [*jo vyakti ke pās rahatī hai*], but even so, as it is separate from life it does not interfere in life...I cannot say whether you get my point or not—whether I even deserve to be understood or not.(Vatsyayan [1983] p. 303)

Ajneya here is struggling for words and words fail him—he almost lapses into incoherence—but it is apparent that he has travelled a long way from the crude atheism of SL. He is struggling to express his belief in a transcendent dimension to life, but does not turn to any of the traditional formulations of such a belief. Towards the end of IS we find Gaura, one of the two main female characters of the book, arguing against Bhuvan that such transcendence is indeed possible. (IS p. 325)(43)

The War was not the only formative influence in Ajneya's experience during these years. In common with many of his generation he was disappointed with the fruits of Independence which was finally achieved in 1947. We see this reflected in some of his critical writing. For example in one passage, part of an essay published in 1960, he compares the thirties to the post-Independence period:

> The young man of 1930-1935 was not jealous of his elders' generation: there was no need for him to be jealous. The knowledge kept coursing through his mind that some great [event] [*kuch bahut baṛā*] would soon be happening in which he would take part. His life was perpetually full of hope [*āśā*] and the call of the unknown future [*anāgata ke āhvāna*]. But the young man of today knows great events happened before [his time]: and when he looks at the previous generation then he does so with the feeling

> that these people took part in those great events. Because of this he also feels that he is separate from those events, he is rootless [*ucchinna*], and is filled with jealousy towards the previous generation. (Vatsyayan [1983] p. 90)

Ajneya's disappointment embraced more than dashed political hopes. It included the fact that he was disturbed by the parlous condition of Hindi literature. He attacked his fellow-writers for the superficiality of their concerns:

> To-day's Hindi literature is mostly a literature of dissatisfaction [*atṛpti*] or you could say of greed [*lālsā*] or wishful thinking, a dream world of wish-fulfilment.... (Vatsyayan [1945] p. 47)

But his complaints go deeper and wider than purely literary issues. In 1945 he wrote of the erosion of the ties that had held traditional society together:

> The point is not simply that our life has ceased to be rural [*dehātī*] and has become urban [*śaharī*]. It is not just the framework of life that has changed but life itself. Now society is neither rural nor urban, now its very organisation [*saṅgaṭhan hi*] is destroyed. There is no thread [*sūtra*] to hold it together in unity. People choose where to live on the basis of convenience and no longer have any living relationship [*jīvit sambandh*], the connection of [what] flows in the veins, with their neighbours. The only link is of geographical proximity.(Vatsyayan [1945] p. 14)

This sense of disappointment is reflected in IS in several ways. Two male characters, Chandramadhava and Hemendra, embody the worst features of westernised urban society. We have already seen how Ajneya was fiercely critical of this. But in addition to this all four main characters are much more detached from contemporary events than Shekhar was. Even though the novel is set in the war years, the war itself serves as hardly more than a back-cloth to the novel itself. In this detachment from society and from events we can possibly discern a modern version of a very ancient pattern. Hindu life is traditionally divided into four stages, student, householder, forest dweller and recluse.(44) The last two stages represent withdrawal from society, in which a man has by now fulfilled his obligations. While few follow this pattern literally to-day, it is not uncommon to find it so to speak transposed into a modern key. People may be deeply involved in public life during their early years but they then withdraw from it, perhaps in disillusionment, in middle and later life. The South Indian Christian theologian M M Thomas has drawn attention to this pattern in the lives of several well known modern figures.(Thomas [1967] pp. 120-6) He observes that

> When Achyut Patwardhan and Jayaprakash Narain (sic) of the Socialist party of India moved away from the ideology of liberal Marxism or socialist secularism, the former in 1950 into Theosophy and the latter in 1957 into the experience of the 'unity of existence' of advaitic (45) mysticism they also resigned from their responsibilities of leadership in party and power politics, that is withdrew from a very significant segment of history.(pp. 121-2)

Ajneya's last two novels seem to reflect something of this trend. In IS there are only four characters. Others appear as shadows on the edges of the story—as coolies or domestic servants, as fellow-residents of a house, or fellow-passengers in a train, but none of them emerge as real people. The story is hardly a story at all, it is a description of a changing pattern of relationships between two men and two women, three of whom are themselves in different ways detached from traditional society and its values. In TEHS this trend is pushed to the furthest possible extreme for the two characters are deliberately cut off from the rest of the world in their mountain hut buried under the snow. In this progressive withdrawal from society our novels may reveal an undercurrent of traditional Hindu thought and life which is not apparent on the surface. Nor is it apparent if each novel is considered in isolation from the other two. In other words it is not only the author's life and background which are at certain points necessary adjuncts to interpreting the text, but each of the novels is important for the interpretation of the others. To read each of them in the light of the other two is a different exercise from reading it as if the other two did not exist. We are arguing here for a modified version of what in biblical studies is known as 'canonical criticism'.(46) A text is to be interpreted not on its own but in relationship to other texts in the Canon. But we use this as a tool only. The texts have to be considered on their own as well.

This contrast between SL on the one hand and IS, and even more TEHS, on the other is striking: it raises profound questions about the relationship of character to event, to action and to story. These we shall have to pursue in Chapter Six and they are germane to the central concerns of this book. They will lead us to address to Ajneya's novels the question implicit in the quotation from M M Thomas, but Ajneya may well have counter-questions of his own which challenge our argument. To say, as he does, that the artist can only change himself, and should not attempt to change society through his writings(47), looks on the face of it like withdrawal from society, but it could be interpreted not as a withdrawal but as a much more profound form of engagement. There are some Christian resonances here: Christ's deliberate embrace of the way of the cross could be interpreted as a withdrawal from public ministry, yet when the Johannine Christ says, 'for their sake I now consecrate myself' (John 17.19), does he not point to a much more profound engagement with the issues which lay at the heart of that ministry? It is also possible to exaggerate the extent of Ajneya's withdrawal. It was only from direct political activity. After leaving the army at the end of the War he made his living for the rest of his life by editing a succession of journals and newspapers, in which he often commented on public affairs. Yet it is also true that he was always a very private person and had only a small circle of friends.(Macve [1991] p. 6) He pointed out himself that living in such a restricted social circle made it difficult to write novels.(48)

Apart from those we have already described there are other parallels in IS to Ajneya's personal life: Bhuvan is a scientist who at one point goes on an expedition to Kashmir for the study of cosmic rays. Ajneya himself was also trained in science and once went on a similar expedition(49), but much more important than this, in a tantalisingly brief sentence Mishra makes reference to the fact that in 1940 Ajneya made the serious mistake of getting married in a civil ceremony and that this marriage was a source of 'great pain' to him.(Mishra [1990] p. 11) In his radio interview he briefly admits that this marriage was a mistake (Lele [1993] p. 161), but says no more about it. Did he join the army partly in order to escape from his unhappy marriage? There seems to be a wholly understandable reticence in our sources about this side of his life. Yet the central theme of the novel is the unhappy marriage of Rekha and her love affair with Bhuvan. Furthermore, during the course of the novel Rekha's divorce is a central issue and the whole question of divorce was very much in the air in 1951, when the novel was published. In 1954 the Hindu Code Bill was promulgated. For the first time this allowed divorce by mutual consent and so gave a new freedom to women.(50) At the end of the novel Bhuvan is about to marry not Rekha but Gaura and it is possible that her character is modelled on Ajneya's second wife.

In the ten years between the publication of IS (1951) and TEHS (1961) what additional developments had there been in Ajneya's life and thought which can shed light on TEHS? The critic R S Chaturvedi says that in these years he recovered his confidence [*āsthā*],(*sc* in a dimension of transcendence) and that this was partly due to periods he spent in a Christian monastery in France and a Zen monastery in Japan.(Chaturvedi [1968] p. 90) The word Chaturvedi uses—*āsthā*—can mean confidence or hope.(Monier-Williams [1899] p. 161) As here, its object is not necessarily clearly focussed but it is often used in a religious sense. If Chaturvedi is right and it was indeed these monastic visits which stimulated even if they did not actually create this recovery, then the word *āsthā* seems appropriate, for Ajneya does not seem to have felt any compulsion to choose between Zen and Christianity. Certainly in TEHS there is evidence of faith in a dimension of transcendence on the part of Selma, but as we shall see it is a faith which lacks definition or particular content.

In 1955 Ajneya toured Europe for a year at the invitation of UNESCO. This visit he describes at length in his second travel book, Ek Būnda Sahasā Uchalī.(A Drop Suddenly Popped Up)(51) His tour included a visit to Scandanavia which made a considerable impact on him and it seems that it was experiences in Sweden that gave him the seminal idea for TEHS:

> A question which I had given much thought to twenty five-years previously when I was in jail and which I had tried to elucidate in some form in my writing—in poetry, in novel, even in drama ! —that same question welled up in a new form. Talk of people committing suicide by jumping from a lift in Stockholm, [and] an unwanted and heated debate with a Swedish poet about life and death [*jīvan aur maraṇa*], brought that question to a focus—what does it feel like to be face to face with death in solitude [*ekānta meṁ mṛtyu se sākṣāt hone par*]? (Vatsyayan [1988] p. 164)

A description of her own experience by a Swedish woman shed a glimmer of light for him on the problem of how to tackle this question:

> This writer was imprisoned for the whole winter in a mountain hut with someone who was seriously ill with cancer—owing to an unexpected snowfall all paths to the hut were blocked. One person waiting for death [*mṛtyu kī pratīkṣā kartā huā ek vyakti*], and another person watching her, trying to cover it up and yet also wanting it—here before me was the perfect example of my problem: cut off from all connections with anything else it was placed in a void [*śūnya*]!(Vatsyayan [1988] p. 164)

In an interview which was given in 1960—just before TEHS was published—Ajneya spoke again of the novel:

> The characters are foreigners. It is difficult and perhaps inappropriate to say what the story [*kathāvastu*] is but the theme [*vastu*] (I hope you are not going to ask me to explain the difference between the story and the theme!) is about being face to face with death [*mṛtyu se sākṣātkār*]. It (shows how) being face to face with death makes one's friends [*apnoṁ ko*] into strangers [*ajnabī*] and strangers into friends, and how death itself is for some people a friend and for others a stranger. This is the theme of the novel. There is a comparison in the book between the East's acceptance [*svīkār-bhāva*] of death, and the West's hostility [*virodha-bhāva*] to it, though what I call the eastern view [*dṛṣṭi*] is symbolised in a western character. But I do not think I should impose what is in the novel on you or on the future reader. The novel will be coming out soon, please read it for yourself!(Vatsyayan [1983] pp. 326-7)

In a later interview, published in the same volume, he says that the novel is about the relationships which develop between the two characters Selma and *Yoke* (pronounced 'Yokay') through their mutual inter-actions, and about the relationship of the individual with time. In this passage the bracketed sections are all Ajneya's own:

> You could say that time [*kāla*] is the chief character. All the characters have their own 'strangers'. With strangers there are two kinds of relationship, first, complete denial, as for example when Yoke tries to deny the existence of death; or second, later acceptance [*svīkār*], confidence or trust [*āsthā yā śraddhā*], or belief which has no supporting evidence [*akāraṇa viśvāsa*], as when Yoke accepts Jagannathan [*Jagannāthan*] as a good man without any evidence as a basis for so doing. Only 'belief which has no supporting evidence' is really trust [*śraddhā*]. Yoke, who denies death, in the end finally (with the aid of trust?) comes before

> another stranger (God?). In this she finds freedom [*svatantratā*] (freedom of choice [*varaṇa*], or freedom even from choice?) Yoke who denies death, and who therefore lives for the moment [*kṣaṇajīvī*], is mortal and kills herself, but in doing so she touches a kind of immortality [*amaratva*]. For 'to die in the presence of a good man' is surely in another way to go on living through the proof of the good man's witness. But even this immortality is left for the reader to guess at, Yoke does not recognise it herself. This immortality too is a 'stranger'. So in the title 'To Each His Stranger' there are 'inner symbols of symbols [*pratīkoṁ ke phir antaḥpratīk*]', and the possibility of the 're-echoes of echoes' that there could not have been in any other title.(Vatsyayan [1983] pp. 330)

His interviewer also asked why Ajneya had chosen a foreign setting and foreign characters for this novel. He says that he thought long and hard about the right context in which to cut his two characters off from the rest of the world. He thought about an earthquake, and even visited Bihar to have a look at a coal mine to see if he could have them buried underground in a mining accident. Then the setting under an avalanche of snow began to seem the most fitting. He could have set this in the Himalayas, but then the problem would have been that all the characters would have represented that point of view which he calls 'eastern'. (Vatsyayan [1983] p. 330-1) These remarks are not entirely consistent with the account in *Ek Būndā Sahasā Uchalī*, but perhaps they refer to the earlier stages of the gestation of the novel in his mind. In that case his visit to Sweden crystallised ideas which were already there.

He speaks to his interviewer more specifically on the characters of TEHS:

> The characters [*pātra*] and the events [*ghatnāeṁ*] are not completely foreign [*videśī*], though to call them foreign is not entirely mistaken. In fact the reason why only the smallest indication of country was given was to put the whole thing in a context which was independent of country. Naked human existence [*mānavīya sattā (yā astitva) mātra*] is put before the reader (Vatsyayan [1983] p. 330)

Thus in this novel the withdrawal from society is pushed to the furthest possible extreme. At the same time the last sentence of this quotation raises a new issue which we have not so far considered: do we actually reach 'naked human existence' by stripping away particularities or by entering more fully into them? That is a very large philosophical and theological question which we opened up in the Introduction and which in the western tradition points to Wittgenstein's dispute with Descartes and his many intellectual descendants. It has important, indeed fundamental implications for theology. Here is evidence that Ajneya would have sided with Descartes' view of the isolated individual monad as the source of thought and against Lindbeck's cultural-linguistic model of religions and cultures, though as we have seen, in other respects he seems to lean more towards Lindbeck's position.(52)

TEHS is much the least satisfying of the three novels and stands apart from the other two in content, though it has more in common in terms of *genre*, for it too is not a straight chronological narrative. Its first two parts belong to the 'stream of consciousness' genre, which we consider in the next chapter, while the third is more of a straight narrative.

We have now placed the three novels in the context of their author's life. We have seen how in his early years he was introduced to important elements in Brahminical Hinduism and to European literature. While other critics have stressed the latter influences upon him we shall concentrate on the former. When we consider in more detail in later chapters the ways in which he re-interpreted his inheritance it will be important to show what elements in it had actually been taught to him. We have seen how he progressed from a youthful involvement in revolutionary violence to a more detached attitude to society as a writer and journalist. We have located him at a certain point in the spectrum of a Hindu tradition which was itself changing during his life-time. We have also located him in the political and social context of his place and time in India and shown that had he lived in some other part of the country he would have been exposed to different influences and been a different kind of writer. We have also shown that the connections with his own life and the text of the novels are many in SL, fewer in IS and non-existent in TEHS and that this progression could be significant in a way of which he himself may have been scarcely aware. Indeed it is precisely this kind of point that an outsider to any culture may be able to see more clearly that the insider. Finally, we have attempted to justify the claim we made in the Introduction against some contemporary western schools of literary criticism, that to set the novels against their background in this way is not merely legitimate but essential for their interpretation.

Before turning to a detailed study of the texts one more preliminary task remains: that is to locate the novels in the context of modern Hindi and European fiction. To that we turn in the next chapter.

NOTES

1. Hinduism has been largely based on face-to-face village communities which depended for their livelihood on agriculture. As such they have much in common with similar societies elsewhere. The traditional Catholicism of Southern Europe is one obvious parallel, but there are others: Indian students can at once relate to the social world portrayed in the novels of Thomas Hardy, for it is very similar to their own background. (Dr. H Trivedi, Professor of English in the University of Delhi, in an interview, February 1991.) Hardy describes rural communities in the age before industrialisation was to transform the life of Britain. When seen in this kind of historical perspective the differences between Hindu and western societies are less than is often assumed.
2. *dharma* cannot be adequately translated by any single English word. It means 'that which is established' and so law, righteousness, custom, virtue, nature. Thus it is the *dharma* of a warrior to fight, of a mother to care for her children, of fire to burn. So here, everyone has their allotted place, with its appropriate *dharma*, within the social order. See also Monier-Williams [1899] p. 510.
   Hindi and Sanskrit words which are used in the text are either explained at the point where they occur, or, as here, in a footnote. If they are used more than once and are important for the argument of the book they are also explained in the Glossary.
3. The English word 'caste' translates two Sanskrit words, varna and jati. *Varṇa* literally means 'colour'. It also means one of the four main social groupings: priests [*brāhmaṇs*], warriors [*kṣatriyas*], merchants [*vaiśyas*] and manual labourers [*śūdras*]. This fourfold division is however largely a literary fiction which over-simplifies a much more complex social reality. Society actually consists of many endogamous sub-groups — *jātis*. A regional caste system will always have Brahmins at the top of the hierarchy, but below it are numerous jatis whose inter-relationships are traditionally defined in terms of degrees of ritual purity. It is common for members of a *jāti* to identify themselves with one of the four *varṇas*.
4. There is a well-known reference to the divine origin of the four *varṇas* in the *Ṛg Veda,* the earliest Hindu scripture:
   When they divided up the Man ...
   His mouth became the brahmin; his arms

became the warrior-prince; his legs
the common man who plies his trade.
The lowly serf was born from his feet.(*Rg Veda* X. 90. 11-12, translated in Panikkar ed [1977] p. 76)

5. Caste distinctions have always been more extreme in South than in North India. In the Punjab they have always been less important than in other parts of the North. This may be partly due to the influence of Islam and Sikhism both of which preached the equality of all people before God. For further discussion of these territorial distinctions see J H Hutton [1963].
6. For this debate see Beteille [1992] pp. 7-10 and 237-49. See also Forrester [1979] pp. 1-5.
7. See below, p. 28, for the way in which Ajneya's grandfather fulfilled this role.
8. Traditionally the Brahmins would teach the basics of Sanskrit to their sons who would eventually follow their fathers in learning and teaching that particular branch of knowledge to which their family was attached. This might, for example, be grammar, a particular school of philosophy, literature, or astrology. For Ajneya's initiation into Sanskrit learning see below, pp. 29-30. This tradition has now largely broken down in India, for it is no longer possible for a traditional Sanskrit *paṇḍit* or teacher to make a living from his knowledge in the way that his forebears used to do. On the other hand, more people now know a little of the language, for it is widely taught in schools.
9. Buddhism rejected discrimination based on caste as more recently did Sikhism and the medieval movements of *bhakti*, or devotion to God conceived in a personal form. The protest was taken up by nineteenth century reform movements and progressive thinkers. See for example Radhakrishnan [1960] pp. 67-92.
10. For a discussion of this see Brockington [1981] pp. 4-5. Also, see the reference given below in note 13.
11. See Lipner [1986] pp. 76-9 for a discussion of the relation between the essential and empirical self in one important school of Hindu philosophy, where the essential self is that which continues while the empirical is specific to a particular birth. Here the same 'basic I-awareness' of human life continues into the state of final release or 'salvation'. 'The liberated *ātman* continues as an identifiable person'.
12. Yet some Hindus have persecuted those from whom they differ. See, for example, Jaini [1979] p. 306.
13. See Hooker [1989] pp. 113-4.
14. See above, p. 3.
15. This literally means 'word to oneself' and is a Sanskrit grammatical term meaning: that form of the verb which implies an action belonging or reverting to self, the terminations of the middle voice. (Monier-Williams [1899] p. 136.)
    Ātmanepad was republished in 1983 together with another book (Likhi Kāgad Kore), under the combined title of Ātmaparak. We shall use this latter work for future references to Ātmanepad.
16. This was jointly edited by a board of three people. For convenience we give the first name only (Lele) when referring to this book in the text. For full publication details see the Bibliography. The book is one of a series in which a number of people who were well-known in various spheres of Indian life

were interviewed extensively and the results published only after their deaths.(Lele [1993] p. v). I am grateful to one of the editors, Dr Gangesha Gungan, for both telling me of this series and for presenting me with a copy of the book of Ajneya's interview.

17. Śikhar se Sāgar tak (From the Mountain-Top to the Sea) by Ramakamal Ray. This adds little to what we learn of Ajneya from our other sources.
18. Mishra published the first edition of this book in 1963, and a second in 1990 in which he brought his biographical chapter up to date. We shall use this latter edition in quotations.
19. For the meaning of this word, see above, note 3.
20. This word can mean spiritual guide or preceptor or, as here, traditional teacher.
21. *Pāṇini* (? 350 BCE -? 250 BCE) is the legendary founder of Sanskrit grammar and the putative author of the *Aṣṭādhyāyī*.
22. The sage *Vālmīki* is the putative author of the original *Rāmāyaṇa* which is therefore commonly referred to by his name.
23. The reference is to the poet Maithili Sarana Gupta (1886-1964) who wrote several long narrative poems based on traditional myths.
24. Ms Ila Dalmia, Ajneya's companion during his later years, in an interview with the author, February 1991.
25. The normal word used in India to describe a Christian minister or priest.
26. Hindustani is Hindi which includes the use of Urdu words. By Hindi purists it is regarded as no real language at all, though it is widely spoken by ordinary people. In the same way it is common to hear English words included in Hindi speech.
27 We recall that Saccidananda was Ajneya's first name: see above, p. 1.
28. For the reason for the absence of a Hindi translation of these words, see Introduction, Note 10.
29. 'Ajneya' literally means 'the unknowable one'. For the way in which our author acquired this soubriquet, see below, p. 39.
30. Traditionally translated from the French as 'Hell is other people'.
31. See, for example, Vatsyayan [1988] p. 40, where in an interview with Karl Jaspers he makes this point.
32. The best study of this subject is to be found in Patel [1983] pp. 163-360.
33. For this and the following paragraphs I am indebted to Brown [1985].
34.
> Indians had found this new mode of travel much to their liking and the result was that, for the first time, English men and women found themselves in really close contact with a large number of Indians. Every critic of Anglo-India was able to bring back at least one tale about the arrogant, and sometimes brutal, behaviour of the English on trains.(Edwardes [1969] p. 194)

35. For caste discrimination, see above, Note 5.
36. He took part in the killing of a British police officer whom he and his colleagues held responsible for the death of Lajpat Roy, a Hindu leader who had died of wounds sustained in a police *lāṭhī* charge. Bhagat Singh escaped arrest on this occasion but on 8th April 1929 threw a bomb in the Delhi Legislative Assembly. He was arrested and eventually sentenced to death.(Gupta [1980] pp. 126-31).

    A *lāṭhī* is a stout bamboo stick with a metal handle. It is still used by the Indian Police.

37. At the beginning of SL Shekhar is in the condemned cell thinking of various events from his past life which come into his mind in a series of disconnected flashbacks which are not in chronological order. One of these describes how a group of people are on the bank of a river standing by the mangled corpse of someone who has just been killed in an explosion, which has also destroyed their purpose.(SL Vol. 1 p. 34) Although Bhagat Singh is not mentioned by name it is reasonable to suppose that this is the incident to which Mishra refers. However, unlike all the other flashbacks in the first part of the novel, there is no further reference to this incident in the main body of the work. Though Shekhar is arrested and spends ten months in jail in the course of the novel, he is later released and we do not learn how he came to be arrested for the second time and sentenced to death. Presumably these events were to be described in the third volume of SL which Ajneya never published, though he always maintained that he had written it and that it would be published eventually.(Vatsyayan [1983] p. 53, and Lele [1993] pp. 50-1)
38. In SL the shop has a more innocent purpose. It is a sign-writing shop which serves as a day-time hiding place for several party members.
39. Even though I was connected with a terrorist party I did not remain a convinced terrorist, but I remained very interested in the question of how the mind of a terrorist is formed.
40. Cintā
41. Vipathagā.
42. He used 'Ajneya' for his creative work, that is to say, his poetry and novels, but for his other writings he used his own name, 'S H Vatsyayan'.
43. For a discussion of Gaura's argument at this point, see below, p. 77.
44. The Sanskrit terms for the four stages as a collective unit is *āśramaḥ*. These four stages of life together with the four castes make up the Hindu social order and are often referred to collectively as *varṇāśramadharma*. The separate terms for the four stages of life are: *brahmacārin* (celibate student of the Vedas), *gṛhastha* (married householder), *vānaprastha* (anchorite), and *saṃnyāsin* (one who has abandoned all worldy concerns).(Monier-Williams [1899] p. 158)
45. This is the anglicised adjective of advaita or non-dualism which in its most extreme form has been the dominant school of Hindu thought in modern times. According to this school there is only one pervasive reality which as *brahman* underlies all external phenomena and as *ātman* is the deepest reality of the human person. *Brahman* and *ātman* are one. See the Glossary under *Advaita Vedānta*, and for a more complete account of the teaching of this school, see Hiriyanna [1949] pp. 151-74.
46. For a description and discussion of canonical criticism see Barton [1984] pp. 89-103.
47. I am now free of my youthful delusion that the writer changes society — that is to say that that is his necessary duty and aim, and is necessarily a social revolutionary. **The writer changes no-one but himself, and solves no problem except that of his art.** (Ajneya's emphases) He has no power of changing society, or if such power is in his works, it is there because in his pure determination to change himself he presents the individual in the form of a indestructible social value or pattern. The establishment of value in society is his true social work.(Vatsyayan [1983] p. 52)

48. Through force of circumstances and my own predilection I have spent most of my life alone. [One can certainly compose] poetry in solitude but for the novel such a life is insufficient. (Vatsyayan [1983] p. 283)
49. Vatsyayan [1955] p. 81.
50. For the background to this debate see Derrett [1978]. Some words from Derrett's Preface form an apt comment on the background to this novel:

    There is no place, even in New Delhi, for the divorced or separated Hindu wife, for whom remarriage is almost impossible, and for whom respectable male friendships are disappointingly hard to come by (such is the 'traditional' i.e., at present immature, psychology of men). This fact is admittedly explained by the time-lag between the woman's rise to her educational and economic opportunities and her husband's readiness to have an independent human being as his life's partner.(Derrett [1978] pp. ix-x)
51. The background to this title is probably *Advaita Vedānta* philosophy in which the human individual is sometimes likened to a drop of water in the ocean. Ajneya is being a little whimsical in this choice of title, but it illustrates in a small way the main thrust of our book for it shows how he drew this title from his own tradition. No English author would have chosen such a title for a travel book.

    For publication details see Bibliography.
52. See above, pp. 8-12 and Introduction, note 24.

2

THE NOVELS IN THEIR LITERARY CONTEXT

In the first chapter we located Ajneya's novels in the context of his life. We also set that life in the larger context both of the Hindu tradition and of the political and social movements in which he was caught up and which did much to shape his thought and writing. In this chapter our task is to locate the novels in their specifically literary context. Just as it was not enough to call Ajneya a Hindu without further qualification, so it is not enough simply to describe our three texts as novels. We first have to ask the general questions of what kind of text a novel is and how it relates to more traditional literary forms which preceded it and which in the case of Hinduism continue to co-exist with it. Next, within 'the novel' thus identified as a general class there is a host of sub-categories. In which of these can we most appropriately place the novels of Ajneya? The answer to this last question has two parts: the novels belong in a European context, for we have already noted how deeply Ajneya was influenced by contemporary European models. Further, while he deliberately chose to publish his novels in Hindi (1) the fact that he published English translations of the last two demonstrates that he also had a wider readership in mind. Yet it is no less clear that the novels belong primarily in the Hindi and therefore Hindu context, and we have already stated that to interpret them within this setting is one of the main aims of this book, their connections with European literature having already been sufficiently explored by Indian literary critics.(2)

In the first part of this chapter we shall be largely occupied with general questions of *genre*: what kind of work is a novel?

What kind of novels did Ajneya write? The importance of these questions can be illustrated from contemporary biblical studies: it is self-evident that in order to understand a particular book of the Bible we first have to establish what kind of book it is. We cannot read a letter as if it were a poem or a prophetic oracle.(3) Nor can we, as our forebears happily did, read the Bible as if it was a single monolithic unity. Indeed it is precisely the collapse of that monolithic understanding, about which we shall have more to say below, which has made the question of *genre* both possible and necessary. Something similar is true for novels in general and for our three novels in particular: before we can begin to interpret them in detail we need first to establish what kind of texts they are. Having decided that we then need to decide how they are connected with other texts of a similar *genre*. At this point we extend the range of the modified form of 'canonical criticism' for which we argued in the previous chapter.(4) Ajneya's novels belong within four different 'canons': they belong with one another as a '(first) canon within the (second) canon' of their author's total literary output; third, they belong within the canon of the contemporary Hindi novel, and fourth within that of the European novel.

First therefore, we ask the question: what is a novel? We answer with the bald and obvious statement that a novel is a kind of narrative. We shall have to give a much sharper focus to that statement in a moment but at this point our purpose is simply to separate narrative from other literary forms, for it is only comparatively recently that it has received the serious attention of both literary critics and of theologians as a separate *genre* in its own right.(5) The fact that other kinds of narrative preceded and often still co-exist with the novel makes it a literary form which at one and the same time marks a link with and a break from the past. The nature of that relationship is important, indeed crucial, for our understanding of Ajneya's novels. We have already seen him allude to it himself when he wrote that is no longer possible to write an epic poem (itself a particular kind of narrative) and that the modern epic is the novel.(6) The relationship between the novel and its narrative predecessors can best be explored by describing the circumstances in which the novel arose. What first made people write — and read — novels? We look at this question first in the context of English and then of

Hindi literary history. We shall find that in each case the answers are remarkably similar.

In Western Christendom it was the Bible, interpreted as a single great drama from Genesis to Revelation, which traditionally provided the overarching story within whose context all human life could be interpreted. In the words of Hans Frei:

> Since the world truly rendered by combining biblical narratives into one was indeed the one and only real world it must in principle embrace the experience of any age and reader. Not only was it possible for him, it was also his duty to fit himself into that world in which he was in any case a member.(Frei [1974] p. 3)

But by the late eighteenth century events had begun to have their own autonomy, and so there was an unconscious move towards the separation of 'the depicted biblical world' from 'the real historical world' in which people actually lived. There followed

> a gradual change to the sense of another temporal reality than the biblical. The self might or might not claim this new historical world as its appropriate home, but in any case the true narrative by which its reality is rendered is no longer identical with the Bible's over-arching story.(Frei [1974] p. 50)

That sense of 'another temporal reality than the biblical' creates the space which is necessary if novels are to be written. Frei's phrase about the narrative rendering of reality implies that stories are necessary in order to give shape and meaning to our world. We would also claim that what they do cannot be done in any other way. In the words of Richard Niebuhr:

> Interpretation of our meaning with the aid of a story is a well-known pedagogical device. So Lincoln told his homely tales and conveyed to others in trenchant fashion the ideas in his mind; so Plato employed myths to illustrate philosophy and to communicate visions of truth that ordinary language could not describe; so Jesus himself through parable tried to indicate what he meant by the phrase "kingdom of God". Yet what prompted Christians in the past to confess their faith by telling the story of their life was more than a need for vivid illustration or for analogical reasoning. Their story was not a parable which could be replaced by another; it was irreplaceable and untranslatable.(7)

In the same way, novels do not simply illustrate truths which could equally well be conveyed in other ways. They are 'irreplaceable and untranslatable'. They point to the fact that we all need stories to give shape to our world and meaning to our lives and that nothing can take the place of such stories. When therefore the Bible read as a single narrative could no longer provide the over-arching framework of meaning for a whole society, it was the novelists who stepped into the breach and created new stories which fulfilled the same role in more modest ways for smaller groups of people, for it was precisely at the time when the traditional role of the Bible began to collapse in the way described by Frei that people began to write and to read novels.(Frei [1974] pp. 142-54). Nor did this only happen in western Christendom. Scholes and Kellogg describe how something very similar happens in societies where the epic poem filled the traditional role of the Bible:

> Epic poems are made in cultures which do not distinguish between myth and history. As soon as the distinction begins to be made ... it can be applied critically to the narratives of the past and will become established in the aesthetic and intellectual norms which influence current literary production. The distinction between fact and fiction...is [now] clearly established.(Scholes and Kellogg [1966] pp. 57-8)

Empirical narrative now replaces epic's loyalty to a traditional story (such as the Bible understood as a monolithic whole) constantly retold, with allegiance to 'reality'. Reality in this sense no longer coincides with the narrative of Bible or epic but has to be discovered by empirical investigation. Sacred texts can now be treated as sources for such investigation when it is applied to the past, and this use patently undermines their sacredness as traditionally perceived, though they can still be understood as sacred in a rather different way.(8) The history of the criticism of the Gospels is an example of this change. Also, fictional narrative now becomes possible. As we have just noted, Ajneya himself showed his awareness of this when he said in his radio interview that the novel was the modern form of the epic and that it was no longer possible to write a long continuous epic poem based on the *Mahābhārata* or *Rāmāyaṇa* in the traditional fashion. In the next chapter we shall see that Shekhar uses an important sacred text — The Laws of Manu [*Manu*] — as a source book for his highly critical investigations into the nature and origins of Hindu society.(SL Vol. 1 p. 150) In other words our novels provide examples of the thesis which Frei, together with Scholes and Kellogg, propose.

The shift from epic on the one hand to both historical investigation and to the novel on the other has another significant effect: the role of the teller of stories undergoes an important change. In the words of a Jesuit scholar, R Antoine:

> The bard or the singer of tales is "the means of expressing the inner life of the community".
> No-one, I think, will question the fact that the *Rāmāyaṇa* bears all the marks of oral poetry. The epic songs relating to Rama were sung long before the idea arose of putting them down in writing. ...The "singer of tales" is the guardian not of a verbal tradition but of a spiritual tradition. He never claims to "create" his songs: he has received them from his forbears together with the technique of singing. He is the people's articulate memory. Memory, here, means fidelity to tradition and never implies purely verbal repetition. The singer can lengthen or curtail his performance, adapt new themes to his narrative and, in general, regulate his singing according to the moods of the audience.(Antoine [1975] p. 16)

Ajneya the Brahmin is still, like the singer of tales, in some sense a guardian of tradition, but Ajneya the novelist is its critic and re-interpreter. This means that he stands in a new relationship to society which makes him more self-conscious than the teller of tales described by Antoine, for he has a different role. This is also true of his readers, for in an oral culture listening to the retelling of a familiar tale is a corporate activity which binds its hearers together in an act of shared remembrance. The reading of a novel is a solitary experience which separates those who have had it from those who have not. Thus the novel is the harbinger of a plural society in which different and even conflicting world-views have to co-exist. In fact the novel not only contributes to making such plurality possible, it also embodies it within its own contents, for as we shall see below, the novel in general and our three novels in particular contain within themselves the clash of different world-views, or at least of different understandings of life in society. The solitary reading of a novel—or any other book—gives readers a certain independence of mind. They are now free to think unfamiliar and possibly revolutionary thoughts which the new literature may suggest. The shift from the telling and hearing of traditional tales to the writing and reading of novels thus has important consequences, and it was still comparatively recent in the society within which Ajneya wrote.(9)

Of course we must not exaggerate this change. Traditional Indian society also knew a degree of plurality to which the different schools of Indian philosophy-theology bear witness, and in the modern period there are Hindi novels which still reflect and re-inforce traditional values.(10) But for our purposes in this book the point is that Ajneya's novels were indeed a new departure in the sense which we have just described. He himself provides indirect endorsement for this suggestion for he was very much aware of the fact that the shift to the novel opened up new possibilities and marked a real change. He describes some of these implications in an essay which he wrote (in English) in 1959 about Hindi literature of the period after 1918. He writes of:

> the search for personality which was, consciously or unconsciously, the main driving force of the literature of the period and the source of its bitterness and absurdities, its exasperations and exaltations.
>
> In a tradition where the age had always been more important than the artist, literature had inevitably been concerned more with the creation of types than of individuals ... As the Hindi writer discovered himself as an individual he became aware that as a creator he was concerned with persons. The realisation was as painful as the discovery had been awkward and embarrassing: the degree of maturity and poise in subsequent writing directly reflects the degree and speed of the adjustment which the individual writer was able to attain with the new situation.(Vatsyayan [1959] p. 84)

This change is reflected in two of our novels: for example, in SL the young Shekhar too complains that education was more concerned with the creation of types than with the development of the individual.(SL Vol. 1 p. 53) Again, both Shekhar in SL and Bhuvan in IS stress the importance of free choice by the individual, especially in the matter of choosing a marriage partner, a view of marriage which is at odds with tradition.(SL Vol. 2 pp. 158-9; IS pp. 73-4) Here we find Ajneya's characters themselves involved in the struggle to become persons in the sense that he described. This shift is of no little significance for Christian theologians, for persons and their relationships have always been at the heart of the Christian vision, as argued, for instance by David Jenkins.(Jenkins [1967] pp. 13-24) In the Introduction we used some more recent theological arguments to enlarge the case for that significance in terms relevant to this book (11). If that case be granted then it follows that a dawning literary concern for the significance of persons in another tradition is a move which opens up rich possibilities for conversation. This is closely related to the shift from epic to the novel which we described above.

Frei, together with Scholes and Kellogg, shows us how the novel as a literary form needs certain conditions in which to take root and grow. These conditions are only possible when the more monolithic world of epic, or of the Bible as traditionally understood, disintegrates. But what of the novel's origins? The soil may be ready but where does the seed actually come from? In particular, why did the novel originate in a Christian context? Robert Alter claims that the antecedents of prose fiction are to be found in the narrative portions of the Hebrew scriptures. (Alter [1981] pp. 23-46) He suggests that:

> Prose narration, affording the writers a remarkable range and flexibility in the means of presentation, could be used to liberate fictional personages from the fixed choreography of timeless events and could thus transform story-telling from ritual rehearsal to the delineation of the wayward paths of human freedom, the quirks and contradicitons of men and women seen as moral agents and complex centers of motive and feeling.(Alter [1981] pp. 25-6)

Here we are back to the shift from epic to fictional narrative, but the shift now happens within the Bible itself. Its narrative forms are sufficiently close to those of the novel for them to be seen as its forerunner and parent. In other words in the act of writing novels Ajneya moved into a framework of discourse which implicitly opened up possibilities of conversation with Christianity, possibilities which could not have been afforded in the same way by the epic poetry which he said it was no longer possible to write. There has of course been an encounter between Hinduism and Christianity which goes back at least a hundred and fifty years. That encounter has already been well studied.(12) Yet in this field the study of novels is still very much a Cinderella. If our argument is sound then novels by their very nature can make available new possibilities of meeting which have yet to be fully explored. This further underlines our claim for the importance of the novel as an area for serious theological study, especially in the field of inter-faith relationships.

We have seen how the novel became available as a literary

form for English writers towards the end of the eighteenth century. How did it become available for Ajneya's use as a Hindi writer? The answer to this question concerns not only form but also language.(13) Hindi is one of more than a dozen major languages of India, but it was only in the early years of the twentieth century that it was forged into the kind of instrument in which novels and other kinds of continuous prose could be written. This was largely the work of Mahavir Prasada Dvivedi [*Mahāvīr Prasāda Dvivedī*] who both made Hindi grammar into a consistent structure and clarified the language so that it could be effectively used for written prose.(Shukla [1940] pp. 333-4) He also established the principles for deciding what words should be included within Hindi vocabulary. Much of that vocabulary is derived from Sanskrit. This development of the language is important: just as Beethoven could not have written his symphonies before the emergence of the modern orchestra with its variety of instruments, so too the emergence of the novel in Hindi or any other language depends on the prior emergence of the language itself as a suitable instrument. Here is a variation on the theology of Lindbeck — culture and language precede what is thought in them.(14)

There are two important differences between modern British and Hindu cultures which we need to bear in mind at this point: first, within Hindu society there are many people who still live in the unfractured and unself-conscious world of epic and myth — a world which in form if not in content is close to that medieval Christian world described by Frei. For them the traditional Hindu stories such as those to be found in the *Rāmāyaṇa* and *Mahābhārata* are unquestioned: they are not 'literally true', for the concept of literal truth implies the possibility that the stories might be true in other ways, and that possibility can only arise when they are questioned. Rather are the stories 'real' for they provide the assumed and unquestioned context within which life has meaning, they define and support social roles, they inculcate in a simple and popular way the values of Hindu thought.(Hooker [1989] pp. 17-49) Many of those who inhabit this mental and spiritual universe are largely illiterate and uneducated — though not for those reasons to be dismissed as unintelligent — but they do not and indeed cannot read novels. Still less do they write them. One of the effects of this is that the readership of Hindi novels is still comparatively restricted. Their print runs are significantly smaller than those of their English counterparts, but with increasing literacy more novels are now being written and read.(15)

The other important difference between the two cultures is this: because of this continuity of tradition, and because of the late development of the Hindi language, that language is much closer to Sanskrit than is, say, English to Latin. Indeed it is often possible to use Sanskrit and Hindi dictionaries almost interchangeably. The meanings of many words hardly change from the one language to the other. We shall therefore find that Ajneya used many words which derive directly from Sanskrit and which for that reason resonate with the Hindu tradition in a very direct way. Because the language — and *a fortiori* the symbolism — which he uses is still so close to its traditional roots he is able to re-interpret his inheritance in a way which would have been much more difficult had the language available to him stood at a greater distance from it.

If by the end of the nineteenth century the Hindi language was available as a suitable tool, how was it that the novel as a literary form became available at the same time? In order for this to happen it needed, just like its European step-parent, congenial soil in which to grow. This it found in the existence of traditional stories in which the vast Sanskrit tradition is especially rich. The two great Epics are full of them and there are many others to be found in the *Purāṇas* — which almost by definition are encyclopaedic collections of traditional stories — as well as in popular oral culture. But while these stories form an important element of the soil in which the novel was able to take root and grow they are not the plant itself. That plant originally grew in western soil in the way in which we have described before being transplanted to India where it has taken root and now flourishes vigorously. This point is readily conceded by Indian literary critics:

> In almost every country there is manifested the natural tendency [*svābhāvik pravṛtti*] to look for and to find the roots of one's own country's traditions [*paramparāoṁ*] in the remote past. Possibly this strengthens national identity [*rāṣṭrīya aham*]. Hindi literature too has not remained a paragon of virtue in this respect. Wherever one finds writing about the birth and development of Hindi

> novels and stories there one finds an eagerness [*utsāha*] among writers to trace their origins as far back as possible. In the *Rāmāyaṇa, Mahābhārata* and [other] great poems there are countless tales [*upākhyāna*] which seem close to the novel [*upanyāsa*]. The tales of *Nala* and *Damayantī, Satī* and *Sāvitrī*, and the stories recounted by the characters found in some *Upaniṣads* seem like short stories. The elements of narrative [*kathā ke tattva*] are certainly present in [such collections as] the *Hitopadeśa, Bṛhatkathā*, the *Jātak* stories, the *Pañctantra*, and *Yogavaśiṣṭha*. Many love stories from the middle period of Indian history can also be put in this category. But in spite of all this we cannot put them in the same class as the modern novel and short story. *Dharma*, morality [*naitiktā*] and didacticism [*updeśātmaktā*] separate them from modern narrative literature [*ādhunik kathā-sāhitya*]. The literary form which is known to-day as the novel and short story is, from the point of view of its purpose [*uddeśya*] and subject matter [*viṣaya-paridhi*], an entirely modern form. Its time of gestation was the second half of the nineteenth century and its birth was made possible as a result of the connection established with European literature through the medium of English. (Varshaneya [1970] p. 9)

Another important element in the soil was the changes brought about in nineteenth century northern Indian Hindu society through the intellectual impact of the West (16). One effect of this was that many hitherto unquestioned aspects of Hinduism were challenged.(17) That statement needs to be read against the background of what we wrote in Chapter One about caste.(18) We shall see that many of Ajneya's characters, especially in SL, are no longer able to fulfil their traditional roles in a changing society which had hitherto been shaped by the caste system. In IS the claims of that society are much looser and more distant but the characters still lack a clear sense of role or identity. This is one of the pressures which forces them to become persons in the sense that Ajneya himself described.

We must now turn to a closer examination of the development of the Hindi novel itself. The first writer of realistic fiction was Prem Chand (1880-1936). He described the world of social reality in a manner comparable to Jane Austen or Charles Dickens. Realistic fiction attempts to portray the ordinary experiences of life as it is actually lived by ordinary people:

> A thoroughgoing realism involves not only a selection of subject matter but, more important, a special literary manner as well: the subject is represented, or "rendered", in such a way as to give the

> reader the illusion of actual and ordinary experience.(Abrams [1988] p. 153)

Prem Chand's first Hindi novel was published in 1918.(19) The context in which he wrote is well described by Peter Gaeffke:

> The rising educated middle class, composed as it was of a mixture of different castes, was unsure of the way in which the future should be shaped...This middle class was also uncertain how to apply the new ideas of freedom, equality and brotherhood to their personal lives, dominated as they were by joint families and the caste councils.(20) There also remained the old evils of Hindu widowhood, child marriage and numerous superstitions.(Gaeffke [1978] p. 37)

Prem Chand's novels are dominated by the need to purify Hindu society by removing these social evils. This was also the great concern of Gandhi, by whose social thinking he was deeply influenced. Indeed several of his novels closely reflect different stages in Gandhi's long career.(21) All his novels were written between the Wars. They graphically and movingly describe the realities of village life: the injustices done to the poor by landlords and money lenders, the constant struggle against the unpredictable vagaries of climate, the effect of city life and its new values on those who had been nurtured within village tradition, the suffering inflicted on women by men, particularly in arranged marriages when these were unduly distorted by economic factors. He was the first Hindi writer to take village life as a serious subject for literary portrayal. While his early novels proposed simplistic and idealistic solutions to the problems he described, his later ones propose no solutions at all. In this they can be called genuinely modern.(22) He is still regarded as the greatest novelist to have written in Hindi. In Ajneya's own view he displayed a breadth of social sympathy unmatched by later writers.(Vatsyayan [1976] p. 36)

After Prem Chand the central trunk of the Hindi novel diverged into two main branches: the first of these consisted of a group of progressive writers who followed Prem Chand in condemning social injustice but who departed from him in that they confined themselves within a doctrinaire Marxist framework. Ajneya himself wrote critically about them on the grounds that their dogma inhibited their creativity.(Vaṭsyayan [1976] pp. 91-9)(23). One of the best known of these writers was Yashpal

[*Yaśpāl*] whose novels certainly exhibit these faults, but more positively, like Prem Chand in his later novels, he changes the significance of the hero. The hero of Prem Chand's last and greatest novel, The Gift of a Cow [*Godān*], is a peasant who spends a life time struggling against impossible odds. He fails in his life's ambition to buy a cow which he can then give to a Brahmin on his deathbed in order to secure his safe passage to the next world. By contrast the hero of one of Yashpal's novels, The Revolutionary [*Deśdrohī*], is a factory worker who organises a strike against an unjust boss, and who eventually dies as a result of the struggle he has led on behalf of the workers.(Yashpal [1967]) In both these cases the hero — if such he can now be called — does not triumph over adversity but is overwhelmed by it. The same is true of Shekhar in SL and to a lesser extent of Bhuvan and Rekha in IS. This degree of similarity suggests that we should not be too rigid in our classification: the boundaries between the different kinds of novel are blurred.

The other branch of the Hindi novel explored human motivation and consciousness from within. This was Ajneya's *metier* and in order to appreciate his achievement we need to set him in the context of two of his immediate precursors. The first was Jainendra Kumar.(24) His novels usually have only a few main characters, as opposed to the galaxy of actors who throng the pages of Prem Chand. Gaeffke perceptively comments that Jainendra is 'describing a society where the individual has [so] little space to develop his personality'.(Gaeffke [1978] p. 45) This comment needs to be read alongside Ajneya's own remarks about the Hindi novelist's discovery of personality which we quoted above. While in Jainendra's early novels some people try to escape from these social restraints, in the later ones they betray a resignation to their fate within them.(Gaeffke [1978] pp. 45-50) We have already observed that the main characters of all three of Ajneya's novels step or already live outside traditional social boundaries. To set Ajneya's novels in the context of others of the same *genre* is to begin to see how radical and innovatory they are. Ajneya's second predecessor in this school was Ilachandra Joshi [*Ilācandra Jośī*]. He was the first Hindi novelist to take seriously the thought of Freud in its implications for the novel, but he failed adequately to assimilate this new knowledge. In the words of one critic:

> In his novels psychology is used on a purely doctrinal level, not on a practical level like Jainendra ... Where mental analysis and the description of the stream of consciousness are used for the life-like depiction of character, there psychology is presented in a natural, spontaneous and practical way, but where naturalness, spontaneity and practicality are absent from the characterisation, there psychology is presented on a doctrinal and unpractical level. (Prabhakar [1966] p. 28)(25)

Ajneya grasped the implications of this new knowledge much more thoroughly than did Joshi and so was able to assimilate it more naturally into his writing. In his first novel he shows how the childhood years of his main character have profound, even determining effects on his later development, and in IS he dares to deal openly with sex, while never descending into crudity or voyeurism. In both of these respects he broke new ground in the field of Hindi fiction. He also did so in another important way: his predecessors all wrote 'straight' narratives in which the author occupies a position of assumed omniscience in the same way as a Jane Austen, a Charles Dickens, or a Prem Chand does. It is one of the marks of the realist novel that the author has a kind of privileged access to the minds of all the characters. But Ajneya's novels mark a break not only from epic but also from this kind of realist fiction. The nature of and reasons for that break we must now explore. To do so we need to set the issue in the English literary context.

The nineteenth-century English novel, somewhat like the British Empire, was able to flourish for so long because other forms of discourse did not lay claim to its territory, but eventually Darwin produced a new account of human origins and by implication of the human future, Freud brought to light hitherto unsuspected sources of human motivation, and historical studies produced new ways of looking at the past. These all in different ways did begin to lay claim to the territory which the novel had hitherto occupied unchallenged:

> The new sciences of sociology and psychology ... disputed with art for the control of the representation of actuality, driving both narrative and dramatic art ultimately away from essentially mimetic or realistic formulations. Before the rise of these latest branches of science, literature controlled the present; just as before the rise of scientific historiography it controlled the past. History was so clearly an art in the ancient world because historiography had not

> become quite scientific enough for scientific history to dispute with artistic history. Just so in the nineteenth century did the novel control the field of present social and psychological reality, while the sciences of society and the psyche were slowly and painfully being born.(Scholes and Kellogg [1966] p. 231)

To this we must add the social, intellectual, and spiritual upheavals subsequent to and in large measure caused by the First World War. The cumulative effect of all these changes was that the novel could no longer continue in its relatively untroubled nineteenth century way. In the words of David Daiches:

> The English novel, from its beginnings in the late seventeenth and early eighteenth centuries to its great popular flowering in the nineteenth, had been essentially what might be called a "public instrument", basing its view of what was significant in human affairs on a generally agreed standard. Its plot patterns were constructed out of incidents and situations which were seen to matter in human affairs equally by writer and reader. Changes in social or economic position or in marital situation were obvious and agreed indications of a significant alteration in a character's state, and such crises marked the crises of virtually all eighteenth- and nineteenth-century plots. The author's attitude to his characters was essentially one of observer; anything significant in his characters' behavior was at once indicated by a publicly observable movement towards some shift in status or fortune...The correlation between internal and external, between moral and intellectual development and appropriate observable action or inaction, was taken for granted. And society was taken for granted. Men lived in a social and economic world which was real, and the most real part of their behavior was that which changed or in some way determined their position in that world.(Daiches [1960] pp. 1-2)

Daiches here fills out the description we have already given of realist fiction which was thus a kind of half-way house between the traditional narrative of the Bible as described by Frei, and the distinctively modern novel which was born when the publicly shared set of common assumptions described by Daiches broke down. Modern English novelists had to cope with new problems which had not crossed the horizon of their much more secure Victorian predecessors. Authors and readers now no longer shared a public world whose values could be taken for granted, and this meant that from now on readers had to be deliberately won over to accept a particular author's perspective.

Thus Virginia Woolf used some of the techniques of lyric poetry and a 'pattern of highly charged symbolic events' to persuade the reader to adopt her point of view, while D H Lawrence

> constructed his plots in such a way as to use social institutions as devices for probing the difficulties which lie in the way of proper human relationships and showed his characters discovering (or failing to discover) their own sense of meaning in those relationships through experiences that are essentially poetic and even mystical in nature and are projected by a quite new kind of fictional symbolism.(Daiches [1960] p. 6)

Further, these authors found that they could no longer use the traditional mode of chronological narrative sequence. In their novels time moves backwards and forwards, sometimes in a flashback technique, in a way which attempts to capture time as it is actually experienced by the characters. Consciousness is now seen as infinitely more complex and mysterious than had been the case in the earlier novels — here Freud and Jung had their influence — and with this, public position and private worth are no longer necessarily related to one another. All these changes led inexorably to the loneliness and isolation of the individual living in a society which seemed increasingly hollow and unreal.

This, precisely, is the world of the characters of Ajneya, and it is for this reason that it is important to see his work not only in the context of modern Hindi fiction, but also in this wider context of the development of the English novel. Indeed he was influenced by D H Lawrence in particular, as well as by other writers, and this influence has been explored by Hindi critics.(eg Patel [1983] pp. 209-24, 277-99 and 318-46) In IS, though not so much in the other two novels, his language at times has a poetic and symbolic quality, and it is here that the influence of Lawrence is most obvious. In all three novels he uses the technique of the flashback, the effect of which is to break the continuity of the action and to disrupt its chronological sequence. Across the three novels external events become progressively fewer in number and of reduced significance when they occur. What really matters is what goes on in the minds of the characters. This makes necessary a re-evaluation of time: time as the characters actually experience it now becomes more significant than time in the sense of measurable chronological sequence. This raises important questions about the nature of time itself, its relation to narrative, and the significance of both as the context within which human life is interpreted. These we shall discuss in Chapter Six.

The novel of the kind written by Ajneya is thus no longer a 'mirror of society' in which the writer attempts a portrait of his age, or of a part of it. It does indeed reflect society, but it does so now not as an end in itself but with a deeper purpose in view: the opening up of the human dilemmas which arise in an age when traditional answers no longer suffice. In the words of a Latin American novelist:

> When we all understood everything, the epic was possible. But not fiction. The novel is born from the very fact that we do not understand one another any longer, because unitary orthodox language has broken down. Quixote and Sancho, the Shandy brothers, Mr and Mrs Karenin: their novels are the comedy (or the drama) of their misunderstandings. Impose a unitary language: you kill the novel, but you also kill the society.
>
> Fiction is a harbinger of a multipolar and multicultural world, where no single philosophy, no single belief, no single solution, can shunt aside the extreme wealth of mankind's cultural heritage. Our future depends on the enlarged freedom for the multiracial and polycultural to express itself in a world of shifting, decaying and emerging power centres.(Carlos Fuentes in The Guardian Weekly 5th March 1989 pp. 8-9).

Here Fuentes reinforces our argument about the change from the world of epic to the world of the novel, but he also takes it an important stage further, for if fiction is indeed 'a harbinger of a multipolar and multicultural world', and if a single novel contains within itself the inescapable disagreements of those who no longer share a unitary language, then the possibilities of cross-cultural conversation which the novel opens up are rich indeed. Further, in extending our argument Fuentes has not moved in a straight line but completed a circle and brought us back to the debate about the theology of religions which we opened up in the Introduction: how is it possible to go on making absolute claims in a world when we now know others are doing likewise? Fuentes assumes that it is no longer possible and indeed that it is actually inhibiting to do so, yet we have argued that dialogue is only possible at all if one is committed, and that authentic commitment is only possible if we are genuinely open and exposed to the 'other'.(25) So we find that contemporary novelists and theologians share a common agenda.

In this chapter we have placed Ajneya in his literary context, a twofold context which embraces both European and Hindi literature. We have seen that as a literary form the novel marks a shift from the unitary world of epic, a shift which Ajneya acknowledges himself when he says it is no longer possible to write an epic poem, and when he describes the changing nature of personality with which modern Hindi writers have had to come to terms. We have also seen that his own novels in particular mark a second shift — away from the assumptions of a common set of values shared by author and readers. He thus has more in common with Lawrence and Conrad than with Eliot and Dickens. To locate his works in this way is to begin to glimpse the rich possibilities which a conversation with them can open up. As we have already suggested, this conversation has two sides: we see him engaging with his own tradition in criticism and in reconstruction. We also see him engaged at the same time with many of the same questions which pre-occupy Christian thinkers at the close of the second millenium: questions of the significance of human life and the place of ethics in a world where in his words we no longer live in 'a religious, God-centred, believing society'.(26) In the next chapter we shall see how these concerns compelled him, as they also compel us, to reshape the parameters within which human life is perceived as being lived.

NOTES

1. Surprisingly, he appears to have written SL in English before publishing it in Hindi. In his first travel book he describes a stay in the Kulu Valley which is in the Himalayan foothills. He says that while he was staying there he translated into Hindi a novel he had first written in English. He also says that he had written this novel in jail where he had spent four years (for which, see above p. 39) and that in it he attempts to portray the life of a revolutionary. This can only refer to SL.(Vatsyayan [1953] pp. 155-6)
2. See above, p. 2.
3. For a discussion of the importance of *genre* in biblical studies, see Barton [1984] pp. 16-8.
4. See above, p. 42.
5. See for example Chatman [1978], Tracy [1981], McConnell ed [1986], Hauerwas and Jones eds [1989].
6. See above, p. 30.
7. From Niebuhr, 'The Story of Our Life', originally published in Niebuhr

[1941] pp. 43-81, reprinted in Hauerwas and Jones eds [1989] pp. 21-44. Our quotation is from p. 23.

8. For the use of Hindu sacred texts as sources for historical investigation see Pargiter [1972] and Hazra [1975].
9. One consequence of the shift from the public recitation or performance of epic poetry to the private reading of novels and other books is that it becomes much more difficult for religions to function as information systems in the way described by Bowker (see above, pp. 10-1), for much more information is now much more widely available. In his radio interview Ajneya draws attention to the change in his own lifetime from poetry which was recited at public gatherings to poetry which was published in books.(Lele [1993] pp. 37-9)
10. Some novels attempt to recover a particular historical episode in novel form and so their authors are not interested in challenging contemporary assumptions in the way that Ajneya was. For two good examples of this in Hindi see Dvivedi [1976] and Nagar [1975].
11. See above, pp. 11-14.
12. See for example Thomas [1970].
13. The same is no less true of the English novel, but to investigate the development of the English language to the point at which it was possible to write novels in it lies outside the scope of our book.
14. See above, pp. 8-12.
15. The best survey of the field is to be found in Gaeffke [1978] pp. 47-72. These pages reveal a steady increase in the number and type of novels published up to the date when the book was published. A visit to any reputable Hindi bookshop in India reveals an increase of titles since 1978. Since about 1975 critical writing in Hindi on the Hindi novel has also burgeoned, though most of it is too recent to have yet been taken into university courses.
16. For a useful overview of the intellectual impact of the West during this period see Brown [1985] pp. 152-72.
17. This questioning was initially confined to the intelligentsia of Calcutta, but it was this area which eventually set the trend for the rest of the country. See Kripalani, 'Modern Literature', in Basham ed [1975] pp. 414-5.
18. See above, pp. 24-5.
19. His first novel was published in Urdu in 1903.
20. These councils or *pañcāyatas* were responsible for social discipline with a particular *jāti*.
21. For details of this see Gaeffke [1978] pp. 38-42.
22. Similarly, the great Victorian novels are usually neatly rounded off with the new social status of the main characters corresponding to their perceived moral worth, but one of the marks of a distinctively modern novel is that the ending is left open and incomplete. This happens in all three of Ajneya's novels.
23.

> Prem Chand's humanism wanted to see the whole of life, and having seen it he gave it his sympathy and through the medium of his sympathy he grasped the [appropriate] dogmas. On the other hand the progressive writer started with the dogma, and from it established a kind of humanism, and because of the dominance of that -ism wanted to establish sympathy with humanity.(Ajneya [1976] p. 36)

24. It was Jainendra Kumar who first referred to our author as 'Ajneya'. For

this see above, p. 39.

25. See above, pp. 11-14.
26. See above, p. 3.

3

REDRAWING THE TRANSCENDENTAL AND SOCIAL BOUNDARIES

In the first chapter we identified and described the context of Brahminical Hinduism within which Ajneya was nurtured, and by looking at his family roots and personal history in that context and in the context of his time we set the stage for examining the ways in which he both challenged and reshaped his inheritance. In the second chapter we located the novels in the specifically literary context of the modern novel in both Hindi and English literature. This enabled us to see that for Ajneya as a Hindi author to write novels at all was still a comparatively recent and essentially new departure. In the present chapter we look specifically at the ways in which the novels redefine the boundaries within which human life is understood as being lived. Traditionally these boundaries marked the frontiers of two separate but inter-related spheres. The first is transcendental: human existence was understood as not being limited to this life alone but as having started before it and continuing beyond it, in this world through rebirth, and in the next through heaven and hell. The second sphere is social: here the key fact is that the internal and external boundaries of the Hindu social system were defined by degrees of ritual purity. In redrawing these boundaries, therefore, Ajneya attacks the whole notion of ritual purity. To reshape the boundaries is implicitly to re-interpret the life which is lived within them. In other words Ajneya is creating a new anthropology the main elements of which will become clear as we proceed. We touched on this subject in the last chapter when we discussed the changes from epic to the novel and from traditional social roles to a new understanding of personhood. The present chapter fills out that argument and takes it a stage further.

In SL Ajneya makes a direct, sustained, and at times detailed assault on both the transcendental and the social boundaries. In IS the mood is different, for the battles of SL have long since been fought and won. Here his main target is the degraded and dehumanising materialism, or 'survivalism' as we have seen him call it (1), which he sees as threatening Indian society and taking root especially in the big cities. In this second novel he is still engaged with his traditional inheritance but in a less direct and more allusive and nuanced way. The references are occasional rather than sustained. In TEHS he has on the face of it moved still further from his tradition, at least as far as its boundaries are concerned, but we shall find evidence that his concern may still be there, if beneath the surface. All this means that for most of this chapter we shall be pre-occupied with evidence from SL. We shall make fewer references to IS and fewer still to TEHS. This balance will change in subsequent chapters, for not all of our themes are of equal significance in all three novels. We deal initially and comparatively briefly with belief in rebirth and in heaven and hell, looking first at the way they were understood in the tradition to which Ajneya was an heir, and then at the way in which he challenged them. The bulk of the chapter will deal with the much larger and more complex subject of the social boundaries as defined by ritual purity. Sacred geography, which we also consider, is a bridge linking together the transcendental and social areas.

We begin by examining how Ajneya reshapes the transcendental boundaries. In the Vedas [*Vedas*], the earliest Hindu scriptures, human life in this world is perceived as being essentially good, rather as it is in the Hebrew scriptures.(2) There are shadowy notions of heaven and hell but these are not developed, and there is no mention of rebirth. This doctrine makes its first scriptural appearance in the Upanishads where it is assumed to be true, rather than argued.(3) It is similarly taken for granted in almost all subsequent scriptures and philosophical systems. The earlier belief in heaven and hell is not rejected but combined with rebirth, so that heaven and hell are now temporary rather than ultimate abodes for the departed.(4) The entail of reward or punishment is sometimes understood as being worked out in them before the soul returns to earth in another form. In the

Purāṇas the heavens and hells are elaborated both in their numbers and in the descriptions of their respective rewards and punishments. However, while all this is to be found in the scriptures it is not always reflected in the lives of ordinary people. Some studies have suggested that belief in rebirth at the popular level is less common than the scriptural evidence might suggest.(5) Our novels support this research for references to rebirth are very few.

There are three important references to life after death in SL and one in IS. At the beginning of SL the young Shekhar is in the condemned cell struggling to discover some kind of permanent significance for his brief life which is about to end with his execution. In particular he wonders what part of him, if any, can survive his impending death. He reflects that even if nothing of himself survives surely his 'spirit of rebellion [*vidrohaceṣṭā*]' and 'ideal of radical revolution [*maulik krānti kā ādarśa*]' will live on.(SL Vol. 1 p. 36) And yet:

> Science [also] says that life [*jīvan*] comes only once, and that no part of human life is eternal [*nitya*], in death the whole of it comes to an end [*avasāna ho jātā hai*], nothing remains which could be reborn.(SL Vol. 1 pp. 36-7)

Here he rejects or at least poses a question mark against the possibility of rebirth and shortly after this we find him rejecting belief in heaven and hell as well though for rather different reasons:

> All around him is suffering [*duḥkha*], poverty, pain, disease, death, everything. The sub-contractors [*ṭhekedāroṁ ne*] of religion [*dharma*] in different countries have exhausted all their creative powers in devising the most fearful and evil torments in hell [*narak*], but they are all in the world, there in his world, and he does not accept them, he rebels and fights against them. (SL Vol. 1 p. 72)

Here social concerns are intermingled with transcendental ones. According to tradition the torments of hell were the punishments justly inflicted in the next world on those who had broken the divinely ordained rules of conduct in this one.(6) Shekhar will have none of this. For him the traditional hells are mere human constructs devised by the all too human 'subcontractors' of religion. The Hindi word corresponding to 'subcontractors' has here the same kind of overtones as the word 'tax-collectors' in the Christian scriptures. It suggests a class of corrupt middlemen who work for a master but dishonestly make extra money for themselves. This insight into the structures of religion enables Shekhar to perceive that the real hells are all around him now in the suffering of the oppressed. Because this suffering happens in this world it is both possible and necessary to remove it. While he is a new student in Madras at a later stage of the novel a specific incident leads him to similar conclusions. He has just joined the Brahmin students' hostel and noticed how their mess is protected from the glance of any low caste person, for if any such even looked at their food it would be regarded as defiled and so unfit to eat. Yet at the same time the students are happy to drive away with a 'shoo' the occasional dog which crept into the mess.(SL Vol. 1 p. 207) In other words people of low caste are in their eyes lower than dogs. Shekhar cannot accept this hypocrisy and refuses to observe the norms of conduct which are required in the hostel. Eventually this refusal to conform becomes too much for the other students:

> [He] began to notice that all the students were looking at him as if he were some kind of strange creature [*videśī jantu*] and it seemed to him that in their hearts they were wondering what he would be in his next birth [*agale janma meṁ*] — a dog [*kuttā*] or a crow [*kauā*] or a worm [*kīṛā*], and as if they were filled with compassion [*dayā*] for his fate. The thought of this 'compassion' made him fume and he thought to himself: 'If I am going to hell [*narak*] where are they going ?'
>
> But their compassion did not soften their hearts to the extent that the thought of his going to hell made them forget their own [prospects for the] other world [*parlok*]. They decided that they would no longer eat with Shekhar and one day he discovered that they had all submitted a petition to the Principal [asking him] to make separate arrangements for him. [They said that] if this request was not granted they would be compelled to leave the hostel. (SL Vol. 1 pp. 207-8)(7)

Here the belief in (or denial of) both heaven and hell and rebirth are in juxtaposition without any attempt being made, or even felt necessary, to correlate them. Both doctrines are rejected by Shekhar not now because he finds them incompatibile with evolutionary theory but simply because of his implicit assumption that all people are of equal worth and dignity. We also note how for him belief in heaven and hell is inseparably interwined with the social norms of purity. We shall have more to say about this connection below, but at this stage we are simply concerned to point out that he rejects heaven and hell, and at least poses a serious question mark against rebirth. Here is a fundamental reshaping of the parameters of human life. In IS we find Bhuvan adopting a similar position in a letter to Gaura but without feeling any need to argue his case as Shekhar had done:

> After this life there is nothing, Gaura; this life is complete in itself [*yahī sampūrṇa hai*] and its end is the final end [*yahī anta hai*].(IS p. 324)

But Gaura cannot accept such a bleak view as the last word on the subject:

> Was Bhuvan right to say that this life alone is everything, that there is nothing after it, no other world [*parlok*], no rebirth [*punarjanma*] ? She could accept that there is no rebirth and no other world either — she could see no necessity for another birth in order to enjoy the fruits of deeds [*karma-phala*] done in this one, for all accounts must be settled in this life and nothing is carried over into another one — she could go along with all that — but is this life alonc really all there is — this life which is circumscribed by the limits of time and space [*deśa-kāla*] which are in turn limited by our consciousness [*cetanā*] ? Was it not true that we lived many lives not one after the other but all at once, that we lived in several worlds [*lokoṁ meṁ*] at the same time — and that we receive the influences of these worlds through several layers of consciousness [*ekādhik cetanā dvārā*] ? Even if we do not always do this, even if it only happens at certain moments of heightened awareness, at certain peaks of energy [*jīvan-śakti ke kṣaṇoṁ ki uttejanā meṁ*] — but if we can enter on another level [*star*], another world, another life...(IS p. 325)

There are perhaps echoes here of what is to be found, for example, in the *Taittirīya Upaniṣad*, which in a long and complex passage (2.1-3.10, translated in Hume [1931] pp. 283-92) suggests that the human self, and therefore our consciousness, is many-layered. The essence of the passage is caught in its conclusion:

> He who knows this, on departing from this world, proceeding on to that self which consists of food, proceeeding on to that self which consists of breath, proceeding on to that self which consists of mind, proceeding on to that self which consists of understanding, proceeding on to that self which consists of bliss, goes up and

> down these worlds, eating what he desires, assuming what form he desires.(3.10.5, translated in Hume [1931] p. 293)

We are not suggesting that this or any other such passage was directly in Ajneya's mind as he wrote, but rather that the kind of thinking here described would have been familiar if not second nature to him. Further, the achievement of the 'heightened awareness' of which Gaura speaks is a stage on the road to the final goal of most Brahminical Hindu philosophical schools. In other words Gaura here is not thinking wholly new thoughts, rather is she attempting to re-interpret tradition. She does this by placing within a single life-span what tradition had extended over many, and by finding in this world alone what tradition had looked for in others beyond it, though the other worlds are still real and impinge upon our consciousness in this one. A direct return to what Shekhar had rejected is no longer possible yet she finds resources in tradition which can be re-interpreted to produce a more credible and satisfying account of life's significance than Bhuvan was able to offer. In Chapter Five we shall see that in TEHS the figure of Selma embodies in a human life (and death) something of what Gaura had been feeling after in intellectual terms.

We now turn to the boundaries of society which is the second and more complex area where our novels reshape the parameters of human life. In Chapter One we briefly described the Hindu caste system as part of Ajneya's background. We must now elaborate that picture, giving particular attention to the place of ritual purity within it. Also, since one of the important targets for Shekhar's assault on his inheritance is the oppression of women, and since the place of women in society is also important in IS, though in a rather different way, we shall also describe the traditional role and status of women in some detail. The concept of purity defines the external boundaries of the Brahminical social system (8) by separating those within it from those outside, who are regarded as defiled and defiling. The land of India is especially pure and traditionally foreign travel was banned.(9) Purity defines the internal divisions in that it marks not only the theoretical boundaries between the four *varṇas*, but the actual frontiers — which are often blurred — between one caste [*jāti*] and another.(10) It is here that the questions of whom one can marry one's children to, and from whom one can accept food without risk of defilement, assume large importance, for these are the two major points at which different groups of people interact, and so where boundaries need to be defined.(11) Inadvertent contact with an unclean person or substance also needs to be guarded against and here too it is the concept of purity which marks the boundaries. Purity performs this defining function in other cultures also (12), but the Brahminical system has two special features which are not found elsewhere: first, in this system those who are defiled do not lose not power or health, as they normally do in other cultures, but status, so that a Brahmin who is defiled is literally degraded and reduced to the status of a *śūdra* until he — the paradigm is male — has performed the appropriate rituals which can alone ensure his re-admission to his proper position in society. The second feature is that some groups are permanently defiled and defiling because of their birth into a group whose traditional occupation is re-garded as unclean.(Dumont [1972] pp. 76-103)

In many cultures beliefs about society also co-incide with and reflect beliefs about the human body.(Douglas [1970] pp. 147-9) It is therefore no surprise to find that Brahmins attach particular importance to the purity of the head, which corresponds to their own position in society, while the feet, corresponding to the outcastes, are regarded as being especially polluting. In this way the Brahmins' pre-occupation with their own bodily purity re-flects their concern for the purity of society.(Hooker [1989] p. 136) As with any such system, what is outside and potentially defiling is always more powerful than the purity within, which therefore needs to be continually protected.(13)

The system of purity extends beyond the social order and the human body to include sacred geography as well. Here too that which is above is pure and that which is below is unclean. Thus the Ganges is believed to flow down from heaven — the realm of perfect and unsullied purity — to earth via the toe of Vishnu [*Viṣṇu*] and the long hair of Shiva [*Śiva*].(14) It thus makes available on earth the purity of heaven. It has a binary opposite in the underworld, the river Vaitarani [*Vaitaraṇī*] which is the ultimate symbol of filth and defilement.(Hooker [1989] pp. 144-50) Our use of the phrase 'binary opposite', a technical term taken from structuralist thought, indicates that the significance of ritual purity can best be interpreted within the framework of a structuralist model. We have already argued that while we reject structuralism as a total system of explanation, we can sometimes use it as a useful tool of interpretation.(15)

The essence of structuralism as a tool of analysis (16) is the claim that a system can be grasped not in its parts but only as a whole in which the various parts are inseparable from one another. Thus within the Hindu caste system the Brahmin at the top of the social hierarchy depends on the services of the sweeper at the bottom to remove nightsoil and other defiling substances. Only so can the Brahmin maintain his purity which is essential for the proper enactment of the rituals which he performs on behalf of society. The sweeper depends on payment by the Brahmin and other high castes for his livelihood. In this way the concept of purity both separates Brahmin and sweeper from one other and yet at the same time binds them together into a system of mutual interdependence. This means that their separate roles can only be properly understood in relation to each other's.

How do women fit into this scheme in which the paradigmatic roles are all male ? Along with the Brahminical social order itself the traditional role of women is classically expounded in the The Laws of Manu [*Manusmṛti*] (17) which insist that

> In childhood a woman should be under her father's control, in youth under her husband's, and when her husband is dead, under her sons'. She should not have independence. A woman should not try to separate herself from her father, her husband, or her sons, for her separation from them would make both (her own and her husband's) families contemptible.(5.148-9)(18)

A wife's loyalty has nothing to do with her husband's qualities, for

> A virtuous wife should constantly serve her husband like a god, even if he behaves badly, freely indulges his lust and is devoid of any good qualities.(5.154)

The demands of subservience and loyalty are re-inforced by the traditional view of women's nature: their understanding is so unreliable that Manu does not permit them to give evidence in court.(8.77) Further, men must always guard their women for

> By running after men like whores, by their fickle minds, and by their natural lack of affection these women are unfaithful to their husbands even when they are zealously guarded here. Knowing

> that their very own nature is like this, as it was born at the creation by the Lord of Creatures, a man should make the utmost effort to guard them.(9.15-6)(19)

At the heart of this low view of woman lies the fact that during her monthly period, and when she gives birth to a child, she is ritually unclean and so others must keep away from her to avoid the risk of defilement. Manu specifies that a man has to perform a special ritual bath whenever he touches

> an outcaste, a *cāṇḍāla* (20), a woman who is menstruating or has recently given birth, a corpse and so on.(Leslie [1989] p. 85, referring to Manu 5.85 and 103)

Not surprisingly, according to Manu, '*śūdra* status is [now] associated directly with the female state'.(Leslie [1989] p. 38, referring to Manu 9.18), and both women and *śūdras* owe their lowly status to sins committed in a previous birth.(Leslie [1989] p. 246, referring to Manu 12.3 and 9) (Therefore when Shekhar questions rebirth he is also implicitly questioning the low status of both *śūdras* and women). When her husband died a wife might, willingly or unwillingly, mount his funeral pyre to die with him. Much more commonly she lived on as a celibate in an ascetic role, for apart from her husband she had no ritual status. Re-marriage was out of the question.(Leslie [1989] p. 141)(21) A woman had no social role apart from that of wife. Her marriage was equivalent in her life to her husband's investment with the sacred thread in his. This was the ceremony by which a boy was initiated into one of the top three or 'twice-born' *varṇas*, and so enabled to begin his traditional education.(Pandey [1969] pp. 111-25) His wife was expected to serve him 'as her sole deity'.(Manu 2.67) Marriage partners were, and apart from some urban and westernised circles still are, chosen by the parents of the two parties, and girls are normally married young, at the onset of puberty. There is thus no place in this scheme for the independent unmarried woman, still less for the independent divorcee such as Rekha in IS.

Julia Leslie points out that there are two poles of a woman's life which are 'represented by two radically opposed concepts'. These are her dangerous and uncontrolled sexual nature [*strīsvabhāva*] and the 'role model of the virtuous and self-effacing wife [*strīdharma*]'.(Leslie [1989] p. 320)(22)

Manu's code has never been comprehensively and literally enforced, any more than Christians have comprehensively and literally followed the injunctions of the Sermon on the Mount. Also, while the code is formally regarded as normative, it has to cope in practice, like any system of law, with many de facto exceptions. Nonetheless the values it enshrines have been and still are widely influential. For example, a Hindi language pamphlet entitled The Role of Women in Indian Culture and in the Law Books [*Bhāratīya Saṃskṛti tathā Śastroṁ meṁ Nārī Dharma*] sold seventy thousand copies between 1967 and 1980. This pamphlet is based on and quotes frequently from Manu. The code finds popular expression in the The Holy Lake of the Acts of Rama [*Ramacaritamānasa*]. Composed by Tulsi Das [*Tulsī Dās*] (? 1527- ? 1623 CE), and written in *Avadhi*, a medieval precursor of modern Hindi, this poem is a recasting of the *Rāmāyaṇa*. It upholds the fourfold social order expounded by Manu and in the character of Sita [*Sītā*], the gentle and faithful wife of Rama, makes Manu's model of the ideal wife widely known in an accessible and appealing way. This is still the most popular and widely read devotional text in the Hindi language area, and Sita is still the role model for countless Hindu wives.(23) Thus the influence of Manu is still powerful and in SL Shekhar recognises its crucial significance, for when he is writing a book criticising the Hindu social system he actually buys a copy of Manu's code, believing that here is to be found the root of the evils he sees around him.(SL Vol. 2 p. 150)(24)

Yet we must not allow either Manu or Shekhar's criticism of him to blind us to the more positive attitudes to society which are to be found in other parts of the tradition. For example, the *bhakti* (25) movements, in which God is worshipped in personal form, have, since the fifteenth century of our era, preached human equality before God in the realm of worship, if not always in social practice, while modern reform movements have challenged the social inequalities enjoined by Manu. More recently, many women were drawn into India's Independence Movement and found in this a liberation from the constrictions of their traditional domestic role. Not least, other Hindi novelists besides Ajneya have challenged the injustices of caste and the oppression of women, if not always in such a radical fashion as he does.(26) All this forms the background against which Ajneya both explicitly in his first novel, and implicitly in his other two, challenges traditional male assumptions about women.

Against this background we can now examine the ways in which the concept of purity is handled in our novels. We divide our analysis into three areas which are implicit in our previous discussion: food, together with the body, including sexuality; human relationships; and sacred geography, which as we have pointed out is also a link with the realm of transcendence. As our discussion has already shown, this division is somewhat artificial since all three areas are inter-related and frequently overlap.

Turning first to food, we find that orthodox eating arrangements are ridiculed at an early point in SL when Shekhar is a boy at home. The family took into their employment a new cook who must have been a Brahmin, though Ajneya does not explicitly say so, for Brahmin families would normally only eat food cooked by another Brahmin. The new cook thoroughly washed the stove and cooking area and

> drew a line with a kind of soap-stone (used as chalk) [*cūne se*] all around it a full arm's length away from himself. Any cooking vessel [*bartan*] coming inside this area had to be rewashed and if the cook stepped outside it he had to wash his feet again before stepping inside. He jumped inside the circle so that no defiling touch [*chūta*] should come within.(SL Vol. 1 p. 66)

Here defilement works rather like an electric circuit: any contact with impurity has to be broken (hence the jump) otherwise it will come into the circle. However, problems arose when the cook actually had to serve the meals he had prepared. This meant that he repeatedly had to step outside the circle and so wash his feet whenever he did so. To enable him to stay inside the circle his brother was taken on to act as waiter, but even so, whatever vessels had once been taken outside the circle could not be brought back in. This gave the resourceful Shekhar his chance: he put his own used dish back into the circle and this simple manoeuvre, repeated several times, rapidly reduced the whole system to chaos. Not surprisingly the new cook did not stay long !(27) Here Ajneya suggests that traditional food regulations are not only immoral in the sense that they are used to re-inforce the low status of the outcaste, as in the hostel in Madras, but they are also inherently absurd.

Food and defilement also figure together in the last part of

TEHS where Yoke is a prostitute (TEHS p. 107) — and so a defiled person — in German-occupied territory (presumably Norway which would fit in with the Scandanavian setting of the book) in the Second World War. It is difficult to obtain even the barest necessities of life. Yoke, with a cigarette hanging from her mouth, comes into a shop where a man called Jagannathan is buying food.(TEHS p. 105) Jagannathan is an Indian name and is one of the few overtly Indian references in the whole book.(28) He manages to buy some cheese and a few other things.(TEHS p. 104) All at once Yoke takes the cigarette from her mouth and sticks it into the cheese he has just bought. Then she takes the cheese from his hand and deliberately lets it fall to the floor.(TEHS pp. 105-6) She runs from the shop with Jagannathan in pursuit. When he has caught up with her she takes a suicide pill and dies in his presence. She says she has done this so that she could die in the presence of a good man, which is what she believes Jagannathan to be.(TEHS p. 109) So her deliberate act of defiling food leads not to her rejection but to a kind of acceptance. This could be an unconscious rejection by Ajneya of traditional Hindu attitudes to purity. However, a note of caution is in order: we can only make this somewhat tentative suggestion about TEHS in the light of SL where the assault against the tradition is so explicit and so powerful. They would hardly occur to one on a first reading of TEHS without the prior study of SL. Yet why does Ajneya build this incident around the defiling of food ?(29)

In spite of their many obvious differences Yoke and Shekhar share a concern for integrity, and here we can discern the first element in the new anthropology which Ajneya is creating. Shekhar sees through hypocrisy in others, and in her confused and unsatisfactory way Yoke is struggling to find her own authenticity. This concern for integrity is pursued in a different way in Shekhar's reaction to a regular practice which he notices in his own home:

> His mother sometimes went and sat apart from everyone else, did not go into the kitchen and ate her food from separate vessels, and if anyone went near her — and nobody did except for Shekhar's younger brothers — she would say, 'Don't come near me, go away and play'. What was all this about ?(SL Vol. 1 p. 130)

What it was actually about of course was menstruation which while it is happening defiles a woman and so puts her in the category of the *śūdras*. As usual Shekhar asks what is going on but he is simply told that his mother is ill. He can see no evidence for this 'illness' and notes how rapidly his mother always recovers. So another element in his critique is the taboo surrounding any open discussion or explanation of menstruation. Shekhar also asks questions of a number of people in an attempt to discover where babies come from. He is fobbed off with disingenuous and unconvincing answers. When he eventually discovers the truth he is filled with horror. A whole series of mysterious incidents, hints and innuendoes suddenly become clear:

> All were strung on a single thread, became clear, he understood them...and all their movement was in one direction, towards a single hateful and sinful act [*ghṛṇit pāp-karma*], which his own father and mother had performed, Sharada's [*Śāradā's*] (30) father and mother had performed, from the beginning of creation [*sṛṣṭi*] every father and mother had performed. This alone is love [*pyār*]. It was for this that he had desired Sharada; this — unspeakable, hateful, unthinkable, sinful... it is better that you should die, that Sharada should die, better that the whole world should die.(SL Vol. 1 p. 191)

This attitude is strikingly in accord with the attitude towards the sex act which is to be found in parts of the Hindu tradition. According to the *Maitrī Upaniṣad*:

> This body arises from sexual intercourse. It passes to development in hell[-darkness] [*niraya*]. Then it comes forth through the urinary opening. It is built up with bones; smeared over with flesh; covered with skin; filled full with faeces, urine, bile, phlegm, marrow, fat, grease, and also with many diseases, like a treasure-house with wealth.(*Maitrī Upaniṣad* 3.4, translated in Hume [1931] p. 419)

This quotation actually refers to the composition of the body but it is plain from the context that the sex act itself is also regarded as unclean. It is strange that Shekhar can reject almost everything else in the traditional system of purity as it affects society and the body, except the conviction that sex is inherently defiling. Yet even here men and women are equated. He points to the fact that this is an act which men and women perform together, he does not point to the loss of semen by the male partner, which is the most powerful traditional reason for regarding the act as weakening (for the man) and unclean.(31) Further, there is a significant change of attitude in IS where we find that when Rekha first offers herself to Bhuvan he does not accept her because he says sex should be 'the highest experience of beauty [*saundarya kī caram anubhūti*]' (IS p. 136), and he does not want to risk destroying this beauty. Perhaps we can see a link here with other parts of the tradition where sex is accepted in a much more open and positive fashion, such as the *Kāma Sūtras* and other similar erotic texts, and the *Gītāgovinda* where the *gopīs'* love for Krishna [*Kṛṣṇa*] is an analogue for the human devotee's union with God.(32)

Pre-occupation with bodily purity and with the purity of food, as in the Madras hostel incident, is often merged with concern to maintain one's purity from being contaminated by contact with people of low caste. When Shekhar is a child one of his playmates is a girl whose real name nobody knows but whom everyone calls Phulan [*Phūlāṁ*]. She is the daughter of a low caste widow who lives next door. Her mother is thus doubly unfortunate.(33) As the two children play they naturally go in and out of one another's homes. One day Shekhar is told by his parents that when he goes into Phulan's house he must accept nothing to eat because she is of low caste. He asks why it is all right to play with his little friend but not to eat with her. In other words he instinctively wants to give a higher value to human relationships than to the ban on sharing food. He also appears to sense that Phulan is in no way inferior to him. He is told not to ask questions but to do as he is told, but a little later he overhears the widow telling her daughter with pride the name of the caste to which they belong.(SL Vol. 1 pp. 62-3)(34) In the condemned cell he reflects on this incident:

> Today he understands the emotion [*bhāva*], today he can also have some idea of the fearful pain [*bhayaṅkar yantraṇā*] which the widowed mother must have suffered. Only after fully enduring it could she fill her being with pride [*abhimāna*], turning it into a defensive weapon. He could also understand the emotion caused by the arrogant insult [*dṛpta avamānanā*] which made her teach the same pride to Phulan. Today he can understand that the problem cannot be resolved in this way, and that such pride is inappropriate, but even though he knows this he is still compelled to feel sympathy [*sahānubhūti*] and understanding [*saṁvedanā*].(SL Vol. 1 p. 64)

In other words in rejecting discrimination on the grounds of caste the now adult Shekhar and the widow share an implicit conviction of the universal dignity of all people. Here our argument moves an important stage further than a simple concern for personal integrity. In that childhood incident Shekhar can now discern a kindred spirit who was stereo-typed by society but still able to discern and so preserve her natural human dignity. There is also a hint here of the theme of our next chapter: the very pain which society inflicted on this unfortunate woman was the source of vision. It was this that enabled her to perceive her true worth. This illuminates a new element in Ajneya's anthropology: the integrity which Shekhar is seeking cannot be found without pain and suffering.

As he sits in his cell he recalls another incident when he and a friend had once walked for twenty miles in blazing heat. They asked a villager for a drink but he directed them to a river three miles further on. He was unwilling to let them drink from the well by his own nearby home, even though they were Brahmins and he was of low caste. (*ie* they and not he would be defiled if they drank). He was afraid that if he gave them water he would get into trouble with other members of his community. But when Shekhar's companion grew angry and pointed out the inconsistency between this man's obstinate refusal to give them a drink, and the defiling way he earned his bread (35), the man proudly insisted that he earned an honourable and honest living. Shekhar reflects that not all people of low caste have this kind of pride (though Phulan's mother certainly had). Many meekly accept the slave mentality which society thrusts upon them.(SL Vol. 1 pp. 64-5)

Thus the food regulations provoke ridicule, as in the incident when as a boy Shekhar upset the absurdly complicated kitchen arrangements of the family cook. The enforcement of the traditional regulations by Brahmins can serve to enhance the pride with which some of the so-called defiled regard themselves, as with Phulan's mother, and the low-caste villager who refused to give Shekhar and his thirsty friend a drink of water during their long walk. The fact that Shekhar's mother cannot enter the cooking area during her menstruation, and the taboo on talking about it or about sex and 'the facts of life', add to the absurdity and injustice which the purity regulations impose. Behind

Shekhar's rejection of all this we have already begun to discern the outlines of a new anthropology: in human life which is now perceived to be limited to this world and to one life in it, what really matters is a total honesty which refuses to accept the kind of rules which create unnecessary and impractical inconvenience and which also result in some people assuming an innate social superiority over others. Conversely, pride in the identity of one's own despised group is applauded as a refusal to be stereotyped by those at the top of the social hierarchy.

The rejection of traditional attitudes towards the purity of food and water, and towards the body, merges into and overlaps with the second area where purity regulations are important: human relationships. Shortly after Shekhar has left the Brahmin hostel in Madras he pays a visit to the south-east coast of India, in order to discover if the stories he has heard about untouchability in the South are really true.(SL Vol. 1 p. 208) He discovers a wounded woman by a path, picks her up and takes her to the Arya Samaj [*Ārya Samāj*] (36) hostel where he is staying. He later reads in a newspaper that she had died from her injuries, and that she was an untouchable who had been beaten up, presumably by Brahmins, for walking along a path that was out of bounds to her. Here is the most extreme example of caste discrimination which it is possible to find: if the rules of purity can lead not only to social degradation but even to murder then they are indeed totally indefensible. Bearing in mind the fact the Ajneya was familiar with the Bible it is possible that this incident may have been modelled on the parable of the Good Samaritan (Luke 10.25-37), to which it bears an obvious resemblance.

In SL the most striking rejection of traditional norms of purity in human relationships occurs at a turning point of the novel. In one of his bouts of despair (which we discuss at a later point in the book) Shekhar had made a half-hearted attempt to commit suicide by making no attempt to get out of the way of an approaching lorry which only narrowly avoided him. To prevent him making another attempt Shashi [*Śasi*] spent the whole of the next night sitting at the foot of his bed.(SL Vol. 2 pp. 164-70) When she returned home her husband Rameshvar put the worst possible construction on her absence. He literally threw her out of the house, in the process inflicting the injury on her from which she was eventually to die. Shattered in body and mind she painfully made her way back to Shekhar's room. The morning of her arrival is clear and bright — 'beautiful and well-oiled [*sundar aur snigdha*]'.(SL Vol. 2 p. 175) This latter word is hardly translatable into English. It is used of a young leaf which still has its new sheen, or of the newly oiled hair on a person's head. Hair is usually oiled after a bath and such newly oiled hair is a mark of purity. Shekhar thinks to himself that were he a musician, a painter, or a maker of images he could capture the heart of the day in one of these arts, but instead he is going to write — hopefully poetry but certainly something — for he cannot remember a day when his 'mind had been washed clean as it is today [*jaisā dhulā huā uskā man āj hai*]'. Thus the external purity of the day and the inner purity of Shekhar's mind co-incide. Then he suddenly hears the painfully slow footsteps of someone dragging themselves up the stairs:

> Such unwillingness, such weariness at dragging oneself forward out of the mire [*daldala*] of life and out of the tangled net of water-weeds — who is this ill-fated wretch [*abhāgā*], who on such a pure [*punīt*] day as this —?(SL Vol. 2 p. 175)

It is of course Shashi whose arrival has been heralded in language redolent of defilement — the mire — which stands in stark contrast to the purity both of the day itself and of Shekhar's mood. She collapses on to the threshold and describes her state in terms of uncleanness:'

> I have been turned out [*parityaktā*] by my husband. I am impure [*kalaṅkanī*]. There is no place for me [anywhere]. Don't ask me in. (SL Vol. 2 p. 176)

Shashi says she has no place to go to because traditionally in Hindu society a woman thrown out of the house by her husband in this way was in a desperately difficult position: suicide or prostitution were real possibilities, though she might sometimes be accepted back into her parental home. Shekhar defies convention and takes Shashi into his room. Indeed, she must have secretly hoped that he would do just this all along in spite of what she actually said, for why else did she drag herself up three flights of stairs to the door of his fourth floor room ? From now on the relationships between the pair are on a new footing. So far Shekhar has talked and written about the need to change society, particularly in its attitude to women, but in taking the rejected Shashi into his home he actually steps outside the moral boundaries of that society and so does she. Ajneya makes this point clear in an apparently trivial incident which occurs a short time later. Some children who live in the same building come and ask Shekhar to make them some kites. He agrees to do so but later the children's parents forbid them to come again.(SL Vol. 2 pp. 197 and 199-200) We recall the incident when Shekhar himself had been forbidden by his own parents to accept any food in the home of the outcaste Phulan. (SL Vol. 1 pp. 62-4) Now it is Shekhar himself and Shashi whom the world ostracises, but this cannot shift Shekhar's conviction that he has done the right thing in welcoming her. In other words he senses that he is responding to a moral imperative which makes higher claims upon him than the traditional norms which he has rejected, and now, significantly, he has to pay a high price in personal terms for the new principles he has espoused. This isolation from society thrusts him more and more on his own inner resources, a situation for which nothing in his upbringing had prepared him. The pursuit of integrity exacts a price of a rather different kind from that paid by Phulan's mother, and points to an unknown future.

Shashi, however, is much less sure of her ground than Shekhar, and frequently reveals this by her asides. When they are preparing for a meal, Shekhar suggests that she should eat first, wash the vessels and then serve him, but she tells him not to let her clean their cooking vessels.(SL Vol. 2 p. 183) He then says he will not eat until she does. Shekhar is directly challenging traditional norms, for a woman always eats after her husband and Manu lays down that when a man has eaten 'he should leave some remainder [*ucchiṣṭam*] for his wife, his servants and his slaves'.(Leslie [1989] p. 222) Admittedly this is hardly a normal domestic situation since Shashi is not Shekhar's wife, but then, in a mock appeal to tradition, he says that she is his guest — implying that she must therefore accept whatever hospitality he offers. Later, Shekhar wants to kiss her, but she restrains him, saying that her lips are *jūṭhe* — polluted because already touched by another.(SL Vol. 2 p. 221) This word usually refers to the left overs of a meal, but Shashi seems to be using it to suggest that it is her own husband whose physical touch has defiled her.

In this incident we find, for the first time in our study, that traditional norms are not simply challenged and rejected, they are ironically reversed. There are important implications here which we examine in a series of similar examples. In IS Rekha says to Bhuvan:

> Actually I have two sides — one full of character [*caritravān*], natural [*prakṛt*] and free [*mukta*]; the other civilised [*sabhya*] and without character [*caritrahīn*].(IS p. 106)

This is a reversal of the traditional understanding of woman, who, as we have seen was only 'safe' for men when her sexual nature was tamed and controlled within the protected boundaries of marriage. But marriage for Rekha symbolises all that is worst in her experience, which is one reason why she refuses Bhuvan's eventual proposal of it.(IS pp. 213-5) She claims that her 'natural' side is not an untamed menace but good — 'full of character'.

To return to SL: by accepting Shashi into his home Shekhar is giving their personal relationship with one another a higher value than the traditional norms of purity. Those norms demanded that Shashi be cast out from society, and she herself seems inclined to accept them as valid. But Shekhar goes even further than defying these norms: he suggests that Rameshvar, who has so brutally enforced them by violently expelling Shashi, in fact belongs not to the world of purity, but to the world of defilement. Shortly after Shashi's arrival at his room he storms off to have it out with Rameshvar. At the point where they are merely exchanging angry words and Rameshvar has called Shekhar a Communist, the latter thinks to himself that

> this is some other world [*duniyā*], another world of mud [*kardama*], slime and black muck [*kālī bāmī*], from which a poisonous vapour is rising.(SL Vol. 2 p. 180)

Throughout this whole incident the traditional rules of purity are not directly attacked, instead they are ironically reversed. What tradition condemned as impure — Shekar's acceptance of Shashi — is defended, while the champion of the traditional understanding of a woman's purity, Rameshvar, is condemned as belonging to the world of uncleanness. Something similar happens in IS. During the complicated manoeuvres over Rekha's divorce, Rekha's husband Hemendra hears that she is pregnant, though he does not know by whom. He writes to her and she is shattered by the contents of the letter. We are not actually told what he has written, but can guess that he says he knows of her condition. She then writes to Bhuvan of the beauty of their love for one another, setting it in the context of the Vedic marriage hymns (37), but adds, referring to the letter, 'Now this dirty finger-nail [*mailā nākhūn*] comes and tears that union from one end to the other'.(IS p. 239) In other words, although he was her legal husband, Rekha interprets Hemendra's intervention as a gross and wounding act of defilement.(38) There is a comparable ironic reversal in the Gospel of John, where the Pharisees, on the eve of the Passover, refuse to enter the court of the Gentile Pilate 'to avoid defilement, so that they could eat the Passover meal'.(John 18.28) Yet in that court stands Jesus, the pure and holy one. In the novel as in the Gospel the reversal is not explicitly stated, it is simply made by implication and left for the reader to discover. It is all the more telling for that. Narrative, much more than other literary forms, lends itself to making points in this implicit and ironic fashion.

There is another, and much more explicit reversal at an earlier point in SL, and this takes us into the area of sacred geography and cosmology. It happens while Shekhar is a student in Madras. He has now left the Brahmin hostel for the reasons we described at the beginning of this chapter. One evening he goes to a local slum colony. An open drain flows through the middle of it:

> It was evening. The water of the drain was gleaming like old copper. If there had not been a bad smell [*durgandha*] it would have been difficult at that moment to say that the water was dirty [*gandā*].(SL Vol. 1 p. 215 p. 44)

Shekhar is surprised to find himself alone.

> As he was thinking, it was as if a wall fell before his concentrated strength and a path [*mārga*] began to appear. He remembered from the Bible the story of Jesus' forerunner John the Baptist. It was in a place like this that the young man must have stood — with frenzied eyes [*unmatta āmkhoṁ*], scattered untidy hair and wiry body, wearing a deer-skin. He cried, 'Come ! I will anoint [*abhiṣek*] you with the water of life [*jīvan ke pānī se*]!' And it was on just such a dirty red evening that the people of low caste, the rejected dregs of humanity [*mānavatā ke ucchiṣta choṭī jāti ke logoṁ ne*], rejected what he said, saying he must be mad; but hearing his continuous crying out they came to see what the water of life was.

> It seemed to Shekhar entirely appropriate that he should remember that on this spot, for what is the water of life ? The water of the Ganges, Jumna, Godavari, Krishna, Narmada has become lifeless [*prāṇahīn*] through continuous washing in *dharma* and *bhakti*. If life, eternal life [*cirantan jīvan*] is to be found anywhere it is only in such filthy drains which flow, long neglected, in the midst of these untouchables who are the foundation of society [*samāj kī nīṁva*]...the water of the so-called holy rivers which fall [from heaven] is overflowing like the knowledge of the pandits [*paṇḍitoṁ kā pāṇḍitya*], its only use is to sprinkle on funeral pyres and carry away bones in its onward flowing stream.(SL Vol. 1 p. 215)

Shekhar's memory of the Bible is a little hazy, but the references in the first paragraph make it clear that he is thinking of the baptism of Jesus in the Jordan by John. This makes him go on to reflect that the traditional waters of Hindu purity — the sacred rivers — are now 'lifeless', and made so by traditional devotional practices, their water only fit for funeral rituals, like the learning of the *paṇḍits*. Here Ajneya goes a stage further than the ironic reversal of roles which we considered above: he now says that the pursuit of total ritual purity is finally self-defeating, for it ends in barrenness and death. True life, Shekhar realises, is now to be found in the filthy drain which flows among the untouchables who are seen as the 'foundation of society'. Here sacred purity is stood on its head. What was believed traditionally to convey life in fact conveys only death. Geography and social order co-incide and that which was at the bottom of both — and so defiling — is now seen instead as the only source of real life. In other words the very thing which for the system was a source of danger is in fact what it needs for its own life. There is a profound insight here which is to be found in other cultures too and which is very close to some Christian perceptions of the significance of the cross of Christ.(39) Ajneya's appeal to the Bible at this point suggests that he regards it as a resource for this kind of reversal in a way that the Hindu scriptures are not, but tantalisingly, it seems that he never explicitly followed up what he said in this passage.

Shekhar makes an implicit appeal to sacred geography in a very different way in an incident which occurs when he is a student in Lahore — after he has left Madras. The term is over and he is going through one of his periodic bouts of depression, loss of meaning and purpose. He wanders into the red-light area of the city, gazing at the seductive women and listening to their voices. Suddenly he is brought to his senses by the voice of someone asking him to buy some flowers. These were no ordinary flowers but lotuses:

> He staggered as if he had been shot, then coming to his senses he covered his eyes with one hand and fled — fled...in that place — bunches of lotus flowers [*kumuda*] ! the lotus which for him had become the symbol of purity [*svacchatā kā pratīk*].(SL Vol. 2 p. 23)

Here is the reverse of the previous incident, which is not surprising because it is the nature of symbols to be multivalent and so capable of different meanings in different contexts. There the filthy drain became a symbol of purity over against the now defiling sacred rivers of tradition, while here one of the key Hindu symbols of the traditional holy lake, seen unexpectedly in a place of defilement, serves to bring the young Shekhar to his senses. Personal memories may also have played a part. Earlier Shekhar has described a childhood boat trip on the Dal Lake in Srinagar, capital of Kashmir. He plucked half-opened lotus flowers and laid them at the feet of his sister Sarasvati [*Sarasvatī*] (SL Vol. 1 p. 20), to whom he was devoted.(SL Vol. 1 pp. 143-4)

Sacred geography is theologically important because it creates the framework within which human life is lived. It assures people that they have a secure and meaningful place in the scheme of things and this is based on the logically prior conviction that there is indeed a scheme there in the first place. Without such a scheme, in other words without a credible cosmology, human beings suffer loss of meaning. Ajneya is much more conservative in his attitude to sacred geography than he is towards the social order. This is doubtless to be explained by the fact that while his assault on the social injustices and absurdities caused by purity regulations was direct and deliberate, sacred geography belonged to the inherited structure of his thinking. He does not seem to have brought it to the level of consciousness. Indeed apart from the incident by the open drain he keeps the traditional framework even though he often gives it a more secular significance. For example, in Hindu mythology there is a holy lake of still water high in the Himalayas. So important is this that it actually forms part of the title of Tulsi Das's recasting of the *Rāmāyaṇa* — 'The Holy Lake of the Acts of Rama'. This lake and others like it are usually described in terms which heighten their symbolic purity. In the original Sanskrit *Rāmāyaṇa* when Rama is searching for the abducted Sita he thinks of her when he is beside the lake of *Pampā*:

> Its water was covered with lotus flowers and was as clear to the eye as translucent crystal, and the floor beneath the water was pure sand. It was full of fish and turtles and the trees on its banks added to its beauty.(*Rāmāyaṇa* 3.75.16-7)

The transparency of the water means that it is perfectly clear, unruffled by the wind, and the 'pure sand' indicates that there is no mud on the bottom. The lotus, as we have just seen, is a common and powerful symbol of purity — as it also is of inner awakening and awareness. The imagery of the holy lake is taken up shortly after the incident in the red light area of Lahore when Shekhar goes to the Himalayas on a solitary journey in search of absolute beauty. He arrives at an isolated snow-bound lake. In the borderland between sleeping and waking he sees a vision of a beautiful goddess dressed in white dipping her feet in the water. Her face resembles that of someone he knows — Sharada, his adolescent sweet-heart in Ootacamund — or Shashi ?(SL Vol. 2 p. 26) Later he reflects that

> He has spent his life in a city — in the dirt [*gandagi*] and crowds [*bhiṛa*] of a city, in its quarreling [*kalaha*] and hubbub [*kolāhala*] and he has learnt to keep so contented [*santuṣṭa*] and quiet [*cupa*] there that apart from being a single unit [*ikāī*] in the city's population he has no other importance. He is a part [*aṅga*] of that dirt and crowd, of that quarrelling and hubbub.(SL Vol. 2 p. 26)

Here we see the first hint of a theme which is to be elaborated in IS where it assumes much greater significance: as we have seen, traditionally the binary opposite of the pure lake and the sacred rivers is the world of defilement symbolised by the polluted river of the underworld, the Vaitarani. However it seems that for Ajneya the Vaitarani is unconsciously replaced by the large modern city which smothers any possibility of spiritual life and perception. When Shekhar tells his neighbours in Lahore of his impending journey in search of beauty they laugh at him: 'He couldn't even recognise the beauty of an ox', and in a striking image they say he is 'a blind creeping worm [*keṁcuā*] of the city's alleyways'.(SL Vol. 2 p. 26)

In IS the life of the metropolis is epitomised by Chandramadhava, who is an uncultured sensualist — his reading hardly extends beyond Peter Cheyney (IS pp. 24-5)(40) — and a manipulator of other people's lives in his own, usually sexual, interests. He believes that 'wherever we find a little bit of pleasure [*sukha*] we should accept it with eager and grateful hands', but he is oblivious to any higher possibility.(IS p. 70)(41) We learn that he and Bhuvan were fellow-students at college.(IS p. 15) After leaving, Chandramadhava travelled abroad in a continual search for excitement [*sansanī*].(IS p. 15) When we first meet him he is a journalist in Lucknow, which like Delhi, epitomises for Ajneya the modern city. He is street-wise and canny (IS pp. 20 and 24) and for this he even evokes from us a sneaking sympathy, for these qualities are necessary in India's big cities where life is a constant struggle for survival and where there is no safety net in the form of a welfare state to support those in need. He knows Rekha, and in fact it is he who introduces her to Bhuvan (IS p. 12), but he is constantly trying to manipulate her life. She loses one job because of his frequent and unwelcome visits. He helps her find another post as a governness in a princely state (42), but then spreads rumours that she has many lovers. This makes some of the prince's employees think she is a loose woman. Their unwelcome advances make her leave this post as well.(IS pp. 46 and 53-4) Chandramadhava had intended this for he had wanted her to be free of her job so that he could ask her to come with him on a trip to the hills.(IS pp. 51-2)

Our sympathy is evoked for the innocent and vulnerable Rekha, an unattached woman with no-one to protect her from the unscrupulous behaviour of men. This is a reversal and so implicit critique of the traditional attitude which was precisely the opposite: it is men who are at risk from the uncontrolled sexuality of single women.(43) Chandramadhava asks Bhuvan to come along as chaperone on his projected journey, but his scheme misfires and Bhuvan and Rekha go without him.(IS pp. 52-7 and 87-94) He declares his infatuation for Rekha in a letter in which he makes it plain that he lives only by his instincts and thinks she should do the same.(IS pp. 91-4) Here is an example of the very kind of animal behaviour which Ajneya so deplored.(44) Rekha writes to Bhuvan and tells him how Chandramadhava had taken her to the Lucknow Residency in a dust storm (IS p. 96) and made unwelcome advances to her. She comments to Bhuvan that she 'ought not to drag him too into this mire [*āpko is kīcaṛa meṁ khīṁcnā bhī na cahiye*]'. (IS p. 96) Both the dust storm and the mud reflect the traditional language of defilement. By contrast when Bhuvan and Rekha finally have sex they do so by the light of the full moon (another symbol of purity) beside a beautiful lake high in the mountains of Kashmir (IS p. 152), a place which Rekha actually refers to as 'the roof of the world [*duniyā kī chat*]', (IS pp. 156 and 158) and which is reminiscent of the holy lake of tradition. A year after their time in Kashmir, and when she is in the depths of despair after her abortion, she writes to Bhuvan:

> A year ago today I was on the Northern Meru [*Meru*], to-day I am on the Southern Meru. On that day I was on the roof of the world and today — what hell [*pātāla*] can be deeper than the one I am in today?(IS p. 269)(45)

Meru was the mythical mountain believed to be at the centre of the world, a place of paradisal purity. The North is the area of auspiciousness, the South of inauspiciousness. In the *Purāṇas* we find that the original Meru is given a binary opposite in the South.(O'Flaherty [1980] p. 81) So here too we see the traditional pattern of sacred geography maintained but in a secular form. This evidence points to the fact that IS is partially open to a structuralist interpretation. Pushed to its theoretical conclusion this would make the characters devoid of any significant life and independence of their own and reduce them to mere cyphers — embodiments and illustrations of the implicit structure which would then constitute the 'meaning' of the novel — an ironic conclusion indeed for an author who made so much of the freedom of the individual. Certainly Chandramadhava, and his boon companion Hemendra, Rekha's homosexual husband, both fit the structure so completely that they have no role or character outside it. They are too bad to be true and are totally beyond any kind of change or 'redemption'.(46) But this is not so of Bhuvan who experiences a real and liberating transformation of which Gaura's love is the cause and agent. This transformation, which we consider later, is further evidence for the new anthropology which we have been exploring.

We turn now to TEHS. On the face of it nothing could be

further than this novel from the pattern of sacred geography which we have just been considering, yet even here there may be hints of it. The snow which forms the ever-present setting of this novel is of course one of the great Hindu and indeed universal symbols of purity. The snow-clad peaks of the Himalaya are traditionally the abode of the gods and we have just seen that it was near those peaks that Bhuvan and Rekha made love. Yoke reflects that her boy-friend Paul is

> above the land of snow... in the fresh air [*khulī havā*] with I don't know who; and I — I am here underneath the land of snow, suffocating [*ghuṭan meṁ*], and in the company of that...(TEHS p. 30)

There could be a hint here of the traditional map of sacred geography, with life and purity belonging to the world 'above' and death and defilement to that 'below' where Yoke finds herself. There is also a hint of what we have already noticed in SL: absolute purity is paradoxically deadly and lifeless. Shortly before Selma's death Yoke, looking out of the window, gazes at the 'untouched [*achūti*] white which is called virgin [*kvāṁrī*] snow':

> There was something in that unblemished whiteness [*achūtī safedī*] which was false [*jhūṭha*], or which seemed false to Yoke. It was probably not the expanse of snow that was false, for its emptiness [*sūnāpan*] was as much an unbroken truth as death [*mṛtyu*]. Perhaps the feeling of falseness was transferred from her own rebellion against Selma's story.(TEHS p. 91)

Yoke's feeling that there is something 'false' about the 'unblemished whiteness' of the snow reminds us of Shekhar's experience by the open drain when he felt much the same about the unsullied purity of the holy rivers of Hindu tradition. Both experiences suggest that the pursuit of total external purity is ultimately barren and self-defeating. This is matched by an opposite experience: when Selma has died Yoke feels that the whole room is pervaded by the odour of death. Her efforts to keep the odour in Selma's room by shutting the door and stopping the crevices with a sheet and a blanket are of no avail. She finally realises that the smell is coming from her own body. Even the snow is filled with it, perhaps because she has touched it.(TEHS pp. 95-6) This could be read as a total rejection of the traditional Hindu view of ritual purity, for here the menace of defilement comes not from without but from within and so there can be no external defence against it. If that is so then the whole elaborate system of boundaries and protection must collapse.(47) In the second part of the book, which is a flashback to Selma's youth, she is isolated in her shop on a bridge surrounded by flood water:

> No sight-seers came. Only floating animals or the carcases [*lāśeṁ*] of animals, as if drawing a line of stench [*durgandha*] after them, passed by under the bridge.(TEHS p. 68)

On the next page the flood water is described as the 'filthy stream of the flood at the end of the world [*pralaya* (48) *ki maṭmailī dhārā*]'.(TEHS p. 69) So the water itself belongs to the world of death and defilement. The photographer, to whom Selma refuses to give any of her own supply of drinking water, eventually drinks from the flood-water, goes mad, jumps into the flood and drowns. Yet the water of the great final flood into which everything dissolves is also the source of new creation, so just as total purity is lifeless and dead, so total defilement is the source of new life.

We now briefly summarise the evidence which we have examined in this chapter: we first noted how in our three novels the traditional beliefs in heaven and hell and in rebirth are rejected, and with them the traditional sanctions for obeying the rules of ritual purity which upheld the hierarchical caste system. Those rules are themselves directly attacked and ridiculed, especially where they result in the degradation of outcastes and women. They are also attacked in a more indirect and ironical way when people (the brutal husbands of married women) and rivers (such as the Ganges and the Narmada) which would normally be regarded as belonging in their different ways to the world of purity are placed instead in the realm of pollution. We have noted something similar in Yoke's response to virgin snow. Traditional structures are here turned against themselves to justify the behaviour of those who have deliberately stepped outside them in the name of a new moral vision. Also important is Shekhar's passionate concern for people of outcaste origin, such as Phulan and her daughter, the woman he finds dying by the path in South India, and those who live in the slum colony through which flows the open drain. The focussing of attention on life as it is lived here and now is bound to involve a sympathy with those who were rejected — and worse — when their lives were interpreted within the parameters of traditional social and transcendental boundaries.

Our examination of the theme of boundaries in IS and TEHS led to two strikingly different conclusions. On the one hand Gaura in IS and Selma in TEHS both in their different ways open up human life to the possibility of what at this stage we simply refer to as 'the transcendent'. Here, like Ajneya himself (49) they want to move beyond the reductionist limitation of human life to this world only which Shekhar's assault seems to imply. Yet on the other hand we found that Ajneya's treatment of sacred geography is, with one or two exceptions, much more conservative than his treatment of purity regulations. We saw that Chandramadhava's singularly unattractive character can been seen as fitting into the geographic scheme, and that if life in the modern city, and people such as Chandramadhava who are its denizens, are indeed irredeemable, then this may be partly because they occupy the lowest place in Ajneya's new hierarchy. Perhaps because he does not appear to have brought this to the level of consciousness it bears a remarkably close resemblance to what he had in other areas of his thought either rejected or transformed.

At this point we can extend the range and depth of our theological conversation with these novels: purity regulations are a prominent feature of the Bible and especially of the priestly books of Ezekiel, Leviticus and Numbers.(50) As with Brahminical Hinduism these regulations serve to mark boundaries, and in particular those between Israel and the supposedly impure world of Gentile life and practice. Regulations of this kind play a particularly important part in the life of the Qumram community. Happily for our purposes it so happens that more is known about the life of this community than of any other which was contemporary with Jesus. In its life the regulations had the function of marking off the community not only from Gentiles but also from other groups within contemporary Judaism whose observance was regarded as unsatisfactory. A further parallel with our theme is that in the view of Qumran the true meaning of the Law was only revealed to its own sacred community whose duty it was to protect it from outsiders. We saw above that Mary Douglas has drawn attention to the similarly defensive frame of mind to be found among some Brahmins.(51) We have seen abundant evidence in this chapter for the way in which Ajneya rejects both the regulations and the attitudes of mind that go with them. It is instructive to compare his attitude to that of Jesus who also rejects the regulations and puts in their place a more inclusive pattern of human identity based on the will of God as Father. While Ajneya might well have questioned the role of God in Jesus' teaching he would surely have endorsed both his attitude to purity and his generously inclusive attitude to people. Indeed, the incident beside the open drain provides strong evidence for believing that this is in fact the case.

Further, Jesus does not try to protect his teaching and turn it into a jealously guarded secret, he proclaims it in the public realm where it becomes dangerous and subversive. This points us back to the point we made in the Introduction where we suggested that Ajneya's novels could be understood as 'testimony' in the public realm in the sense proposed by Paul Ricoeur.(52) Indeed to publish novels which challenge tradition is by definition a public act which invites a public response.

The parallels do not end here for we have also noted that Shekhar pays a price for his rejection of the norms of ritual purity, a price which involves him in suffering. This is a theme which runs in different ways through all our novels and it leads to the purification of vision. This is another potential area of consensus, for while the Christian scriptures criticise traditional rules of external purity they have a very different attitude to the inward kind: 'Blessed are those whose hearts are pure; they shall see God.'(Matthew 5.8) This is the theme to which we turn in the next chapter.

NOTES

1. See above, p. 4.
2. See Walker [1968] Vol. 2 p. 562. Walker's two volumes, of which we shall make frequent use, contain a wealth of information not readily available elsewhere, but his incidental judgements on many aspects of Hinduism are

extremely negative and need to be discounted.

3. Faith in rebirth seems to be accepted in the Upanishads without further argument. Scholars generally assume that it formed part of the religion of the indigenous peoples of India, which influenced Vedic religion quite heavily.(Klostermaier [1990] p. 203)
4. We have already referred to this phenomenon: see above, p. 26.
5. See, for example, Ayrookuzhiel [1983] pp. 139-44, Gosling [1976] p. 163, and Fuller [1992] pp. 245-52. This evidence also seems to be in harmony with Ajneya's own views: see above, pp. 3-4. In one of his other books he spells out some of its consequences:

   > There was a time when it was meritorious to put one's own life at risk for the sake of ants or bedbugs, there is a time when it is anti-social to feed bread to crows and monkeys because there is not enough bread for human beings.(Vatsyayan [1976] p. 18)

   The meaning of this is that rebirth enabled people to see life in a continuum embracing human beings, animals and insects, for even an insect might eventually be reborn as a human being. If rebirth is rejected then human life here and now becomes the all-important focus for moral responsibility.
6. For some examples of this see Hooker [1989] pp. 114-5.
7. A crow, because of its black colour and because it eats carrion, is, like a dog, especially defiled and defiling, as is a 'worm'. The Hindi word which this translates is a generic term for which the slang 'creepy-crawly' is probably the nearest English equivalent. 'Next birth' is the normal phrase for 'next life in the succession of rebirths'.
8. The essence of the Hindu social order is encapsulated in the Sanskrit compound *varṇāśramadharma,* which can be translated as 'the sacred ordering of the (four) castes and of the (four) stages of life'. See also Chapter One, note 44.
9. In his autobiography Gandhi describes how he fell foul of this rule before he went to England as a student, and again on his return.(Gandhi [1966] pp. 34-6 and 75-6) This illustrates the fact that most forms of Hinduism are linked to the land of India in a way that Christianity is not linked to the land of its origin.
10. For the difference between *varṇa* and *jāti,* see Chapter One, note 3.
11. See above, p. 24.
12. Purity regulations were important for the ancient Hebrews and there are many examples of them in the book of Leviticus.(Douglas [1970] pp. 54-72)
13. This produces a defensive frame of mind which Mary Douglas captures in some words which describe a group of Brahmins in Western India:

    > The ritual life of the Coorgs...gives the impression of a people obsessed by the fear of dangerous impurities entering their system. They treat the body as if it were a beleagured town, every ingress and exit guarded for spies and traitors. Anything issuing from the body is never to be re-admitted, but strictly avoided. The most dangerous pollution is for anything which has once emerged gaining re-entry.(Douglas [1970] p. 147)
14. Vishnu and Shiva are the two main deities who are worshipped by Hindus all over India to-day. See Danielou [1991] pp. 149-249, and for a briefer account, Walker [1968] Vol. 2 pp. 574-6 and 406-9. For the myths which describe the descent of the Ganges from heaven to earth, see Walker [1968]

Vol. 2 pp. 326-8.

15. See above, pp. 15-7.
16. For two useful summaries of structuralism see Bowker [1973] pp. 86-115, and Eagleton [1983] 104-26.
17. The Laws of Manu were '[P]robably composed sometime around the beginning of the Common Era or slightly earlier'.(Doniger and Smith tr [1991] p. xvii) They are the foundation document of all Brahminical law and all later systems are based on them. 'Manu' means simply 'man' but is also the actual name of a number of prestigious characters of myth. This name was probably attached to the code in order to enhance its authority.
18. This and other quotations from Manu are taken from Doniger and Smith tr [1991].
19. The last sentence is not entirely clear. A better translation is:

    > Knowing their disposition, which the Lord of creatures laid in them at the creation, to be such, (every) man should most strenuously exert himself to guard them.(Bühler tr [1886] p. 93)

20. A *cāṇḍāla* is a man born from a *śūdra* father and a Brahmin mother, a breach of caste norms which was traditionally regarded as the most reprehensible of all.(Beteille [1992] pp. 19-21)
21. The remarriage of widows was permitted lower down the caste hierarchy.
22. This division is reflected in

    > the traditional twofold classification of female deities: the 'terrifying' or 'fierce' [*ugrā*] goddesses such as Durgā, Kalī or Cāmunda; and the 'gentle' or 'pleasing' [*śāntā, saumyā*] ones such as Pārvatī, Satī, Lakṣmī or Rādhā. It is no surprise that the former group are usually depicted as wild, destructive females with rampant appetite and sexuality, and the blood of battlefield, sacrifice and menstruation. In contrast, the latter group consists of ideal goddess-wives whose powers of chastity, fertility and prosperity -- derived from their husbands and thus subordinate to them -- are in turn the fundamental source or *śakti** of their husbands' powers within the scheme of *dharma*.(Leslie [1989] p. 320)

    **sakti* literally means 'power' or 'energy' and

    > is the term applied to the wife of a god, and signifies the power of a deity manifested in and through his consort. The deity and his wife represent the dual aspect of the divine unity, and together symbolise the power of the godhead.(Walker [1968] Vol. 2 p. 336)

23. Sita, the wife of Rama, insists on accompanying her husband when he is unjustly sentenced to fourteen years of exile in the jungle. There she is abducted by Ravana [*Rāvaṇa*], the demon king of Lanka [*Laṅkā*]. After a long search and a great battle she is eventually rescued by Rama and his allies, but before being accepted back by Rama, who is now doubtful of her sexual purity, she has, at his insistence, to pass through a fire ordeal. In later versions of the Epic, notably that by Tulsi Das, it was only a shadow Sita which was abducted by Ravana. The fire ordeal now signifies the change back from the shadow to the real Sita, who is thus able to function as a perfect role model for Hindu wives, her purity no longer open to question. For details of this see Whaling [1980] pp. 247-50. Also, see below, note 43.
24. We provide the relevant information about Manu's code here and in note 17, rather than at the first reference to it in our text (p.56), since here the

code is central to our argument while there it was not.

25. For a description of these movements see Klostermaier [1990] pp. 210-75.
26. We have already given some examples of this. See above, pp. 63-4.
27. To understand this last incident we need to set it in the context of a traditional Hindu meal: the family eat sitting cross-legged on the floor of the kitchen. Thus we must assume that Shekhar was in this position but near enough to the line the cook had drawn to seize this opportunity to cause mayhem!
28. The name Jagannathan means 'Lord of the world' and is sometimes applied to the gods Vishnu and Shiva.(Monier-Williams [1899] p. 408). Ajneya himself writes of this incident:

> Jagannathan is a symbolic name, whatever language you care to translate it into. It is not a symbol of Indianness but of faith [*āsthā*] -- and it is only in faith that the views of East and West can meet...Jagannathan's appearance at the end of the novel is not the entry of a clearly defined human being, it is only a sign of this, that Yoke has arrived somewhere.(*'Apne Apne Ajnabī—lekhak ki dṛṣṭi meṁ'*—Ranvir Rangra, *Jñānodaya* July 1969 p. 19, quoted in Patel [1983] p. 345)

A key word in this quotation is *āsthā* which we have here translated by 'faith'. We have already commented on this word in a similar context (see above, p. 44) and we shall have more to say about its theological implications at a later point in the book.

29. We argued on page 54 that our novels belong within four 'canons', the first of which is as a trio within their author's total literary output. If we accept that each 'canon' creates a context in which a distinctive interpretation of each text is possible then we are justified in reading TEHS in the light of SL, as we do here. Also, if we read TEHS not specifically in the Indian but in the wider literary context which its translation into English makes possible, then we can also expect to find meanings which are not apparent in its original setting.
30. Sharada was his adolescent sweet-heart in Ootacamund.(SL Vol. 1 pp. 160-78.
31. The belief that the loss of semen in the sex act diminishes a man's strength is deep-rooted and widespread in India.(Carstairs [1957] pp. 84-7) One of the words for someone who has renounced marriage and become a *saṃnyāsin* is *ūrdhvaretas*--'he who retains his seed'.(Monier-Williams [1899] p. 222)
32. The *gopīs* are 'cowgirls' or 'milkmaids' who were devoted to Krishna. The *Kāma Sūtras* of *Vātsyāyan Mallanāga* is a treatise on 'the science of love', probably composed around 500 CE.(Keith [1966] pp. 467-70). The *Gītāgovinda* is a long poem devoted to Krishna who

> is the object of passionate love that inspired some of India's greatest poets to unrivalled masterpieces, like Jayadeva who wrote the immortal *Gītāgovinda*.(Klostermaier [1990] p. 231)

The *Gītāgovinda* actually gets a mention in SL. Shekhar's father overhears him singing a few lines of it to himself and angrily asks where he has read it. Shekhar -- who is never at a loss for words -- replies that he hasn't, but has overheard his father singing it himself ! This earns him several slaps and the comment from his father that these days boys 'only learn dirty things [*gandī-gandī bateṁ hī sīkhte haiṁ*]'.(SL Vol. 1 p. 183) This of course makes

Shekhar all the more eager to read the book for himself. It is on his father's shelves and he manages to look at it when no-one else is about, though without actually understanding it, for at this stage he has not yet discovered the nature of the sex act.(SL Vol. 1 pp. 182-3)

33. As belonging to a low caste and as a widow, though since she was of low caste the ban on remarriage would have been much less strict than it was for Brahmin widows. See above, note 20.
34. She uses the word *jāt* which is an abbreviated form of *jāti.* For this see Chapter One, note 3.
35. Shekhar's companion says: 'He probably carries human excrement on his head all day [*din bhar to mailā ḍhotā hogā*].'
36. The is one of the reforming movements within Hinduism which was founded in the nineteenth century. For details of its origins and history see Sarma [1944] pp. 164-92.
37. Rekha says:

    The Vedic marriage hymns are beautiful if you think of them as beautiful and pornographic if you think of them as pornographic. I remember [one of them]: 'I join my bones to your bones, my flesh to your flesh, my skin to your skin...' What they say is right, and we joined eyes to eyes, lips to lips, breast to breast, life to life, love to love, and yes, passion to passion.

38. Hemendra is first mentioned when Bhuvan asks Chandramadhava to tell him of Rekha's background. According to Chandramadhava people said she had been in love with someone whom she could not marry. Then, with a broken heart, she had accepted Hemendra, the man chosen by her parents, but 'She could not give him what she should have given to her husband [*use vah na de sakī, jo pati ko denā cāhiye*].'(IS p. 27) Later she tells Bhuvan in a moment of anguish how Hemendra had promised eternal fealty to a boy in Delhi, and even told her that he had only married her at all because she looked like this boy.(IS p. 112) Thus we learn that Hemendra is homosexual, or possibly bisexual -- we know he has been living with another woman in Malaya.(IS p. 27) His employers are about to transfer him from Malaya to North West Africa where he will be in an all-white community. He will therefore have to legalise, at least for appearance's sake, his relationship with the woman with whom he has been living. It is for this reason that he will have to divorce Rekha.(IS p. 188)
39. Mary Douglas comments: 'Religions often sacralise the very unclean things which have been rejected with abhorrence.'(Douglas [1970] p. 188) She gives examples of this from several different cultures.(pp. 188-210) We touch here on the theme of paradox: in the terms of Christian faith and theology, Christ is the master who behaves like a servant, the mighty king who is powerless on the cross, the holy one who appears to be defiled, the innocent one who is condemned. These paradoxes (and there are others) are similar in structure to Ajneya's use of paradox in the passage we are considering.
40. A writer of popular and sleazy detective novels in the nineteen forties and fifties.
41. In philosophy and indeed in the general usage of Hindi the word *sukha* means 'this worldly pleasure'. Chandramadhava's use of it here is an implicit confession that denies the possibility of any higher form of joy or ultimate bliss -- for which the normal word is *ānanda.*

42. British India covered about two thirds of India's territory (for the extent of which see Introduction, note 2). The remaining areas consisted of semi-independent states which were governed by hereditary rulers. These states were incorporated into India at the time of Independence. The rulers' constitutional power had now gone but the Indian government continued to pay them substantial privy purses which enabled them to continue living in style. Rekha is now employed as governess for the children of such a family.
43. We must not exaggerate this point. By no means all male characters in myth were paragons of virtue in their behaviour towards women. Ravana, the demon king of Lanka, who abducted Sita, is a case in point.
44. See above, p. 4.
45. For the role of Mount *Meru* in classical mythology see Walker [1968] Vol. 2 p. 184. The North is auspicious because when the sun is in its northern course the hours of daylight are increasing, when the sun is in its southern course they are decreasing. So the South is traditionally associated with death.

    In Ajneya's English translation of this passage he has 'North Pole' and 'South Pole' instead of 'Northern' and 'Southern *Meru*'. Evidently he thought that the reference to *Meru* swould not be understood by his English language readers, but his translation completely misses the point. Lovers would hardly regard either Pole as a place of paradisal bliss !(Ajneya [1980] p. 280)
46. In Chandramadhava's case we see evidence for this in his crude attempts to manipulate Rekha, in his lack of interest in the high culture which so attracts Bhuvan and Gaura (IS pp. 81-2), in his fondness for the bottle(IS pp. 184-5), in his superficial attitude to his own profession of journalist (IS pp. 20-4), and in his callous and indifferent attitude towards his wife and children.(IS pp. 191-3) His character is devoid of any depth and in the end he becomes a Communist. Ajneya's own hatred of Communism was well-known. It is as if he poured all that was bad into Chandramadhava and Hemendra. For further comments by a leading Hindi critic on the character of Chandramadhava, and to the flaw in Ajneya the novelist to which this points, see below, Chapter 5, note 10. For hints of a possible redeeming feature in Chandramadhava's character, see above, p. 96.
47. Here again, this is a reading of TEHS in the light of SL.
48. In Hindu mythology the world regularly comes to an end with a great flood or fire [*pralaya*], and is then renewed, often out of the waters. In other words just as human life is repeated again and again through a series of rebirths, so too is the world destroyed and then 'reborn' again and again. Thus in the context of the present passage, the great flood is the ultimate in terms of defilement, for all boundaries have disintegrated, yet it is also from those same waters that new life and new worlds are eventually born.
49. See above, pp. 3-4.
50. For this paragraph I am indebted to Riches [1980] pp. 112-44. For a fuller comparison of the theme of purity in the Christian scriptures with the traditional Hinduism which Ajneya attacked, see Hooker [1989] pp. 132-91.
51. See above, note 13.
52. See above, p. 14.

4

SUFFERING AND THE PURIFICATION OF VISION

The central theme of the last chapter was Ajneya's assault on the traditional understanding of ritual purity which defined both the internal and external boundaries of the Hindu social order. We noted at the end of the chapter that there is a parallel with the attitude and practice of Jesus towards the rules of ritual purity of his own time and place. In both cases the protest was made on behalf of a more generous and inclusive understanding of humanity. This was a further element in the consensus to which we have already made frequent reference. An important difference is the fact that Jesus seems to have drawn his protest from his understanding of God as father, while for Ajneya, at least in SL, God was denied along with the oppressive social order in whose support the traditionalists invoked his name. However, Gaura in IS questions Bhuvan's denial that there is anything beyond this life, and Selma in TEHS seems at the end of her life to have discovered a faith that there is indeed something more. Moreover, while our author has nothing good to say about purity in an external and ritualistic sense he has a much more positive interpretation of the concept when it is understood inwardly. He believes that it is possible to attain an inner purity of vision and that this makes possible a special kind of clear-sightedness into human situations. He understands this not as a natural endowment but as something which is achieved through suffering. We devote this chapter to an explication of this subject. Its importance is explicitly emphasised in different ways in the introductory sections of both SL and IS, before the texts of the novels actually begin. Within all three novels it constantly recurs as an important theme.The Introduction to SL is written over Ajneya's signature and does not form part of the text of the novel itself. Its opening sentence reads:

> In suffering [*vedanā*] there is a power [*śakti*] which gives sight [*dṛṣṭi*]. He who is in agony [*yātanā*] can become a seer [*draṣṭā*]. (SL Vol. 1 p. 7)

Ajneya goes on to say that SL is the fruit of ten years labour and is still incomplete (1), and that it is the attempt to put into words a 'vision' (he actually uses the English word) which he saw in a single night. This was the night in which he was arrested and feared that he might be sentenced to death. He refers to this experience elsewhere and clearly it was seminal.(2) A month after it happened he began to write what was to be the first draft of SL. He tells us in the Introduction that the whole novel is 'a record of personal suffering' -- he again uses the English words.(SL Vol. 1 p. 10) He also quotes from a well-known essay by T S Eliot, again in the original English:

> There is always a separation between the man who suffers and the artist who creates; and the greater the artist the greater the separation.(3)

He makes the same point about the fundamental significance of suffering in IS, but in a rather different fashion. On a fly-leaf before the novel begins he puts two stanzas of poetry. The first is the transliteration of part of a poem by Shelley:

> Many a green isle needs must be
> In the deep wide sea of misery,
> Or the mariner, worn and wan
> Never thus could voyage on.(4)

The second is from a poem of his own:

> Suffering: she burnishes [*māṁjatā hai*] us all: and though
> To let go [*mukti denā*] herself she may not know
> Those whom she holds [*māṁjatā hai*] she teaches
> All others to liberate [*mukta rakheṁ*].(5)

The quotation from Shelley is an apt description of Bhuvan for whose philosophy of life pain is central. Indeed Chandramadhava describes him in characteristically sardonic fashion as having 'a doctrine of pain-worship [*Bhuvan kā duḥkha-pūjā kā ek siddhānta hai*]'.(IS p. 43) Ajneya's own lines encapsulate the life and character of Rekha who suffers much but refuses to tie Bhuvan to herself, eventually 'liberating' him so that he can marry Gaura. In a rather different way the dying Shashi gives Shekhar his freedom at the end of SL, and so the poem can also be read retrospectively as applying to the first novel as well as to the second. In TEHS there is nothing corresponding to the introduction and poem at the beginning of the two earlier works, but there are hints that the ageing and dying Selma has suffered much and that this has given her an insight which the much younger Yoke does not possess and which indeed she cannot tolerate. All these points we elaborate below.

In giving such a central place to pain and suffering Ajneya is doing nothing new, for they are also important elements in Brahminical Hindu thinking. This can be demonstrated in the first instance by a glance at vocabulary. Sanskrit has two rhyming monosyllables which are often used together: *sukha* and *duḥkha*. These respectively mean pleasure and pain of a general and this-worldly kind. The pain may be anything from mild discomfort to intense agony or grief. Other words can also be used to refer to suffering in this general sense: *kaṣṭa*, *pīṛā* and *vyathā* all have a similarly wide range of meaning, while *kleśa* is more limited and intense, meaning anguish or pain, as do *vedanā* and *yātanā*. This last word is also used more specifically for the pains of hell. These Sanskrit words are part of Hindi's common coinage and Ajneya uses them all. He also uses the common Urdu word for pain, *darda*.(6) This wide range of vocabulary reflects the fact that the subject of suffering has a prominent place in Indian thought. Indeed, it is the starting point for the philosophical-theological quest. For example, a standard introduction to *Advaita Vedānta* philosophy states:

> (The aspirant) because he is burnt by the fire of birth and death and other this worldly torments, goes to a *guru* who is well-versed in knowledge of *Vedānta*, just as a man afflicted by a burning headache runs to a pond to assuage his pain.(Tripathi [1975] p. 13)

In similar vein the first lines of the standard introductory work on *Sāṁkhya*(7) philosophy read:

> Because of the torment of the threefold suffering, (there arises) the

> desire to know the means of counteracting it. If (it is said that) this (desire -- i.e., enquiry) is useless because perceptible (means of removal are available), (we say) no, since perceptible means are not final or abiding. (*Sāṁkhyakārikā* 1, translated in Larson [1979] p. 255)(8)

Often it is not simply suffering which must be transcended but pleasure and pain together which are seen as a 'pair of opposites [*dvandva*]', along with, for example, heat and cold, love and hate (in the sense of attachment to or revulsion from particular objects), and wealth and poverty. The aim of much traditional spiritual discipline is to rise above and so be unaffected by these pairs. The need for such transcendence is taught in the *Gītā*:

> Content to take whatever chance may bring his way, Surmounting all dualities (*dvandva*), knowing no envy, The same in failure and success, Though working [still] he is not bound. (*Bhagavadgītā* 4.22, translated in Zaehner ed [1978] p. 268)

We know that Ajneya read this text during the course of his education. He also refers to it critically in the Introduction to SL.(SL Vol. 1 p. 8)(9)

Our account of the place of suffering within Brahminical Hindu thought is confirmed by other sources, for example:

> One's goal should be liberation (however this may then be described) from the seductive thrall of this world. The *Gītā* says that this world is 'the abode of sorrow' (8.15); Raman Maharshi has described it as a 'wild and terrible forest' and a 'prison'. The wise person realises that even our earthly pleasures contain the seeds of their own decay, for as soon as we are gratified boredom sets in or we grow anxious that something will snatch the cause of our gratification from us. In short, like Tweedledum and Tweedledee, *sukha* or pleasure and *duḥkha* or pain are inseparable, with *duḥkha* dominating the relationship.(Lipner [1994] p. 240)

Thus suffering, sometimes on its own, and sometimes as one side of the coin of which worldly pleasure is the other, is the starting point in the quest for true reality. Indeed it is what makes the quest necessary, but suffering does not purify vision, rather does it impair it. To be caught up in suffering or in pleasure, and so to allow them to influence one's inner being is precisely what being ensnared in the pairs of opposites means. Thus the whole point of the quest is not to make use of suffering but to escape from it in order ultimately to be unaffected by it. Here we begin to see that in his novels Ajneya is offering a radical challenge to this traditional understanding.

We now set out the salient points of this challenge. Later in the chapter we elaborate on them, with references to the relevant passages in the novels. A remarkable fact is that it is mainly, though not exclusively, women whose vision is purified. We saw in the previous chapter that Ajneya is especially concerned with the suffering of women. In describing it he draws on traditional vocabulary but gives it a new twist. For example at a certain moment in the Brahminical Hindu marriage ceremony the couple circumambulate the sacred sacrificial fire and the bride pours parched grains into it.(10) This act of offering an oblation is called *homa*. A synonymous term is *āhuti* which means 'offering oblations with fire to the deities'.(Monier-Williams [1899] pp. 162 and 1306) We shall see below that Shashi refers to her own unhappy marriage as being both *homa* and *āhuti*. She uses these terms to suggest that in her marriage she was figuratively speaking burnt up and destroyed. It is by no means unusual in Hindi to refer to the woman's role in marriage as sacrificial in a less extreme and literal sense (11), indeed in all cultures wives and mothers have offered themselves in this way for the sake of their families. It has added force in the Hindu context where, as we have seen, tradition allows the woman no independent identity apart from her husband.(12) But Ajneya uses the traditional terms to describe marriages which are so disastrous for the female partners that they can be described as living deaths. He also uses the same terminology more positively outside the context of marriage when, as we shall see below, Shekhar (in SL) and Bhuvan (in IS) reflect on the great sacrifices which Shashi and Rekha respectively make for them, sacrifices which neither man feels able to accept.

Sacrifice can perhaps be seen as pushing to its logical extreme another kind of common Hindu language which is used to describe married life from the woman's point of view: this is the language of maintenance. Women interviewed by Mary McGee said that the maintenance of family well-being [*saubhāgya*] was the purpose of the many votive observances [*vrata*] which they took on themselves. Well-being embraces the good health, prosperity and long life of husband and children. It also includes the birth of a son which is particularly important for Hindu wives. Such observances, which usually involve fasting, are a normal part of the domestic routine of Hindu wives and mothers. In this domestic context sacrifice can be seen as the most extreme form of maintenance.(13)

There is another area of the man-woman relationship where Ajneya may be using a traditional frame of reference though without recasting it: in IS Rekha refuses Bhuvan's offer of marriage, saying that she does not want to control his future, while at the end of SL Shashi realises that she is dying and so will only be part of Shekhar's life for a time. Both of these women as it were set their menfolk free, and as we shall see, it is the purified vision which their suffering bestows which enables them to see they must do this. This echoes Ajneya's stanza on the fly leaf of IS. Yet there may be something more here and that is an unconscious echo of *Sāṁkhya* philosophy where the whole of reality is divided into two principles: *prakṛti* which constitutes the whole of material reality as well as key elements of human consciousness, and *puruṣa* which is pure spirit. In the basic *Sāṁkhya* text to which we have already referred:

> *prakṛti* is invariably regarded as existing to bring about the liberation of spirit -- not only liberation from *prakṛti* as such in a post mortem state, but liberation in various ways from *prakṛti*'s influence in this life.(14)

This point is made in the classic text by a series of analogies in the most important of which *prakṛti* is compared to a dancer who shows herself to *puruṣa* and then leaves the stage, her task completed. It is important to see this in the context of the Indian understanding of dance whereby the performer puts across her message through a series of stylised, highly skilled, and essentially self-effacing symbolic gestures, mainly of hands and eyes, the meaning of which a sophisticated audience readily understands. *Puruṣa* may be either beguiled by and so drawn into prakrti 's dance, and so caught up into the pairs of opposites, or else set free by *prakṛti*. In *Sāṁkhya* philosophy *puruṣa* is not male but asexual, yet the pattern of relationships between Bhuvan and Rekha in IS, and less strikingly between Shekhar and Shashi in SL, are remarkably akin to the pattern we have just described. Further, while we shall see Shashi and Rekha using the traditional language of sacrifice and self-offering to describe their relationship with men, this is not reciprocated. There is no suggestion that men sacrifice themselves for the sake of women. This is again reminiscent of *Sāṁkhya* where *prakṛti* exists for the sake of *puruṣa*, but the reverse is not true. We are not suggesting here a direct and conscious link in the mind of Ajneya, but *Sāṁkhya* assumptions are all-pervasive in the Sanskritic tradition and it would therefore be very odd if they were not part of the half-conscious background of his thinking. There is a parallel here with his use of sacred geography which we examined in the last chapter. There too we argued that his assumptions had not been brought to the level of conscious reflection.(15)

This setting free of men by their womenfolk has other resonances with tradition of a rather different kind. There are several points in our two main novels where a Christian reader expects conflict: this first happens towards the end of SL when it appears that Shekhar is almost in spite of himself about to be drawn into revolutionary violence. Shashi is very troubled, but instead of trying to prevent him from becoming more deeply embroiled with the revolutionaries it is at this very point that she realises she must let him go. And in IS when Chandramadhava introduces Gaura to Rekha with the deliberate intent of stirring up jealousy between them, and so creating trouble for Bhuvan, he is baffled when the two women in fact establish a good relationship. Indeed, at the end of the novel Rekha bestows her blessing on Gaura as Bhuvan's bride when she gives the girl the ring her own mother had given to her.(16) The Christian reader is also struck by the uncritical ease with which Gaura finally accepts Bhuvan as her husband and Dr Ram Chandra [*Dr Rāma Candra*] accepts Rekha as his wife, for both Gaura and Dr Ram Chandra are aware of Rekha's previous relationship with Bhuvan. Here too there may be an unconscious echo of something which is not uncommon in the tradition. For example in the *Rāmacaritamānasa* of Tulsi Das there is a moment when Rama, now in exile, meets Kaikeyi [*Kaikeyī*], the person who was directly responsible for his loss of the throne of Ayodhya and for the sentence of fourteen years' exile imposed on him by his father. Yet Rama is totally accepting of Kaikeyi, warmly embraces her, and simply attributes what has happened to fate. The point of this re-action is that as the ideal king he would be expected to have transcended jealousy and anger. While none of Ajneya's characters are in any way 'royal' figures, it is possible that in the examples we have considered in this paragraph the memory of tradition may have half-consciously overriden the realism of the novels.(17)

Finally, we draw attention to a single word which is crucial to the understanding of our first two novels: *tapasyā*.(18) This means 'the practice of austerity' and is derived from the verb *tap* which means 'to give out heat' -- as the sun for example -- 'to suffer pain', 'to torment oneself', 'to undergo voluntary austerity'.(Monier-Williams [1899] p. 436) *Tapasyā* is usually practised by remaining in one posture for a long time and always with some particular goal in mind, such as attaining supernatural power. Indeed a standard Hindi dictionary describes it as 'the pain undertaken in order to secure a desired goal'. One traditional form of this was for a person to subject himself to 'the five fires', *ie* he sat between a fire in each of the four quarters while the scorching heat of the sun beat down on him from above.(19) Such practices were normally though not always the preserve of men.

Turning now to the texts of our novels we consider first of all the question of suffering in general. This is an important part of the context because not all suffering leads to the purification of the sufferer's vision. The young Shekhar first becomes aware of suffering on a wide scale during the First World War when he comes across some old newspapers which are used for wrapping purchases in the bazaar. There are references in them to German atrocities and Shekhar asks if God is reponsible for the war -- a reasonable question for a small boy to ask since he had already asked 'Does God do everything ? [*sab kuch Īśvar kartā hai* ?]' and been given an affirmative answer.(SL Vol. 1 pp. 83-4) One day he sees a *tāṁgā-vālā* (a man who drives a pony and trap for hire) beating his horse which collapses and dies of hunger. He asks if people die like that when they die of hunger, but again he gets no answer.(SL Vol. 1 pp. 84-5) At this time the family are living in Srinagar, the capital of Kashmir. The Viceroy pays a visit and the people complain that they are starving because of rising prices. Shekhar asks why they are starving, but again, no satisfactory answer is forthcoming.(SL Vol. 1 p. 87) Later, when the family are in Lucknow the River Gomati floods and he goes out in a boat with his father. He asks why the traders, also out in boats, take their wares to the rich areas but not to the poor -- which are lower lying and so more badly flooded. Here many people have drowned and there is no-one to help the survivors.(SL Vol. 1 p. 67) When he goes to Madras as a student the extremes of caste discrimination found in that part of the country cause him much distress, as we saw in the previous chapter. He is also made much more acutely aware of the suffering of women, which he sees as largely caused by their traditionally allotted role of subservience to men.(SL Vol. 1 pp. 216 and 220)

Thus for the young Shekhar suffering raises the question of theodicy -- why does God let it happen ? It also raises the question of social justice when that suffering is inflicted on human beings by others, or when the rich ignore the sufferings which natural disasters bring on the poor. Either way it moves him to passionate anger and persuades him, as we saw in the last chapter, that the traditional hells of scripture were the inventions of the 'sub-contractors' of religion and that real hell was to be found in the social injustice which he saw all around him.(20) His rejection of tradition also involves him in suffering of a much more personal kind. We saw above that in the Introduction to SL Ajneya describes this novel as a 'record of personal suffering'. Almost every page of it confirms this claim: Shekhar is constantly at odds with his family and indeed with the rest of the world. He compares traditional education to the hammering of metal into shape by a smith (SL Vol. 1 p. 53) -- a metaphor which certainly implies the pain in his own experience of such education. He is deeply hurt when he overhears his mother saying that she does not trust him.(SL Vol. 1 pp. 25 and 179) His relationships with girls and women are never permanent. Shanti [*Śānti*] and Pratibha Lal [*Pratibhā Lāl*] die (SL Vol. 1 pp. 100 and 189), his sister Sarasvati leaves home to get married (SL Vol. 1 p. 146), while Sharada's family lock up their house and leave Ootacamund in his absence.(SL Vol. 1 p. 178) Worst of all, Shashi dies from the blow inflicted on her by Rameshvar.(SL Vol. 2 pp. 251-3)

At the beginning of the second volume, when Shekhar is on the train from Madras to Lahore, 'he is fleeing from his defeat [*parājaya*], he is fleeing from his pain [*darda*]'.(SL Vol. 2 p. 9) This sentence appears to sum up the whole of his experience up to that point. There is no hint yet of his pain being transmuted into vision, and he very soon finds that he is at odds with his fellow-students in Lahore (SL Vol. 2 pp. 12-21) as he had been with those in Madras.(SL Vol. 1 pp. 195-208) He is alienated from his fellow-workers in the Congress camp where he is arrested (SL Vol. 2 pp. 33-45), from hypocritical social reformers such as Amolak Rai [*Amolak Rai*] (SL Vol. 2 pp. 150-7), from the corrupt and venal world of publishing (SL Vol. 2 pp. 129-31), indeed from just about everyone except for Shashi and for three fellow-prisoners whom he meets in jail. He does not go home for his mother's funeral (SL Vol. 2 pp. 133-5) -- an unthinkable omission in Hindu as in any other society. He renounces any thought of marriage (SL Vol. 2 pp. 157-8) so that he can be free to pursue his 'mission' -- he actually uses the English word (SL Vol. 2 p. 141), and he refuses to consider any sort of normal employment.(SL Vol. 2 pp. 119 and 139) All this sets him at odds with society, its norms and its expectations, and increasingly involves him in the pain of isolation.

The possibility of suffering actually being transformative, and so of having a positive value in the forging of personality, is first hinted at in SL in the character of the outcaste widow Phulan whom we considered in the last chapter.(21) It is set out explicitly in the character of Madansingh [*Madansiṃh*] whom we consider below, further developed in Shashi, and comes to its full flowering in IS in Rekha, and in TEHS in Selma. Its clearest theoretical statement is to be found in some words of Bhuvan in IS. We have already seen that Bhuvan agrees with Shekhar in the claim that this life is all there is.(22) In the same passage he goes on to spell out some positive consequences which can spring from this rejection of the traditional view:

> The pain [*darda*] of this life is not precious [*mūlyavān*] because it receives compensation [*puraskār*] in some other life; it is precious because there is no other life beyond this one, because its value is not a matter for weighing and measuring, by deciding what one should get through the balancing of accounts. The value is for the personality [*vyaktitva*] which passes through that suffering, and is in that condition of suffering.(IS p. 324)

In other words the rejection of the traditional transcendental framework within which suffering was interpreted opens up the possibility of seeing it as something which may have value for the personality of the sufferer in this life. Bhuvan's claim is exemplified with particular clarity in the character of Madansingh, whom Shekhar meets in jail. He is an archetypal figure, an old man with a long white beard, the epitome of wisdom, but a wisdom of an unconventional kind which has been aquired in an unconventional way.(SL Vol. 2 pp. 62-3) When Shekhar meets him he has already been in jail for twenty-one years. When he first arrived there he was completely illiterate, but he has taught himself to read and write 'and in this place I have tried, weeping, to know those great things without which no-one can live'.(SL Vol. 2 p. 63) On the walls of his cell he has written his own *sūtras*. This is a key term from the tradition and means in the singular a short aphorism. Different series of such *sūtras* form the basic texts of all traditional branches of knowledge. Thus, for example the *Yoga Sūtras* of Patanjali [*Patañjali*] are the foundation text of *yoga*.(23) This self-taught old man is therefore the antithesis of Shekhar on whom the adult world had tried and failed to impose its own kind of education. Even so, he respects Shekhar because he has been to college.(SL Vol. 2 p. 63) Madansingh is implicitly equated with the great wise men of tradition, the primeval Rishis [*ṛṣis*] to whom the *sutras* and even the Vedas were originally revealed.(24) Significantly, he tells Shekhar that the production of each of his *sutras* has caused him to weep for hours.(SL Vol. 2 p. 64)

Here for the first time we find an explicit link between pain and vision, a link which is reinforced and enlarged when the old man gives a redefinition of *tapasyā*. He says that 'to remain sitting unmoved is not *tapasyā*, *tapasyā* starts from being unable to sit unmoved'.(SL Vol. 2 p. 64) Here is a critique of the traditional kind of *tapasyā*, which as we have just seen, normally did entail staying in one posture for a long time, and subjecting oneself to discomfort and pain in order to obtain spiritual power. At the same time Madansingh's new definition endorses Shekhar's insatiable curiosity and mental restlessness, an attitude very different from the stillness of mind which in the tradition was a precondition of being a recipient of revelation.(SL Vol. 2 p. 64)(25) This difference is underlined by an extended meditation on and reshaping of part of the creation narrative in Genesis.(Vol. 2 pp. 85-7)(26) It is unclear from the context whether we are meant to attribute this to Shekhar himself or simply to regard it as an interlude by the author. In this recasting of the story God creates the heavens and the earth, the heavenly bodies, vegetation, birds and animals, and finally man. He creates woman out of two tears of man. But throughout this process God remains dissatisfied because creation does not move. The serpent, which God has also created, sits and laughs because he knows why it does not move, but he keeps the secret to himself. Eventually the woman gives birth to a child and presents him to the man who asks God, 'What is this creation [*sṛṣṭi*] which you did not make yourself ?'(SL Vol. 2 p. 87) God does not answer so the man asks the snake, 'the guardian of knowledge [*jñāna ka rakṣak*]', and at once the earth begins to move, the stars to shine, the sun to rise and set, the clouds to thunder. The snake had claimed to be the equal of God in knowledge, but evidently he did not know about procreation. He now realises that his claim was false because God has snatched knowledge from him, while God says that his creation is now complete but that man has won the victory: 'I consist of knowledge [*jñānamaya*] and am complete [*pūrṇa*]. I seek for nothing. Man has the passion to enquire [*jijñāsā*], therefore he makes the universe move'.(Vol. 2 p. 87)

It is not clear whether Ajneya is appealing to the Genesis account or mocking it, but that hardly matters, for the curiosity which he (or Shekhar) wants to legitimise is better grounded than he seems to have recognised. In both Hindu and Christian traditions there were formative periods when the asking of questions was encouraged. The Upanishads are full of them as are the Psalms and the Gospels.(27)

In this context of the legitimising of questions then, we return to Madansingh, who says, 'If there is any significance [*sār*] in what I say it is there for this reason: what I have not learnt through reading, I have tried to know through suffering [*sahkar*]'.(SL Vol. 2 p. 73) Later on Shekhar makes another biblical reference, comparing the old man to 'the curse-afflicted first man [*śāp-grasta pratham mānava*]', to whom God says 'you will live only by the help of your pain [*apne duḥkha ke sahāre hī tū jiegā*]'.(SL Vol. 2 p. 83) This seems to be a meditation based on or prompted by parts of Genesis 3.17-19.

Shortly after this conversation, when Shekhar is waiting to hear from Shashi in an agony of impatience -- has she agreed to the marriage arranged by her mother or not ? -- he is reflecting on Madansingh's words about *tapasyā* and applies them to his own waiting: 'Pain is *tapasyā*, but real *tapasyā* is the desire to know [*jijñāsā*], because that is the greatest pain of all.'(Vol. 2 p. 84) His reflections lead him to a further re-casting of Hindu tradition:

> Without pain [*vedanā*] there is no knowledge and then alone is knowledge [*jñāna*] of non-human origin [*apauruṣeya*] -- it is not found in human intelligence [*buddhi*], it arises in pain [*vedanā*], in *tapasyā*. It is not the nectar [*amṛta*] which comes from the churning (*sc* of the ocean), it is some immeasurable thing which descends [*vah avatīrṇa honevālā koī aprameya hai*]... this is the way in which the ancient Rishis must sometimes have found that knowledge in the form of *sūtras* [*vah sūtra-baddha jñāna*], which is now the Veda -- which was known -- revealed all at once with the aid of some inner light -- in this way suddenly waking from the *tapasyā* of pain [*pīṛā kī tapasyā*], staggering under the burden of revealed knowledge [*prajñā*] they must have cried -- 'of non-human origin [*apauruṣeya*]'.(SL Vol. 2 p. 84)

Several points in this passage require further elucidation: the word *apauruṣeya* which translates the phrase 'of non-human origin' is a technical term which refers to the belief that the Vedas were revealed to but not invented or composed by the primeval Rishis.(28) 'The churning of the ocean [*manthan*]' refers to a well-known myth in which gods and demons together turned a mountain upside down and wrapped a snake round its base. By pulling each end of the unfortunate snake in turn they were able to twist the apex of the mountain, so churning the muddy bottom of the ocean which was thereby forced to disgorge its treasures. Among these was *amṛta*, the nectar of immortality.(29) Myths are sometimes held to be of secondary status and so not have the authority of the Vedas.(30) This may be the reason why Shekhar rejects this analogy in describing Madansingh's authority and links him instead directly with the original Rishis. But pain is now made central to the aquisition of real and ultimate knowledge [*prajñā*] and Madansingh as an archetypal bearer of such knowledge is a remodelling both of an ancient Rishi and of the Adam of the Genesis story. Here then is a creative blending of the Hindu and biblical traditions each of which in its original form Ajneya seems to have found wanting.

We turn now to the way in which Ajneya interprets the pain of Shashi and of Rekha. Shekhar first becomes really aware of the kind of person Shashi is when he goes to her home after the death of her father. This happens before he is arrested and so before he meets Madansingh. The neighbouring women come to the house and offer the conventional sympathy in the traditional way, but Shekhar feels a deep empathy with the bereaved family so that their pain becomes his own. He realises that

> he is plunged into grief [*viṣāda*], that their pain [*duḥkha*] is his own pain -- and a spring of deep compassion [*samvedana*] welled up from somewhere within him.(SL Vol. 2 p. 30)

He says to Shashi: 'The shadow of pain [*dukha (sic) kī chāyā*] is a kind of *tapasyā* : by means of it the soul is purified [*ātmā śuddha hotī hai*].' To this Shashi, no doubt detecting a touch of narcissism in Shekhar, replies: 'Pain purifies the soul only of the one who tries to remove it, no-one else's.'(SL Vol. 2 p. 33) She thanks him for coming and sharing her pain, but then rebukes him for wanting to rest in its shadow: 'pain is everywhere [*duḥkha sab jagah hai*].' Here is an important connection between the general suffering to which we have already referred and the purification of an individual's vision by means of suffering. For Shashi there is an inescapable link between the active attempt to remove the suffering of others and the inner purification to which Shekhar wants to lay claim. She makes no appeal to traditional interpretations of suffering and would no doubt have agreed with Madansingh who criticised the Indian tradition for being too inward looking and individualist in its attitude, with the result that the quest for salvation tends to separate the seeker from society.(SL Vol. 2 pp. 82-3)

It is the memory of Shashi's words on this occasion which leads Shekhar to make an apparently unimportant decision which has fateful consequences. After her father's funeral he has returned to college in Lahore and along with many other students enrolled as a volunteer to help in the arrangments for a session of the National Congress Party, which is to be held in a large tented encampment. He is given a position of authority over some of the other volunteers and one night he has to make a tour of the sentries. He finds one man uncomplainingly beginning his third consecutive stint in the torrential rain -- his two replacements having successively failed to turn up. Their irresponsible attitude to duty is one that typifies Shekhar's experience in the camp, an experience which no doubt reflects the disillusionment with the Congress Party which was felt by many young Punjabis of the time.(31) Remembering Shashi's words about removing the pain of others Shekhar takes this man's place. While he is standing there in the rain the police arrive looking for a member of the camp staff who earlier that evening had insulted a CID officer. Far from being to blame for this Shekhar had actually saved the officer from further trouble (SL Vol. 2 p. 40) just before he replaced the sentry, but since he happens to be near the spot where the original incident took place he is the one to be arrested. As he is taken away in the police car he thinks again of Shashi's words that pain purifies only the soul of the one who tries to remove it. He then adds his own gloss to her words: 'Purification (*sc* of the soul) is to be found not in suffering with another, but in suffering in their place [*śuddhi dūsare ke sath duḥkhī hone meṁ nahīṁ, dūsare ke sthān par duḥkhī hone meṁ hai*].(SL Vol. 2 p. 43) A little while later he asks himself:

> Is he someone of whom that can be said ? Is a new chapter opening for his soul ? Is he (now) a complete man [*pūrṇa puruṣa*] -- a victor [*vijetā*] -- master of circumstance ?(Vol. 2 p. 45)

Here we catch a glimpse of what Shekhar means by the ideal human being who stands in contrast to the one who was fleeing from his humiliation and defeat on the long train journey from Madras to Lahore at the beginning of this volume.(32) It is striking that completeness and victory are directly linked with the voluntary embracing of suffering by taking someone else's place. There is a Christian resonance to this in belief about the atoning work of Christ on the cross. We shall see below how Shekhar explicitly develops this point in relation to Shashi's marriage to which we now turn.

While he is in jail Shashi sends word that her marriage has been arranged against her will. After hearing this news Shekhar is in his cell pondering the words of the marriage ceremony. He recalls that in it an offering is always poured into the fire. The word 'fire' gives him the clue: a wife's soul is always 'a sacrificed soul [*hutātmā*]'.(SL Vol. 2 p. 69) Yet in a traditional marriage the man is unworthy of such an offering. Shekhar makes a mental list of the qualities which are normally regarded as essential for a good marriage -- education, wealth, family, good manners, character, good looks, reputation (SL Vol. 2 p. 70), and then asks himself if these qualities really 'make a man [*ādmī banātī haiṁ*]', and whether

> these and these alone give a man that portion of divinity [*devatva kā vah aṁś*] which makes him entitled to write on his balance sheet the merit [*puṇya*] of someone's lifelong *tapasyā*.(Vol. 2 p. 70)

We note both the difference between the qualities which society expects of a husband and those on which Shekhar had reflected in the back of the police van. We can also detect a possible touch of sarcasm in his description of the woman's traditional role in marriage as 'lifelong *tapasyā* '. A little while later Shashi writes to him of her marriage as being a sacrifice [*homa*] in terms similar to his own thoughts about her. She adds that that no-one will see her sacrifice.(SL Vol. 2 p. 79) Shekhar asks himself whether Shashi can be right. He agrees with her that in such a situation there must be pain but says that the question is who should bear it. He then asks himself whether this is

> the doctrine of substitutionary suffering [*pratinidhik yantraṇā*] which he had read somewhere in a book and rejected as unacceptable [*agrāhya*] -- that our pain [*yātanā*] can be the atonement [*prāyaścit*] for someone else's sin [*pāp*]? Is every person [*pratyek vyakti*] the Jesus Christ [*Īsāmasīh*] of someone else, the cross-bearer [*krūs ḍhonevala*] of someone else ? Is this the first and last gleam of light in this hell of torment [*yātanā ke is kumbhīpāk*]?(SL Vol. 2 p. 80)

We have already seen that Ajneya learnt this principle from the 'Bible classes' of his teacher, Professor Banade (33), but here he re-interprets and extends it. The doctrine of penal substitution as traditionally expounded by many Protestant Christians is immoral, for it suggests that Christ on the cross bore the penalty of human sins so that God's justice might be upheld while the sinners went free. Shekhar is rightly uneasy about this notion, but by taking it out of its juridical context and by making pain rather than penalty the key concept he gives it a powerful moral content. Ten months later, when Shekhar is released from jail, he goes to visit the home of the now married Shashi. She is crushed and lifeless.(34) He asks her to sing for him as she had done in the past, but she says that now she no longer sings.(SL Vol. 2 109-13) Shashi herself confirms his first impression of her married life at a much later point when she is visiting him just before being thrown out of her own home by her husband:

> I was not miserly [*kañjūsī*] in obliterating myself -- I gave with an open hand -- sacrificed [*homa kar diyā*] myself and saw that everything was burnt up -- reduced to dust.(SL Vol. 2 p. 169)

Turning now for a moment to IS we find that a similar situation arises when Gaura asks for Bhuvan's advice about the marriage her parents are arranging for her but which she does not want to accept. He tells her that no-one can tell anyone else what to do at such a moment, for guidance is a matter of 'inner light [*bhītar kā ālok*]'.(IS p. 73) This is much the same as Shekhar had written to Shashi from his prison cell (SL Vol. 2 p. 78), but Bhuvan goes further than Shekhar had done and opens up new possibilities which have not so far occurred in the novels. He tells Gaura that one should not 'extend the personality [*use ikāī se bāhar prasṛt karne*]' in marriage until one's own 'personal development [*vyakti kā svatantra vikāsa*]' is complete and that when one finds the right companion one should go ahead without asking anyone's advice.(IS p. 74) Here is an example of Ajneya's emphasis on freedom of choice in the context of the moral independence of the individual to which we have already referred.(35) This is a far cry from the traditional way of arranging marriages in the society in which he was nurtured.

Gaura toys with the possibility of 'self-sacrifice [*apne ko utsarga kar denā*]' to her parents' 'will [*icchā*]', a choice which as she points out has the 'whole of tradition [*sārī paramparā*]' behind it.(IS p. 76) But Bhuvan writes back saying that 'genuine self-sacrifice is the work of a free individual [*saccā balidān bhī svādhīna vyakti kā karma hai*]'.(IS p. 76) Here Bhuvan refines the language of sacrifice beyond anything found in SL. In doing so he reminds us of the kind of language in which Christian theology speaks about the cross, though Bhuvan does not set his reflections in an explicitly Christian context as Shekhar had done when he asked if we were not all called to be Christs to one another in a mutuality of pain-bearing.

We return now to SL and to Shashi who has just said that she indeed sacrificed herself freely in marriage. Now however, she begins to glimpse the possibility of some kind of meaning in her own life beyond the deadening barrenness of her marriage to Rameshvar: gathering new strength

> just as the sacrificial fire [*homāgni*] flares up again from a new

> offering [*āhuti*] being poured on to it, she said: 'But in you is that life [*jīvan*] of mine which I am and which is my "I".'(SL Vol. 2 p. 169)

Then she tells Shekhar: 'Now I am nothing, I am only a shadow [*maiṁ ab kuch nahīṁ hūṁ. ek chāyā hūṁ*]', and adds 'though formless I am your self, (and one) to whom you cannot give a name [*aur amūrtta hokar maiṁ -- tumhārā apnā-āp hūṁ jise tum nām nahīṁ doge*]'. He hesitatingly asks if in this she finds '*siddhi*'--a word which was traditionally used for the goal of the spiritual quest -- and 'fulfilment [*sampūrti*]'.(36) But this is too much for Shashi who claims only 'satisfaction [*santoṣa*]', a much more modest and this-worldly goal.(SL Vol. 2 p. 169)

We now leave the role of women in marriage and examine another group of passages where suffering is linked with the idea of self-consciously choosing a particular purpose in life. When Shekhar has been released from jail and is renewing his relationship with the now unhappily married Shashi, he decides to devote himself to writing. There comes a critical moment when he is in despair about producing anything worthwhile. At this point Shashi asks him if he can write for her. She asks him if there is not 'satisfaction in suffering for his aim ? [*kyā uddeśya ke lie kuch kleśa bhogne meṁ tṛpti nahīṁ miltī* ?]'(SL Vol. 2 p. 126) The better he writes the more he will find 'outward trouble [*kleśa*]' but 'inward peace [*śānti*]', and she will share in them both. She tells him to show her everything he writes -- and she asks to see his previous compositions as well.(SL Vol. 2 p. 127) Shekhar sorely needs this kind of support for in setting himself up as a 'total and ideal rebel [*ek sampūrṇa aur ādarśa vidrohī*]'(SL Vol. 1 p. 29) he has set himself against the whole of society. We have already seen how he has refused to opt into that society by getting married or by looking for any normal kind of employment.(37)

In setting himself so totally at odds with traditional society and its norms he has taken on himself the burden of self-consciousness. What this means becomes clear when we compare him to Rama-ji [*Rāma-jī*], the second of the three important characters whom he met while he was in jail.(38) This man was under sentence of death for having murdered his sister-in-law and her lover whom he discovered were having an affair in his brother's absence. He lived unself-consciously within the parameters of traditional village values according to which it was right for a man to kill those who had dishonoured the family in this way. At one point Shekhar reflects that a simple unsophisticated person such as Rama-ji can actually cope better with life's problems than he can himself.(SL Vol. 2 pp. 90-4) In other words Shekhar by contrast can and must stand back from his life and reflect on it, and this involves him in agonising choices. He can no longer, like Rama-ji, unthinkingly accept a traditional niche in a largely static social order where roles and duties are clearly defined and so can be accepted without question.(39) He is instead driven to find significance in his 'mission' -- for which we have already seen him use the English word -- or 'purpose' for which he uses the Sanskrit and Hindi word *uddeśya* which means 'capable of being described' and so 'goal' or 'aim'. This word now begins to occur frequently (40) and what is unusual in its use in the central part of the second volume of SL is that Shekar's very being now depends on him having such an aim, for this alone can give him what tradition can no longer provide, the foundation for a meaningful life, the life which in the novel he is attempting to describe in narrative form. We shall see in a later chapter that without such a purpose, and without the prospect of it attaining a measure of success, Shekhar remains vulnerable to loss of meaning and to despair.

This is an example of the kind of pain of isolation reflected in the work of some of the twentieth century English novelists to whom we referred in Chapter Two.(41) We can also relate it to the pain experienced by the Christ of the Gospel narratives, for Christ too bears the burden of having a purpose to fulfil, a burden which brings suffering.(42) We are not suggesting here that in some crude sense Shekhar is a 'Christ-figure', we are simply pointing out that the pain of attempting to fulfil a purpose against opposition brings him within a frame of reference which is at this point close to the Gospels. At the same time we must beware of making the contrast with the Hindu tradition too stark: there are many prophetic figures who had to endure the opprobrium of their contemporaries in order to bring new insights to bear on the life of society.(43)

When Shekhar has been drawn into the circle of revolutionaries and he and Shashi move from Lahore to Delhi for their own safety, the wells of inspiration dry up and he finds he can write nothing, but again Shashi urges him to continue, mentioning Madansingh, Rama-ji, and Mohasin [*Mohasin*] (the third of the characters whom he met in jail) as possible subjects, and telling him too that he can write her story as well.(SL Vol. 2 pp. 217-8) Shekhar then reflects on Shashi's qualities:

> What Shashi says is right. When is she ever wrong ? because in her every word is found the gold [*kañcan*] which comes from burning oneself in the fire of suffering [*apne ko tapākar*] -- just as there used to be in Baba's (*ie* Madansingh's) words...Shashi is the same age as he (Shekhar) but what profound discrimination [*vivek*] she has, what noble compassion [*praśasta saṃvedanā*], what depth and clarity of knowledge [*viśada jñāna*] -- of true wisdom [*prajñā*] (SL Vol. 2 p. 218)

Jñāna and more especially *prajñā* are two key traditional terms for that transcendental knowledge which was the goal of the philosophic quest, while *vivek* is the faculty which, in at least one school of philosophy, enables the aspirant to distinguish the truth which pertains to that quest from the untruth which does not.(44) Shashi -- a woman -- has reached the final goal not by following the traditional path (which offered very little scope for women), but through the fires of her suffering. Shekhar puts her on the same level as Madansingh both directly in the intensity of her inner experience and indirectly in her achievement, for to reach *prajñā* is on a par with composing *sūtras*. We find something very similar in the character of Selma in TEHS, though here it is obscured by several factors: Selma is described through the eyes not of a Shekhar but of Yoke who is increasingly hostile towards the older woman, so much so that eventually she makes a half-hearted attempt to strangle her.(TEHS p. 52) Moreover Selma's impending death from cancer, and the author's pre-occupation with death, tends to crowd out the evidence for Selma's transmutation through pain. Yet there are hints that this has actually happened. For example, Yoke confides to her diary the observation that Selma has

> no kind of hostility [*virodha*] within her -- not towards me, nor towards my murderous feelings [*hiṃsra bhāvoṁ*], nor even towards death [*mṛtyu*] itself...even more unacceptable and unbearable is the...compassion [*kāruṇya bhāva*] that streams out, soothing [*salākar*] everything.(TEHS pp. 35-6)

Yet later, when Selma eventually tells Yoke the story of her earlier experience when she was marooned on a bridge during a flood, we learn that at that time the very meaning of life for her lay in the fact that

> she was alone, and on the other side was everything that was not her, and with which her only link was hostility [*virodha*]. This hostility was the only firm point of reference [*dhruvatā*], and she must keep firm hold of it.(TEHS pp. 72-3)(45)

In other words Selma then had the same barren attitude to life and to death as Yoke does now. On a much smaller canvas this reminds us of Shekhar's total hostility to the adult world and all that it stood for. Between the two moments of Selma's life described in these quotations from TEHS there has been a profound inner change, for compassion towards all has now replaced hostility. The source of this change in outlook is affirmed when Yoke interrupts Selma in the telling of her story:

> You go on about pain [*duḥkha*] and suffering [*kaṣṭa*]-- but how can they be true [*saca*] if you don't even know [*bodha*] them ?
>
> Selma was silent for a while. Then she said: 'That is exactly what I say too -- but in a different way. The truth of pain lies only in knowing it.'(TEHS p. 93)

Yoke is exasperated by the fact that, entombed in their mountain hut, she is overcome with fear and anxiety while Selma appears to be totally unmoved. Selma in her reply is thinking back to her past experience, the transmutation of which enables her to rise above the fear of death now. Here it seems Selma has indeed transcended the 'pairs of opposites' and even time itself, yet apart from the fact that she is a widow (TEHS p. 91) we are given no direct clue as to the nature of the pain she has undergone. In her transcendence of ordinary experience she seems to be a reversion to the heart of the Hindu tradition, many of whose aspects Ajneya had so emphatically rejected in his first novel. In her compassion towards all there may also be Buddhist influence: we recall that Ajneya had stayed in a Zen monastery in Japan and that this had a profound effect upon him.(46)

We now return to SL and to Shekhar, who after comparing Shashi to Madansingh goes on to ask himself:

> Why is Shashi not the leader [*netā*] herself, why is she content to

> take the unimportant role of an obedient follower in Shekhar's life. Why in order to lead him forward does she continually sacrifice [*āhuti*] herself, obliterate herself [*apne ko miṭā rahī hai*] ? Can he accept such a great self-sacrifice [*ātma-balidān*] ? What guarantee is there that what is produced by such a great act of renunciation [*tyāga*], its ultimate value [*ātyantik mūlya*], will be equal to its giving ? And even if it is how can he accept its cost ?(SL Vol. 2 p. 218)

Here the language of a woman sacrificing herself for a man is again redolent of tradition but it is used for a different end. Instead of describing the traditional role of a woman in marriage, which was, as we have seen, the maintenance of the family's well-being [*saubhāgya*] (47) it points to Shashi's dedication -- outside marriage -- to the making of Shekhar and to the fulfilment of his purpose. Shashi interprets her self-offering in terms of the eternal nature of woman, whom she compares to the earth which can only bear fruit by suffering.(SL Vol. 2 pp. 218-9) Here she is close to tradition: Sita, consort of Rama and one of the great suffering women of Hindu myth, was born from the furrow -- which is what her name means -- and at the end of the *Rāmāyaṇa* returns to the earth from which she had emerged at the beginning, her purpose complete.(48) Perhaps too we can see a hint here of *Sāṁkhya* philsophy, where *prakṛti*, her task accomplished, sets *puruṣa* free and vanishes.(49)

Shashi's transformation through suffering reaches a climax towards the end of the book when Shekhar notices that her very face is changed:

> He had noticed before that Shashi's eye-lashes seemed transparent [*pārdarśī-sī*], but now it seemed that her whole face [*samūcā ceharā*] was transparent, as if the agony [*yātanā*] suffered in silence for so long had purified [*śodhkar*] that clear skin [*svaccha tvaca*] even more and given it an inner radiance [*āntarik kānti*]...Shashi's face is not an afflicted face, and certainly not in this moment of tranquility [*praśamana*] -- but looking at it suddenly one was compelled to think of the experience [*bodha*] of some vast and shining [*śubhra*] suffering [*vedanā*], suffering which like moonlight [*cāṁdanī*] would cleanse and move one.(SL Vol. 2 pp. 220-1)

This transformation of the human body by an all-pervasive inner radiance is an ideal which is found in Indian art, though there the body is always male and the radiance is the fruit of deliberately imposed *tapasyā*.(50) Again, there are hints of something similar in TEHS where Yoke makes reference to the transparency of the dying Selma's skin and to her radiance [*kanti*] (TEHS p. 33), but in her hostility she sees this in the context of the (probably) approaching death from suffocation of both Selma and herself. Should she have seen it instead as the outward evidence for a profound inner change ?

At the very end of SL Shashi spends hours standing outside in the cold and damp waiting for Shekhar's return. He has gone across the river Jumna with one of the revolutionaries to test out some revolvers which the revolutionary had entrusted to his keeping a few days earlier. Since the couple are living in accomodation which the revolutionaries have provided Shekhar could hardly have said no to this request, so here we see him drawn into potentially violent action almost in spite of himself. Shashi had expressed deep anxieties about the revolvers, saying it was all right to put oneself at risk, but wrong to be always ready to kill others.(SL Vol. 2 p. 234) At this point we detect the first sign of a rift between the couple. Shekhar is finding himself drawn into potential violence almost in spite of himself. He rashly assures Shashi that he will be back from the testing by evening (SL Vol. 2 p. 236), but does not come. The doctor had said that she must have complete rest (SL Vol. 2 pp. 186-7), avoid cold and damp, and not be subjected to mental strain (SL Vol. 2 p. 227), yet her long and anxious vigil inflicts just these things upon her. However, when Shekhar does eventually return she says that during her agonising wait she had realised much that she had not seen before -- and that through anxiety [*ghabrāhaṭ*] one sometimes gets *divya-dṛṣṭi* -- a traditional word which describes the supernatural vision attained by the *yogin*. She now realises that her 'task is complete [*merā kāma pūrā ho gayā*]'.(SL Vol. 2 pp. 239-40) Here is one of those points where we expect conflict but do not get it, for instead of a clash of wills about the legitimacy of violence, we find that Shashi so to speak bows out of Shekhar's life. Shortly afterwards she dies. She had wanted to find some fulfilment in living for him and this she has achieved. There may be unconscious echoes here of the dance of *prakṛti* in *Sāṁkhya* philosophy to which we referred above, but also the claim to have fulfilled one's task is traditionally the kind of remark which an old Hindu mother might make on her deathbed (51), but Shashi is not an old woman. Here she lays claim to having achieved a kind of fulfilment, but by a route which is very different from anything in tradition, even though there may be hints of tradition in the words she uses.

In IS the situation is more complex because the theme of the purification of vision through suffering is developed at greater depth and with more elaboration than was the case in the earlier work. The basic patterns within which this development is worked out are relatively simple: when Bhuvan first meets Rekha he discovers that she has suffered much through her unhappy -- and unconsummated -- marriage to the homosexual (52) Hemendra.(IS p. 27) When Bhuvan takes her to the Jantar Mantar (53) in Delhi she recalls that it was there that Hemendra had, so he told her, sworn eternal fealty to a boy. She is overcome with anguish at the memory which this place has evoked. She cannot bear it when Bhuvan mentions the evening star which reminds her of that terrible night.(IS pp. 111-2) However, through telling Bhuvan what had happened she is delivered from her pain and fear.(IS p. 117) Here is the healing of suffering through sharing it with a sympathetic listener, a healing of memory, a theme which does not explicitly occur in SL. Here suffering is not transcended as in tradition nor redeemed by being given a new significance. Its power to hurt is removed by reliving the story of its origin. We examine this theme in greater depth and detail in Chapter Six.

Apart from the torment of her unfulfilled marriage a subsidiary theme in Rekha's life is that she suffers from being a solitary woman -- when Bhuvan first meets her she is living apart from Hemendra (IS p. 27) -- in a society which allowed no such role for women. She is often the victim of both unfounded rumour and of the unwelcome attentions of men who think she is 'fair game'.(IS pp. 46, 54, and 222) She and Bhuvan also suffer greatly because of her abortion. The circumstances which led to this are important as well as the event itself, but before considering this we need to recognise that abortion in Hindu tradition is regarded as abhorrent and unthinkable. It is uniformly condemned in the classical texts, and these assume the context of marriage.(54) Bhuvan and Rekha are of course not formally married to one another, but when they make love in Kashmir there is a hint that though they are not married according to the (to them irrelevant) norms of society, nature is the true witness [*sākṣī*] which sanctifies their union.(IS p. 156)(55) At a pause on their journey down from the mountain top they are talking of their unfulfilled ambitions, Rekha's to be a musician and Bhuvan's to be a surgeon. Rekha says she will 'teach him the lute -- and he will be a great surgeon too'.(IS p. 161) By speaking of 'him' without any previous reference she is hinting that she thinks she is, or hopes she may be, pregnant. There is no thought in her mind at this point of having an abortion. This arises in the context of her impending divorce. She realises that if Hemendra discovers that it is Bhuvan by whom she is pregnant he will not only have the legal right to initiate divorce proceedings himself, but will be able to implicate Bhuvan as well. It is to spare Bhuvan from this possibility that she decides to have the abortion. Although it is performed by a reputable surgeon, it goes disastrously wrong. She has it in Srinagar and suffers a near fatal haemorrhage. In fact Bhuvan only gets her to hospital in the nick of time.(56) Rekha never really recovers from the physical effects of this disaster and her health is permanently broken. The emotional shock to Bhuvan is considerable and to understand this we have to underline the fact that this novel was published in the India of 1951, not in the Britain of the nineteen nineties. We also have to read it in the context of the traditional Hindu horror of abortion to which we referred above. To destroy a possible son -- which is what Rekha had assumed her unborn child would be -- is totally at odds with both her own and Bhuvan's deepest instincts.(57)

Bhuvan is totally shattered when he realises that Rekha has not only had the abortion but had it for his sake. He cannot accept such a terrible self-offering (IS pp. 260-2), nor indeed could his literary creator, for Ajneya writes elsewhere that Rekha's tragedy is that her self-offering remains incomplete.(58) We note here a parallel with Shekhar who had similar difficulties to Bhuvan's in accepting Shashi's very different kind of sacrifice made for his sake.(59) Earlier, Bhuvan had reflected on the wider theme of women's self-offering to men when Rekha first offered to make love with him:

> Suddenly an emotion [*bhāva*] of profound gratitude towards Rekha overwhelmed him: how can this woman surrender [*utsarga kar ke de saktī hai*] everything, asking no gift in return, wanting no

> security [*surakṣā*] -- indeed scorning all possibility of security ? Why ? Is it because she loves Bhuvan and wants to give him something [*kuch*] ? Not just something but everything, her very self [*apnā āp*]. What irony [*viḍambanā*] there is in a woman's power [*śakti*] that her greatest gift should be her own dissolution [*laya*], her own destruction [*vināśa*]. But how can there be a supreme gift without dissolution ? In the bolstering of the ego [*aham*] there is no surrender [*samarpaṇa*]; only in the surrender of the ego is there true surrender.(IS p. 137)

Here Bhuvan is by implication totally rejecting a traditional view of woman as sexually voracious. After the abortion his work takes him away from Rekha and for months he cannot bring himself to write to her in answer to her many letters.(IS pp. 262-3) He still cannot accept what she has done -- here we see the strength of the traditional attitude to abortion -- and she thinks he is blaming her. She realises that if he continues to do so her suffering will be rendered meaningless: 'Pain creates but my pain has remained barren [*vyathā sṛjan kartī hai, merī vyathā bāṁjh rah gaī hai*]'.(IS p. 268) Only if he no longer accuses her can their relationship still give meaning to her life. Here we see a new dimension to Ajneya's concept of the purifying of vision through suffering, for at this point the vision depends on someone other than the seer, in fact it depends on the maintenance of a relationship between two people. We recall that for Shekhar meaning depended on reasonable success attending the purpose he had set himself, his 'mission'. Rekha has no such purpose: meaning for her depends on her continuing relationship with Bhuvan. It is this that makes his continuing silence more than she can bear. Eventually he does write and says that he cannot hold her guilty for he is just as guilty himself:

> and when I realise this great self-sacrifice on your part was an expression of your love for me, I feel like sinking into the earth. (IS p. 262)(60)

Eventually Bhuvan finds his own inner healing through the loving sympathy of Gaura who realises that he is suffering from some great anguish though she does not know its cause.(IS p. 276) In bringing himself to tell her the story of the abortion he finds relief. This happens when he has gone to stay with her family in Mussoorie, a well-known hill station. At first he refuses to let her light a fire because, as he later explains, since the abortion he

> sees faces in the fire -- faces of dead infants -- and my own face too because I died with him.(IS p. 296)

There had been a fire in the room in Srinagar when Rekha had her near-fatal haemorrhage and the memories were too close, but after unburdening himself of the story to Gaura Bhuvan can bear to look at the fire again, just as Rekha could bear to look at the stars after having told him the story of her disastrous marriage to Hemendra. But Bhuvan finds more than Rekha had done in reliving her painful experience: what he finds is not simply healing but something very close to forgiveness, and this is a theme which occupies a much more prominent place in TEHS.

In this latter novel Yoke can neither stand nor understand the unmoved serenity of the older Selma with whom she becomes increasingly angry. This anger reaches its climax with her half-hearted attempt to strangle Selma.(TEHS p. 52) But the anger is tempered and indeed transformed by the theme of forgiveness. This first appears when Selma asks Yoke why she is always pre-occupied with death [*mṛtyu*].(TEHS p. 24) Yoke replies angrily, instantly regretting her outburst, but cannot find it in her to ask for forgiveness. Selma at once changes the subject, 'bestowing forgiveness [*kṣamā*] as indirectly [*parokṣa*] as I had requested it'.(TEHS p. 24) When Christmas comes Yoke comments in her diary that it is the 'day of forgiveness, peace [*śānti*] and goodwill [*sadbhāvanā*] to humankind'.(TEHS p. 33) After another of Yoke's outbursts it is, significantly, Selma who asks for forgiveness.(TEHS p. 43) The theme reaches its climax in the first part of the book after Yoke's attempt to strangle Selma. The next morning she says: 'Forgive me for last night, I was out of my mind.' Selma replies: 'It is I who should ask for forgiveness -- for putting you in such a position.'(TEHS p. 54) She goes on:

> I want you to forgive me and not only that, I want you to be able to say from your own mouth that you have forgiven, because in this way you too will have peace in the future.(TEHS pp. 54-5)

Though we are not explicitly told, it is clear that it is in order to help Yoke to discover that peace for herself that in the second part of the book Selma tells her of something which had taken place many years previously, and of which what they are now experiencing together is a kind of re-enactment.(TEHS p. 62) She had been marooned by a flood on a bridge with two men. The bridge was large and on its central span was space for three shops, which were separately owned by herself and the two men. Selma's attitude to the men -- like Yoke's later attitude to herself -- was one of unrelenting hostility. Yet her antagonism is qualified by an important glimpse of the future. In the first chapter of the book we learn that her name was Akelov (TEHS p. 9), but in this flashback it is Dahlberg (TEHS p. 68), while one of the two men on the bridge is called Jan Akelov.(TEHS p. 69) So long before we are actually told we know that Selma will eventually marry Jan. In spite of their dire situation Selma continues to be what presumably she had always been up till then, a business woman who always drives a hard bargain. She refuses drinking water to one of the men and as a result he dies.(TEHS pp. 70-5) When she insists on Jan paying her for some meat she gives him he flings the money in her face, drawing blood.(TEHS pp. 79-80) Later he comes and asks for forgiveness, but Selma does not trust his motives and meets him with a poker in her hand, and this reminds us of Yoke's attempt to kill Selma earlier in the book (though later in the chronological sequence of events). Selma does not trust Jan's motives and says: 'You came to beg forgiveness but aren't you just insulting me again ?' To this Jan replies: 'How can you forgive ? One who does not understand his own powerlessness [*becāragī*] cannot forgive another person.'(TEHS p. 83) Unconvincingly, Selma twice proposes marriage to Jan. The first time he refuses, but the smile on his face when she asks him for the second time shows his acceptance -- and this is even more unconvincing than the original proposal.(TEHS pp. 89-90)

As we have seen, in the final part of this short novel Yoke, long since released from the hut under the snow, is a prostitute in Nazi-occupied Europe. In a food shop she deliberately stubs out her cigarette on a piece of cheese which has just been bought by Jagannathan. She runs off with this man in pursuit, stops and takes a suicide pill, and then dies in his arms asking for forgiveness.(TEHS pp. 103-109) We have already examined this incident in the context of ritual purity (61), we refer to it again here to illustrate the theme of forgiveness which Ajneya develops throughout this novel.

A final element in the depth of insight achieved through pain is the gift of foreseeing the future. This gift is most richly developed in the character of Rekha in IS. It is especially clear in her singing which thus occupies a place of large importance: there are several moments in the story where she is invited to sing and where her words point further into the future than the action has so far reached, and further indeed than the characters themselves can see at that time. For example, shortly after she has first met Bhuvan he asks her to sing when the two of them are strolling with Chandramadhava by the River Gomati in Lucknow. She sings a Bengali song by Tagore (62) about someone who has been playing a flute all night long. Morning is near and the singer addresses the flute: 'Into whose hands shall I entrust you my flute ? [*baṁśī, tumheṁ kiske hāth sauṁp jāūṁ* ?].'(IS p. 29)(63) This implies, as we learn later, that Bhuvan was the flute into which she was to breathe new life and which eventually she entrusted to the hands of Gaura.(IS p. 146) When Chandramadhava takes her to meet Gaura for the first time she sings about decking a bride in festal garments and we realise that she is talking about Gaura.(IS pp. 180-1) This insight is confirmed when she tries to give to Gaura the ring her own mother had given her.(IS p. 182) Gaura refuses to accept it at this point but later in the book, when she is eventually engaged to Bhuvan she gladly does so.(IS p. 329)

The gift of foresight which suffering conveys is apparent in IS in other ways besides singing. Much of the dialogue between the characters is conducted through letters or through note-books which they write for one another -- as if to suggest that they can more easily say the really important things through the written rather than the directly spoken word. In one such letter Rekha tells Bhuvan that she has had a dream in which she realises that she will be part of the pattern of his life only for a time. She will be a part of the pattern but not the whole of it.(IS p. 146) We recall that Shashi had said much the same to Shekhar.(SL Vol. 2 p. 251) Further, at an early stage of their relationship, Bhuvan and Rekha take a boat to an island in the River Gomati. Bhuvan makes sandcastles and the pair of them play at being Robinson Crusoe and Man Friday. As they leave, Rekha insists on him destroying the sandcastles.(IS p. 120) Looking back we can see that this is prophetic of the course of their relationship. In all these ways

Rekha sees further into the future and so more deeply into the significance of the present than any of the other characters.

We now briefly retrace the route by which we have travelled in this chapter which depends on the argument of its predecessor, for it is the fact that Ajneya's characters explicitly reject their inherited framework of belief and of social order that enables them to see new possibilities in suffering. Here Bhuvan's words which we quoted earlier in this chapter (64) are pivotal. The new possibilites, hinted at in Phulan, are first articulated by Madansingh and by Shekhar's own reflections on him. These reveal a critical reshaping of traditional vocabulary. Madansingh's *sutras* are not given to him by 'transcending the pairs of opposites' but are wrung from his tears. For him *tapasyā* is not passionless withdrawal but the passionate desire to know, a desire which is linked by Ajneya and perhaps by Shekhar himself to an imaginative and possibly also critical re-interpretation of part of the Genesis creation story. In Shashi too we see a re-interpretation of traditional terminology. Through her suffering she has achieved *jñāna, prajñā* and *vivek* -- all of which are key terms in the philosophical tradition.

Shashi opens up further possibilities for Shekhar. When her father dies he wants to claim that sharing in the family's pain is a kind of *tapasyā* which purifies the soul. She abruptly tells him that 'Pain purifies the soul only of the one who tries to remove it'. It is these words that move Shekhar to take the place of the sentry in the pouring rain. He himself links this to the Christian doctrine of Christ taking the place of others on the cross. Closely linked with this is another transformation of traditional Hindu terminology: the use of sacrificial terms to describe the self-offering of Shashi, first in being 'burnt out' in her own unhappy marriage, and then in her life with Shekhar. In IS this theme falters somewhat in the character of Rekha: when she offers herself in sex to Bhuvan he refuses, but interprets her offering not in the traditional language of the sexually voracious woman but in terms of sacrifice. Yet Rekha's supreme sacrifice is to have the abortion of her unborn child for the sake of Bhuvan, an offering neither he nor his literary creator can accept as worthy. When writing to Gaura Bhuvan says that to be worthy a sacrifice must be freely offered. This raises the question of the nature of freedom which we consider in the next chapter.

That theme of freedom is closely interwoven with the subject of the present chapter, indeed Ajneya's fragment of poetry at the beginning of IS makes an explicit link between suffering, purification and the setting free of others. Both Shashi and Rekha 'release' their men and in doing so perhaps reflect the release of *puruṣa* by *prakṛti* in *Sāṁkhya* philosophy. There is also here a hint of *yoga* for both Shashi and Rekha foresee the release of their men through what Shashi explicitly calls *divya-dṛṣṭi* -- another traditional term. To Shashi this comes in a single hour, during her long and agonising wait for Shekhar's return from testing the revolvers. In Rekha's case it happens on several occasions, through her singing and in some of her letters. This theme of prophesied release outweighs the possibility of conflict which we also have seen hinted at in several of these situations. TEHS is shorter and much less complex than either of the first two novels. Here conflict is much more openly recognised. Indeed it is a central theme of the book. It is linked with something very like *divya-dṛṣṭi* in Selma. She does not see into the future -- except in veiled references to her impending death from cancer, but there are suggestions that her suffering has enabled her to come to terms with her own past and so to be transformed from being very like Yoke is now -- hostile to others and the prisoner of her fear of death -- into the serene old lady who is fearless in the face of death and who seems indeed to have transcended the pairs of opposites. In other words she is a throw-back to a much more traditional kind of vision than is to be found in the characters of either Shashi or Rekha. Yet all three are women and so implicitly challenge the tradition which on the whole only spoke of the *divya-dṛṣṭi* and transformation of men. Another important theme in TEHS is the theme of forgiveness: Jan forgives the young Selma and the old Selma forgives Yoke. We saw the importance of forgiveness in a different context towards the end of IS when Rekha needed Bhuvan's forgiveness for the abortion to have continued meaning in her life.

Thus in all this material we can discern a radical re-interpretation of some of the key themes of Brahminical Hinduism. We also find a re-interpretation of certain elements of Christianity, in particular of the Genesis story in the case of Madansingh, and of the penal substitutionary doctrine of the atonement in the case of Shekhar relieving the sentry in the pouring rain and then wanting to take Shashi's pain upon himself. The theme of forgiveness which we have seen in the later stages of Bhuvan's relationship with Rekha, and more extensively in TEHS, also has obvious resonances with Christianity.

NOTES

1. We recall that his projected third volume was never published. See above, Chapter One, note 37.
2. Vatsyayan [1988] p. 12.
3. Ajneya is evidently quoting from memory. What Eliot actually wrote was:

   > The more perfect the artist, the more completely separate in him will be the man who suffers and the mind which creates; the more perfectly will the mind digest and transmute the passions which are its material.(Eliot [1951] p. 18)

4. These are the opening lines of 'Lines Written Among the Euganean Hills'. The complete poem can be found in Bloom ed [1966] pp. 105-15.
5. The complete poem of which this is a stanza was composed in 1949. The Hindi text can be found in Ajneya [1986] Vol. 1 p. 238. The English translation in our text is taken from Ajneya's own translation of IS, Islands in the Stream [1980]. 'Holds' is not a strictly accurate translation of *māṁjatā hai* in the third line. This word actually means 'burnishes', the word Ajneya uses to translate it in the first line. But evidently 'holds' is a better word in the total context of the poem's meaning.
6. We have already pointed out that Ajneya, like most educated North Indian children of his generation, was taught Urdu as a boy. We have also pointed out that he often used Urdu words in his novels. See above, p. 30-1.
7. For a brief summary of the tenets of this philosophy in so far as they are germane to this book, see below, pp. 112-3.
8. This is the first couplet of the *Sāṁkhyakārikā* of *Śrī Īśvarakṛṣṇa*. The interpretation which follows is based on Pandit Gaura's exposition of both the text and of one of its main commentaries, that by *Gauṛapāda*.(Gaura [1975] pp. 2-3)

   The 'three-fold suffering' or three forms of pain are first, *ādhyātmik*, which arises from some cause within oneself, second, *ādibhautik*, which is caused by an external sentient agent, and third, *ādidaivik*, which is of external but non-sentient origin. Gauda explains that there are three ways of attempting to remove this pain. They are first, 'visible remedies' such as 'the use of medicine or the enjoyment of a beautiful woman' but these can only bring temporary relief. (We note that this relief is only for men). The same limitations apply to the second method, which is the performance of Vedic sacrifices. These can eventually take the offerer to heaven, but belief in rebirth has the effect of making heaven merely a place of temporary enjoyment. It cannot be the final goal, because the soul has to return to this world for further 'births'. This takes belief in rebirth for granted.(For an account of this belief, see above, pp. 74-5) Thus the first two methods of obtaining relief from pain are rejected as inadequate. Therefore the only reliable -- because permanent -- means of release is the third. This is the scripturally based knowledge of final reality, a reality which transcends heaven and hell. This leads to the pursuit of saving knowledge and vision [*darśan*]. Thus the transcendence of pain is intimately linked to the traditional framework within which human life is interpreted, a framework which, as we saw in Chapter Three, Ajneya explicitly rejected.

9. He claims that the 'fatalism' [*niyativāda*] of the revolutionary is 'a step beyond the way of works of the *Gītā* [*Gītā ke karmayoga se ek sīṛhī āge hotā hai.*]'. We also know that he read the *Gītā* as a boy.(See above, p. 32)
10. For a full description of the history and content of the marriage ceremony see Pandey [1969] pp. 153-233. The bride's act of pouring offerings into the fire is described in the same book, p. 218.
11. Pandey says that Hindu marriage 'involves a great compromise and mutual sacrifice', though he does not suggest that this is actually stated in the marriage rite.(Pandey [1969] p. 233) However, such language is common currency as a description of married life. (Dr Satyendra Srivastava, Faculty of Oriental Studies, Cambridge University, in an interview with the author, 3rd January 1992.)
12. See above, pp. 80-3.
13. McGee, 'Desired Fruits: Motive and Intention in the Votive Rites of Hindu Women', in Leslie (ed) [1991] pp. 71-88.
14. Dr J J Lipner, Faculty of Divinity, Cambridge University, in an interview with the author on 25th March 1994. The following paragraph is indebted to Lipner, 'On Women and Salvation in Hinduism: Paradoxes of Ambivalence', in Smart and Thakur (eds) [1993] pp. 160-80.
15. See above, p. 94.
16. It is not only this Christian reader who finds the relationship between Gaura and Rekha unconvincing. In one of his essays Ajneya himself writes:

    > A scholar-critic has said that the female characters of IS are unnatural and impossible because they are not jealous. In my view jealousy is the result of imperfect vision and of immaturity. At a certain age -- and an age can also be mental -- jealousy can be natural; but I think that a child can also grow up. For a young girl -- even the heroine of a Hindi novel ! -- to grow up is not particularly unnatural.(Vatsyayan [1983] p. 70)

    We do not find Ajneya's remarks convincing: we believe, like his critic, that jealousy has deeper roots than he suggests. It cannot simply be dismissed as a passing phase of adolescence.
17. > First of all he embraced Kaikeyi, inclining her to gentler thoughts by his sincerity and devotion, then falling at her feet he comforted her, laying all the blame on fate, and destiny and providence... 'the world is ruled by God, blame no-one'. (*Rāmacaritamānasa* 2, C 244, translated in Hill [1952] p. 260)

    The background to this incident is as follows: King *Daśaratha* of Ayodhya had three wives and four sons. Rama was his son by the first wife and *Bharat* his son by the second, Kaikeyi. The latter had once saved the king's life and as a reward he rashly promised her that she could claim any two boons she chose whenever she wanted. When the king was getting old he decided to hand over the kingdom to Rama, his eldest son. On the eve of his coronation

Kaikeyi claimed her two boons, which were first, that Rama should go into exile for fourteen years; and second, that Bharat should be king in his place. All of which suggests to the western reader that Rama had ample grounds to be very angry indeed with Kaikeyi ! (*Rāmāyaṇa* 1.7-9, translated in Griffith [1963] pp. 96-100.)

18. Although favoured by Ajneya, *tapasyā* is less commonly used in Sanskrit and possibly in Hindi than *tapas*.
19. See, for example, Laws of Manu 6.23 (translated in Doniger and Smith [1991] p. 119).
20. See above, p. 75.
21. See above, pp. 86-7.
22. See above, p. 77.
23. *Yoga* is a very old method of spiritual, bodily, and mental concentration and contemplation. It consists of bodily postures and control of breathing as well as spiritual techniques. As a method it is used in almost all religous traditions of Indian origin. For a fuller description, see Klostermaier [1990] pp. 358-67.
24. The Rishis were regarded by later generations as patriarchal sages or saints, occupying the same position in Indian history as the heroes and patriarchs of other countries, and constitute a peculiar class of beings in the early mythical system...according to orthodox Hindu ideas they are the inspired personages to whom these [Vedic] hymns were revealed.(Monier-Williams [1899] pp. 226-7)
25. For a description of this quietening of the mind as a spiritual ideal, see *Bhagavadgītā* 5.19-24.(translated in Zaehner ed [1978] p. 273)
26. This imaginative reconstruction of the Genesis narrative was originally published almost exactly word for word as an independent short story in 1934. It is conveniently available in the volume containing Ajneya's complete short stories.(Ajneya [1989] pp. 207-15.)
27. The classic instance of persistent (and unwelcome) questioning finding its reward is to be found in the *Kaṭha Upaniṣad*, where the young *Naciketas* asks his questions of Death.(translated in Hume [1931] pp. 341-61) For some biblical examples of questions see *eg* Psalms 13:1 and 79:10-11; Mark 2:8-9,18 and 24.
28. Vedic tradition did not consider itself the result of human thought: it related its content to a revelation received by seers and sages in meditation and trance, it aimed at maintaining and duplicating these states of mind through yogic practices, and it exempted Vedic teaching from criticism by declaring its origin *apauruṣeya*, not man-made but eternally present.(Klostermaier [1990] p. 344)
29. For an account of this, see O'Flaherty (ed) [1975] pp. 273-80.
30. Hindu Scripture is formally divided into two categories: *śruti* -- 'what is heard' -- refers to the Vedas, which are usually held to include the Upanishads. For the way in which these Scriptures are held to be revealed, see note 39 above. The Epics and *Purāṇas*, which are the main repositories of myth, are included in the second -- and secondary -- category of *smṛti* -- 'what is remembered' -- which is further from the original source of revelation, and so of lesser authority, than *śruti*. Yet in practice myths play a much more important role in Hindu life than this relationship implies. For a discussion of this see Lipner [1994] pp. 183-4.

31. We recall that Ajneya himself had been a volunteer officer at the Congress session of 1929. See above, p. 36.
32. See above, p. 115.
33. See above, p. 35-6. He remained in close touch with Banade until the latter's death in 1981.(Lele [1993] p. 94)
34. Shashi's lifelessness is very much like that of a similarly unhappily married woman in one of Ajneya's short stories, *Gangrene*, which was first published in 1934. It is now available in Ajneya [1989] pp. 207-15.
35. See above, p. 6.
36. *Siddhi* means the complete attainment of an object, and so by extension, final emancipation or perfection. *Sampūrti* means fulfilment or completion but usually in a more secular sense.(Monier-Williams [1899] pp. 1173 and 1216.)
37. See above, p. 116.
38. The other two were Madansingh and a Muslim prisoner called *Muhammad Mohasin* who remained unfailingly cheerful however harshly he was punished, and who sometimes used to sing for Shekhar's benefit.(SL Vol. 2 pp. 66-7and 88-9)
39. This was what largely pertained in the traditional caste system, for a brief description of which see above, pp. 24-5. For the changing social and intellectual context which made the emergence of a literary character such as Shekhar possible, see above p. 58.
40. In SL Vol. 2 this word or its opposite, 'having no aim [*niruddeśya*]', appears only once in pp. 1-113, twice in pp. 167-253, but no less than 36 times in pp. 114-66. For Shekhar's use of the word 'mission' see above, p 116.
41. See above, see pp. 66-7.
42. See for example, Luke 12.49-50.
43. One such was the famous philosopher-theologian *Rāmānuja* who is said to have risked the wrath of the local Brahmins by climbing the tower of a temple and preaching to the crowds of pilgrims below.(Walker [1968] Vol. 2 p 286).
44. *Jñāna* means 'knowledge, (esp.) the higher knowledge (derived from meditation on the one Universal Spirit)'; *prajñā* means 'wisdom, intelligence, knowledge....true or transcendental wisdom', and *vivek* means 'the faculty of distinguishing and classifying things according to their real properties'. (Monier-Williams [1899] pp. 426, 659 and 987.)
45. We shall see in the next chapter that this attitude of hostility is modelled on the Existentialist philosophy of Jean-Paul Sartre. See below, p. 148.
46. See above, p. 44.
47. See above, pp. 111-2.
48. See *Rāmāyaṇa* 7.97.13-20, translated in Griffith [1963] p. 520. See also Hooker [1989] pp. 291-9.
49. See above, pp. 112-3.
50. For a discussion of this theme see Hooker [1989] pp. 212, and 246-7. See also Rowland [1967] p. 28, and Moore [1977] p. 108.
51. Dr Satyendra Srivastava, Faculty of Oriental Studies, Cambridge University, in an interview with the author on 3rd January 1992.
52. Hemendra's sexual orientation remains obscure. For the relevant evidence see Chapter Three, note 38.
53. An eighteenth century astronomical observatory in Delhi, the ruins of which are often visited by tourists.

54. Lipner, 'The Classical Hindu View of Abortion and the Moral Status of the Unborn', in Coward, Lipner, and Young [1989] pp. 41-69.
55. The writer comments:

    Let the sun, the sky and the wind be the witnesses, and the grass spread beneath them, and the rocks. Let their witnesses be the countless divinities of intermediate space, and the stunted trees and shrubs.

    Hindu tradition recognises eight religiously licit kinds of marriage, one of which is

    gāndharva or 'Cupid's' form of marriage which originated in mutual desire. The couple had had sexual intercourse or were cohabiting and wished to ratify their union. This has a modern ring to it, but this kind of marriage was not encouraged. (Lipner [1994] p. 268)

    This form of marriage may perhaps have been in Ajneya's mind at this point.
56. Bhuvan had left Rekha in Srinagar. She had the abortion in his absence. He returned after receiving a letter from her and it was then that he found her desperately ill and took her to hospital.(IS pp. 161 and 208-9)
57. It is still not easy to discuss this subject openly in India, as the following comment illustrates:

    In preparation for a visit to two well-known Indian universities, shortly after completing this chapter, I offered the present topic (among others) to the relevant departments for possible seminars/ public lectures. I was not too surprised to discover that, in both cases, this topic was politely singled out for exclusion on 'cultural' grounds.(Lipner, note 1 of the essay cited in note 54)
58. Ajneya claims that

    Rekha is the most mature character of <u>Islands in the Stream.</u> I have already written that in my view she is also the most important character of the novel. She is the most faithful to her feelings and most merciless to herself.

    Perhaps this much can be extracted from the story, that Rekha always wants to remain true to her feelings. She takes her responsibility towards what is within her to the limit of self-offering. At the point where this is great strength of personality, a climax of personal development, there too is its defeat. For mere 'self-offering for that which is within oneself' is not enough. There is something outside and greater than oneself. To make such a total sacrifice for that is really (*sc* to reach) a fully developed and mature state of character. Rekha's tragedy is that her self-offering remains incomplete. (Vatsyayan [1983] p. 73)
59. See above, pp. 127-8.
60. This seems a strange metaphor for Bhuvan, a man, to use. Is he half-consciously thinking of Sita, who in the *Rāmāyaṇa* was actually swallowed up by the earth from which she had originally emerged ? See above, p. 128 and note 48. Bhuvan's name means 'a being, living creature, man' but also sometimes 'the world, earth'.(Monier-Williams [1899] p. 760)
61. See above, pp. 83-4.
62. Rabindranath Tagore (1861-1941) was the most famous and influential Bengali writer of modern times. Since Rekha had been brought up in

Calcutta (IS p. 27) it was only natural that she should know Tagore's poetry.

63. While Ajneya gives his Hindi translation of this poem in a footnote he quotes the original Bengali in the text. The line we have translated reads: *bāṁsi tomāy diye jābo kāhār hāte.*

64. See above, pp. 116.

5

THE PURSUIT OF FREEDOM

At the end of the last chapter we pointed out that the theme of the purification of vision through suffering is closely related to Ajneya's understanding of freedom. This is especially clear in the stanza of his own poem which we have already quoted and which he places on the fly leaf of IS:

> Suffering: she burnishes [*māṁjatā hai-*] us all: and though-------To let go [*mukti denā*] herself she may not know Those whom she holds [*maṁjatā hai*] she teaches All others to liberate [*mukta rakheṁ*](1)

Here the link between suffering, purification (burnishing), and freedom is explicitly made. We also saw in the last chapter how this stanza is, so to speak, enacted by Shashi in her liberation of Shekhar at the end of SL, and more profoundly in IS by Rekha in her refusal to hold on to Bhuvan by marrying him. We pointed out the possible parallels in these events to *Sāṁkhya* teaching where the analogy of the dance is used for *prakṛti* 's freeing of *puruṣa*. We noted in addition that Shekhar urges Shashi freely to choose her own path when she is being pushed against her will into an arranged marriage, and that in IS Bhuvan urges Gaura to do much the same, telling her not to feel bound by the choice of a husband which her parents have made for her. We saw too that the purification of vision endows Shashi, Rekha and Selma with an insight into present circumstances and sometimes into the future which other characters do not possess. Such insight enables those who do possess it to rise above the constraints of their present circumstances, and so can be called a kind of freedom. We saw that in TEHS the theme of purification of vision through suffering is less explicit than it is in the two earlier works, though still very much present. The links of this chapter with its predecessor are therefore close, but freedom also has an independent significance in its own right.

We begin by sketching out some of the material which we shall be examining in greater depth and detail later in the chapter, and as a way into it we pose the question: what do Ajneya's characters want to be free from ? In the case of Shekhar our initial answer must be: traditional education and the socialising of young children within its constricting framework. This he sees as harmful and stunting to human potential. When he goes to college in Madras a social dimension is added to his rebellion: people of low caste or outcaste origin, and women, are unfree. Their roles are defined by a tradition which puts them at the bottom of the social hierarchy. Others who have a higher status within that hierachy are unfree in less obvious but no less real ways. These include the effete students of Lahore who in their westernisation lay claim to a kind of freedom, but one which is devoid of moral values and constraints. Similar to them are the people who run the Congress Camp where Shekhar is arrested, those who belong to the corrupt world of publishing, and self-styled and essentially hypocritical social reformers such as Amolak Rai. None of these are oppressed in the way that women and outcastes are, indeed it is often they who are the oppressors, but they are inwardly unfree either because they embrace an inadequate philosophy, or else because they cannot accept in their own lives the implications of the better one which they claim to follow.

It is the moral powerlessness of such people, and indeed of the society he sees all around him, which pushes Shekhar into the path of total revolution. The student Raghavan [*Rāghavan*], who is one of his circle of friends in the college at Madras, is a typical example of such powerlessness: having answered Shekhar's call for social change he then feebly accepts the marriage arranged by his parents to a girl he has never seen. Shekhar's angry outburst at Raghavan illustrates his impatience and contempt for this kind of spinelessness: in the passage we quote Raghavan has just admitted that he is twenty and so in principle old enough to choose a marriage partner for himself. He is just about to explain why he could not actually do this when Shekhar interrupts him:

> Shekhar could no longer control his anger. 'Aren't you ashamed to say you are old enough ? You are twenty years old and you still haven't got the guts to say no to an enforced marriage. You don't want to get married, so why can't you just say you won't...Are you just a sheep or goat that people can lead off with a rope round its neck and then offer up in sacrifice ? You are a man [*ādmī*], a man !'(SL Vol. 1 p. 222)

This outburst comes near the end of the first volume of SL. The second volume is mainly concerned with Shekhar's imprisonment and then with his deepening relationship with Shashi. It is here that the links between freedom and the purification of vision are closest. In IS the situation is different: Bhuvan, Rekha and Chandramadhava stand apart from the constrictions of the traditional social order in a way that none of their counterparts in SL was able to do. Gaura is closer to that order but even she enjoys a freedom to which Shashi was unable to aspire. All four characters of IS are now islands in the shifting stream of life. As we shall see, as an image of the freedom of the individual in society this is modern in content but traditional in form. We shall see that in IS and to a lesser but still important degree in SL nature has a large importance as the place where alone true freedom can be glimpsed even if not finally grasped. Thus, as we saw in Chapter Three (2), Rekha claims to have two sides to her personality, one which is civilised and constricted and the other which is free because it belongs to the world of nature. The mountain lake beside which she and Bhuvan eventually have sex is an idealised example of that world. In both of these novels the freedom which nature affords is set over against the debilitating constraints of civilisation [*sabhyatā*] of which the modern metropolis is the embodiment and symbol. Chandramadhava (in IS) is a characteristic product of the metropolis where he enjoys a distorted kind of freedom which lacks any moral basis. When he visits Europe he rejoices in the freedom of society especially with regard to women, comparing it favourably to what is possible in India. In all this he is rather like the westernised Manika [*Maṇikā*] and her circle at the beginning of SL Vol. 2. Shekhar is disgusted with this group, who consume large amounts of alcohol, are loose in their sexual morals, and ape the worst of western ways.(SL Vol. 2 pp. 12-9) This kind of freedom is a parody and counter-image of the aspirations of the best of Ajneya's characters.

We have already noted on more than one occasion how TEHS stands apart from the first two novels. One element in this difference is the fact that the setting is European rather than Indian, and that a central theme of the book is a debate with the Existentialist philosophy of Jean-Paul Sartre, to which we have already alluded. That debate is not central to this book, but unless its main lines are clarified our interpretation of the Brahminical Hindu roots of Ajneya's understanding of freedom in this novel will be distorted. The chief elements of Sartre's philosophy with which Ajneya was engaged can be summed up in the following terms: human life is in the last analysis meaningless and absurd. There is no God, and we are all caught up in anxiety, disgust with life, and a preoccupation with death. Freedom of choice is a curse which is an inescapable part of the human condition. Therefore to say 'we are free' is tautologous, it is simply to say 'we are human' in different words. In such a world each individual is always in a potential state of conflict with others who are threats to one's own freedom. Every individual has to take the risk of this conflict and by their own free choice create their own values.(3)

In TEHS these attitudes are embodied in Yoke and implicitly challenged by Selma who does not share them. Thus she points out that she and Yoke are manifestly unfree because they are in a hut buried under a snow drift, and neither of them has chosen the other's company. She comments: 'Nothing is in anyone's power. The only thing in anyone's power is to recognise this fact. [*kuch bhī kisī ke bas kā nahīṁ hai. ek hī bāt hamāre bas kī hai -- is bāt ko pahacān lenā*].'(TEHS p. 27) She cannot choose to die alone, as she had planned, and Yoke cannot choose to be absent when she dies. Yoke displays a typically Sartrean hostility towards Selma, an attitude which was shared by Selma herself when she was marooned on the bridge earlier in her life. She was 'converted' from this barren stance into the serene and untroubled character who is buried under the snow drift with Yoke. It is precisely to afford Yoke a similar opportunity of 'conversion' that she tells this part of her own story. Yoke's 'conversion' happens -- most unconvincingly -- when she commits suicide at the very end of the novel. Yet while the central importance of this debate with Sartre needs to be recognised in order to understand this novel, it does not conflict with our view that the roots of Ajneya's own understanding of freedom are to be found in his own tradition. Indeed to a degree he supports this claim himself, for he says that in this book Yoke represents a western attitude in the face of death and Selma an eastern.(Vatsyayan [1983] pp. 326-7) Patently, Selma enjoys an inner freedom in the face of adversity which Yoke does not. The content and significance of this we shall have to discuss.

The Brahminical Hindu roots of Ajneya's view of freedom can be seen most clearly in all three novels in the vocabulary and images which he uses. We shall see that all this evidence points in the same direction: to the kind of absolute freedom which is the goal of the isolated individual who is cut off from society. This means that the novels are in this respect somewhat paradoxical. On the surface they reject much that was sacrosanct to Brahminical Hindus, and as such the first two outraged conventional society when they were first published, but while the actual content of the freedoms claimed was new and indeed revolutionary, their inner patterns are very traditional. To make the same point with the aid of a metaphor: Ajneya served up to his first readers a heady and intoxicating brew which no-one had offered them before. He served it in a western vessel, for the novel is a western literary *genre*, yet the material of which the vessel is constructed bears the stamp 'made in India'.

To make this case more fully we first look at the words which Ajneya most commonly uses for freedom. They are all of Sanskritic origin and often used in Hindi as well. The most frequently used is *mukti*, which literally means 'setting or becoming free'.(Monier-Williams [1899] p. 821) Together with its various cognates it occurs 26 times in SL, 51 times in IS and five times in TEHS.(4) We give some representative examples of its use: it is used to refer to Shekhar as a little boy struggling to escape the grasp of a servant who had been ordered to bring him to his father, and getting his leg free (SL Vol. 1 p. 113), to Rekha's release from Hemendra when the divorce has gone through (IS p. 252), to India's independence from Britain (SL Vol. 2 p. 44), to Shashi's 'releasing' of Shekhar at the end of SL (SL Vol. 2 p. 253), and to the freedom of Rekha's personality when it is turned towards nature rather than civilisation.(IS p. 112). All these examples of the use of *mukti* are secular in that they refer to release from ties that bind and inhibit people in this world and in this life.

A second word which is derived from the same root and has the same basic meaning is *mokṣa.* In modern Hindi usage this retains the significance which it has in the philosophical tradition where it is commonly used for the ultimate human goal of transcendent liberation from all the ties that bind the inner being [*ātman*] of an individual to this world. Significantly, it is literally part of the very last word of SL. Shekhar, about to face execution, is pondering on the fact that Shashi, though now dead, is with him as his 'eternal inspiration -- eternal because free -- and giver of freedom [*cirantan preraṇā -- cirantan kyoṁki mukta -- aur mokṣadā*]'.(SL Vol. 2 p. 253) This is the highest value which Shekhar can give to this word. He had already said in the early pages of the novel that he had been 'made' by Shashi (SL Vol. 1 p. 16), and here he is referring to what she has done for him in quasi-transcendental terms. This is not the final liberation of which tradition speaks, for Shekhar would have repudiated that as a possibility, but his thought here is moving in that direction and indeed echoes, if unconsciously, *Sāṁkhya* philosophy.(5) He seems to be implying that what Shashi has done for him is to give him the only kind of genuine release which is really possible.

Ajneya makes frequent use of three other important words for freedom. The first of these is *svatantratā*, which with its cognates occurs 15 times in SL, only once in IS, but 22 times in TEHS. It is synonymous with *svādhīntā*, (22 times in SL, 28 times in IS, none in TEHS), and can refer to an individual or to a collective body. The adjectives of which these two words are the abstract nouns mean respectively 'self-dependent, self-willed, independent, free, uncontrolled' (Monier-Williams [1899] p. 1275), and 'dependent on oneself, independent, free, being in one's own power or control'.(Monier-Williams [1899] p. 1277) They are generally used in a mundane rather than in a transcendental sense and are frequently used in modern Hindi to refer to political freedom.(6) Our third word, *svacchanda*, is rarer, occuring only 11 times in SL, once in IS and not at all in TEHS. It means 'of one's own free will, choice or fancy, uncontrolled, spontaneous, uncultivated or wild'.(Monier-Williams [1899] p. 1275) In modern Hindi it is used to translate the western literary term Romantic -- in the narrow sense of 'to do with the Romantic Movement' rather than in the larger sense of 'to do with romantic love'. The fact that all three words begin with the prefix *'sva'* meaning 'one's own' is important and suggests that their basic meaning is individualistic.

In our novels these three words are normally used in a secular sense, but with occasional hints of a transcendent dimension. Thus when Shekhar's parrot, whose acquaintance we make below, escapes from its cage, Shekhar reflects that the birds live in another world apart from his own, a world in which there is *svacchandatā* and *svatantratā*.(SL Vol. 1 p. 61) Selma can tell Yoke that there is no such thing as 'freedom of choice [*varaṇa kī svatantratā*]' (TEHS p. 100), while when Bhuvan tells Gaura that we must not run away from the risk of freedom and that the exercise of freedom requires courage, he uses *svādhīnatā*.(IS p. 76) Each of the four words we have considered suggests the absence of or release from that which binds, constricts, or inhibits, and in the case of the last three, being under one's own control as opposed to being in the power of others. We shall see below that in addition to this verbal usage the imagery Ajneya uses also points to these same areas of meaning. Thus vocabulary and imagery alike provide a ready-made context for describing the individual who longs to be delivered from constraints. We saw in Chapter Three that in certain key respects Ajneya reshapes the boundaries which define human identity. In these respects therefore his view of what it means to be human is shaped in opposition to important elements of his own tradition, and in particular to traditional views of transcendence and of ritual purity. In the present chapter also the constraints against which his characters revolt are largely imposed by tradition. So the theme of opposition continues. Yet the freedom which is Ajneya's ideal is always that of the isolated individual who can find true freedom only in the realm of nature, not in society. Our view that this kind of individualistic freedom has its roots in that very tradition which in other respects Ajneya and his characters reject, is endorsed in SL by Madansingh, whom we considered in detail in the last chapter. In a conversation with Shekhar he criticises the other-worldly individualism of the Indian philosophical tradition:

> It seems to me that our Indian life [*jīvan*] and philosophy [*darśan*] is introverted [*antaramukhī*] and individualistic [*vyaktivādī*] -- for example, we only regard something as a means for release [*mukti kā sādhana*] if as far as possible it draws us away from society and says 'know thyself [*ātmānaṁ viddhi*]'. The result of this individualism is that we understand sin and merit [*pāp-puṇya*] too in exclusively individual terms. Thus our devout people [*dharmātmā log*] regard even feeding milk to snakes as a meritorious act. Yet from a social point of view this is violence [*hiṃsā*].(7) On the other hand western life and philosophy is completely contrary to ours. It is extroverted [*bahirmukhī*] and related to society [*samājvādī*] (8)...neither of us can forget the other's ideal [*ādarśa*]. It is especially necessary for us to reform our ideals because we are the underdogs [*nīce*].(SL Vol. 2 p. 83)

We saw in Chapter Three that Ajneya rejects both the 'sin and merit' and the 'release' to which Madansingh refers, for these were parts of the transcendental framework within which Brahminical Hindu thought set human life. Yet he retains the individualism and withdrawal from society to which Madansingh also refers, although in a secular form. Some of his Indian critics also attack this individualism, though they do not trace its roots to his inheritance in the way which we shall attempt to do. The fiercest and most persistent of these critics, the Marxist Namvar Singh, constantly opposed Ajneya for his bourgeois romantic individualism (9), while Ajneya himself had no sympathy for Marxism as his creation of the character of Chandramadhava demonstrates.(10) Indeed when giving the first hint of his eventual conversion to Communism Chandramadhava reflects that:

> when he now thought about people he rarely visualised them as unique individuals.(11) He always added an adjective indicating class [*jātivācak*] to them...to go beyond personality [*vaiyaktiktā*]...was a considerable achievement; to be able to be impersonal [*nirvaiyaktik*], to be able to hate in an impersonal way, to despise everything without pain [*darda*] -- how splendid that would be. (IS p. 190)

Another critic, Devesh Thakur, comments that while individual freedom is the key to IS, no thought is given to how this freedom affects others, or to the fact that every individual is inescapably a member of society. (Thakur [1975] p. 116) Om Prabhakar says much the same thing, pointing out that while Shekhar searches for freedom, his quest is only for himself and not for society. He adds, in more general terms, that while all the critics praise the language of Ajneya's novels, many of them accuse him, among other things, of individualism and escapism.(Prabhakar [1966] pp. 68-71) This critical consensus is impressive and important. We shall return to it at the end of the chapter.

We turn now to Ajneya's use of the imagery of freedom, and this will lead us to the same conclusions as our discussion of his use of vocabulary. For the convenience of analysis we can divide his images into four main groups: height, flight, experiences connected with water, and absorption into a larger whole. The boundaries between these four are not always as clear in the texts as they are in our analysis, and some of the material we shall be examining belongs in more than one category. We shall consider them in turn, in each case first looking at the place of the image within those areas of Brahminical Hinduism with which Ajneya was familiar, and then investigating his own use of it.

We first consider height. We have already seen how the ideal world of purity is associated with height and we pointed out that in IS the pure lake on the mountain top where Bhuvan and Rekha eventually make love may well have its unconscious origin in the *Rāmāyaṇa*.(12) We also saw how Rekha compared this place to the Northern Meru.(13) In the sacred geography of the *Purāṇas* Meru is at the centre of the earth, the place where earth and heaven meet. Around it in concentric circles are the seven continents which are separated from one another by seven seas of (starting from the outer circle), salt water, sugar cane juice, spiritous liquor (!), clarified butter, sour milk, full cream milk, and pure water. We note the ascending scale of purity the nearer we get to the centre.(14) Independent of this particular mythic geographical framework the Himalayas are perceived as being the abode of the gods and goddesses. Some of them have their own heaven -- that of Shiva is Mount *Kailāsa* and that of Vishnu is Mount *Vaikuṇṭha*.(Monier-Williams [1899] pp. 311 and 1020) Mircea Eliade has shown that this association of height with sacredness is universal. The high places of Canaanite worship are obvious parallels, as are Mount Sinai and the hill of Golgotha. Eliade points out that

> High places are impregnated with sacred forces. Everything nearer to the sky shares, with varying intensity, in its transcendence. "Height", "what is higher" becomes transcendent, superhuman. Every ascent is a breakthrough, as far as the different levels of existence are concerned, a passing to what is beyond, an escape from profane space and human status.(Eliade [1958] p. 101)

When Ajneya's characters long for freedom from the constraints of their present existence they sometimes describe their longing in terms of height. Thus when Shekhar is reflecting in the condemned cell both on his own plight and on the human condition in general, he remarks that 'there is in humanity some upward striving power [*mānava meṁ koī urdhvagāmī śakti hai*]'.(SL Vol. 1 p. 35) Later he reflects on the mysteriousness of the events and thoughts which open up the path of the future for him. It is impossible to discern the source of their power:

> When I wonder what is the source of the perpetually upward-looking inspiration [*ūrdhvamukhī preraṇā*] which keeps on charting my life's course, keeps on drawing it upwards [*utkarṣaṇa*], towards some unattainable mountain peak [*śikhar*] which transcends the imagination [*jo kalpanā meṁ dikhtā nahiṁ*] and remains hidden somewhere above the highest clouds -- then I get no clear answer.(SL Vol. 1 p. 68)

At other points the imagery of height has an explicitly sexual content: thus during Shekhar's adolescence the family are making a trip in a boat on a lake in Kashmir. He is alone on the roof of the cabin while the rest of the family are below. He gazes at the rising moon and then:

> A strange feeling arose in my mind. The moon is a girl [*kanyā*] and the dark beauty of this earth is her garment. But the girl is so beautiful that this garment has no right [*adhikār*] to cover her, therefore the moon has cast it aside, and has arisen uncovered [*nirāvaraṇa*] above the horizon. And how beautiful her spreading beauty makes that discarded garment.(SL Vol. 1 p. 23)

Such erotic imagery is common in Sanskrit courtly poetry (15), from where we may assume Ajneya derived it, but our point here is that Shekhar's dream is rudely shattered by a voice:

> 'Shekhar, it's time to come down !' This was his sister's voice. And from that moment on, whenever I see some overwhelmingly beautiful sight [*atyanta sundar dṛśya*], and forget myself in an

> upward-climbing [*ūrdhvagāmī*] intoxication [*unmāda*], then a piercing voice summons me and says: -- 'Shekhar, it's time to come down !'(SL Vol. 1 p. 23)

Here we see clearly that Shekhar's longings elude his grasp. That happens in a rather different and much more painful way at the end of his adolescent love affair with Sharada, whom he meets when the family move to Ootacamund in the Nilgiri Hills in South India. The young couple regularly meet on a hill top with a tree on it.(SL Vol. 1 p. 178) So here too the imagery of height has sexual overtones. The relationship with Sharada comes to an abrupt and unexpected end when Shekhar one day finds her house locked up and the family gone he knows not where.(SL Vol. 1 p. 178) At the beginning of the second volume he sets off on his strange journey in pursuit of absolute beauty and this takes him upwards to the Himalayas.(SL Vol. 2 pp. 24-8) The image of height re-appears half way through this volume when he has emerged from jail. He rents a small room on the fourth floor of a house. It was here that he welcomed Shashi after her rejection by Rameshvar.(16) The room is described in detail and Shekhar reflects that for the first time he is living on his own, 'a single independent unit [*ek svatantra ikāī*]' (SL Vol. 2 p. 117) of that society about which he now feels impelled to write. He goes on:

> He remembered that he had once read some article about the benefits of living on the top floor of a house. What were counted as benefits he had forgotten, but he could think them out afresh for himself ! Fresh air [*svaccha vāyu*], solitude [*ekānta*], distance from the hubbub of the city, a feeling of detachment [*taṭasthatā kā bhāva*] from society...as a child he used to think that people who lived on mountains were nearer to God [*Īśvar*]...Shekhar laughed to himself; then, having reached this high level of life [*ūṁce jivan-star*] he began to wonder what he could write that was worth sharing with others.(SL Vol. 2 p. 118)

There is a hidden touch of irony here, for Shekhar wants to write about society and its reform, yet his whole attitude bespeaks an individualistic detachment from it. So this passage is a graphic illustration of the points about Ajneya made by the Indian critics to whom we referred above. We can also discern in Shekhar's words a parallel to Rekha's use of a different imagery of height -- the Northern Meru -- to reflect on her sexual experience with

Bhuvan.(17) We note that in all these examples height symbolises the fact that an individual, or a couple who are in love, are separating themselves from the constraints of society and aspiring to a realm of quasi-transcendent freedom which is hardly distinguishable from isolation. This reminds us of the word *kaivalya* which suggests total separation from all worldly ties and which *Sāṁkhya* philosophy posits as the final goal of *puruṣa*.(18) Once again we do not suggest that Ajneya was directly thinking of this concept while he wrote about height, but he is moving in the same circle of ideas and conceives of freedom in similarly individualistic terms. Finally, we recall that the first part of TEHS is set in a hut buried under a snow drift in the mountains of Scandanavia. Ajneya tells us elsewhere that he pondered for a long time on the setting for the novel and at one stage considered the possibility of a coal mine in which two people were to be cut off from the outside world by a fall of rock.(19) His choice of setting was governed by the need to isolate his characters. Yet both the height of a mountain top and the depth of a coal mine can be interpreted as images of transcendence.(20)

Our second image is that of a bird in flight. One well-known Hindu symbol of the soul's journey through life is that of the white swan [*haṃsa*] which flies towards the Himalaya in the rainy season, in order to escape -- in popular belief -- from the mud and filth which the monsoon brings to the plains. A bird is a symbol of the soul in other religions too.(21) In the Hindu tradition the significance of the flying bird is characteristically enhanced by its association with purity. There is a beautiful use of this image in *Meghadūtam*, a long narrative poem of Kalidasa (22), which evokes its significance with particular clarity. This poem is addressed by a lover to a monsoon cloud which he begs to take a message to his beloved on its way northwards. He refers to the 'royal swans [*rājahaṃsāḥ*]' which will accompany the cloud:

> regal swans longing for Manasa-lake, gathering tender lotus-shoots for the way will be your companions in the sky even up to Mount Kailasa's peak.(*Meghadūtam* 11, translated in Rajan [1989] p. 139)

The holy lake and Kailasa we have already considered in the context of height, and we also note that the holy lake, the lotus-stems, the unstated because assumed whiteness of the swans and of Mount Kailasa, are all symbols of purity. Further, in both Sanskrit and Hindi *paramhaṃsa* -- 'great white swan' -- is often used as an honorific title for those who have already reached the ideal of ultimate liberation in this life.(23) Such people -- they are normally men -- are the greatest among those who have renounced the ties of home, family and society by becoming *saṃnyāsins*.

The image of flight is used in both SL and IS to refer to freedom aspired to or freedom lost, but never to freedom enjoyed. We are reminded of the words addressed to Shekhar by his sister when he was on the top of the cabin of the boat: 'Shekhar, it's time to come down!' In other words for Ajneya freedom can never be a secure possession, it is always at risk, and is ultimately elusive. We turn first to the use of the image as a symbol of aspiration. When Shekhar is a boy his father buys a bird each for his three sons. Shekhar's bird is a parrot. His parents teach it to repeat the word *Sītārāma* but Shekhar teaches it to laugh. There is a scarcely veiled reference here to Shekhar himself. His parents and the rest of adult society try to impose on him a mindless education which is just like teaching a parrot to repeat something. One day the young Shekhar tries forcibly to feed the parrot with pepper. It refuses to oblige and instead fastens its beak painfully on his finger. He wrenches his finger free and in doing so inadvertently lets go of the parrot as well. It flies off to the top of a nearby tree, gaining confidence when it realises it is no longer confined in its cage. It was never recaptured:

> Those birds disappeared from Shekhar's life. After that no more birds were brought into the house. But did they disappear from Shekhar's heart as well ? Shekhar saw that besides his own world there in another in which the birds live, in which there is liberty [*svacchandatā*], in which there is faith [*viśvāsa*], in which there is love [*sneha*], in which there is an unbounded freedom [*abadh svatantratā*] to think or play, in which there is only one rule, 'Be what you are'...and that world became for him a heaven [*svarga*], a greatly longed for dream, the door into release [*unmukti*] from all his agonies, his help in his loneliness.(SL Vol. 1 p. 61)

That longed-for world takes on a material form in the jungle, the world of nature untamed and unspoiled by humankind. Shortly after this incident Shekhar goes into a garden one evening. He is overwhelmed by the song of the birds all around him and asks himself:

> 'Is this the jungle [*jaṅgal*]?' because he had heard that the home of birds is the jungle. The answer came, 'No, this is a garden [*bāga*].'
> 'Then what are jungles ?'
> 'They too are just like this, only much bigger than gardens. But trees and fruit-trees are not planted in order [*sajākar lagāe*] as they are here, they grow uncultivated all over the place [*apne-āp ulṭe-sīdhe*].' The boy thought to himself, how unconfined [*unmukta*] that place will be, where everything will be free [*svatantra*], even these plants will grow and blossom and bear fruit freely [*svacchandatā se*]...and then in his imagination heaven [*svarga*] took a visible form, and he found a name for it -- the jungle.(SL Vol. 1 pp. 61-2)

This passage needs to be understood in its Indian context where even today much of the land outside the centres of human population is still untamed and uncultivated. This was even more markedly the case when SL was first published (1941-44). To read it against the imaginary background of the gentle English countryside which has been almost entirely brought under human control is to misunderstand what Ajneya is saying. Reflecting on this incident in his prison cell Shekhar says:

> Even today the jungle is for him what cities never were nor will be...today that first dream of his has come down from that high mountain top [*ucca śikhar*], the jungle is no longer heaven [*svarga*] for him, but even so there are many things which nourish that love for the jungle, and even today when imprisoned in the cage he ponders on the jungle.
> Like the parrot he too will not beat his wings against the cage in case they get hurt, because he too has learnt from experience that hurts [*coṭ*] come, but is his soul [*ātmā*] too bound, can it too be wounded, can it too not beat its wings ?(SL Vol. 1 p. 62)

The incident of the escaping parrot gave the young Shekhar his first glimpse of what we might call 'the transcendent'. It also reminds us of the much more mature and sophisticated Rekha's remark to Bhuvan on the two sides to her personality.(24) This is not only true of Rekha: all through these two novels freedom is to be found in the world of nature, whereas the civilisation [*sabhyatā*] of the big city stifles and constricts. So too do conventional social practices, especially arranged marriages. For this Ajneya uses the symbol of a bird winged in full flight and brought to earth, and this speaks powerfully of freedom lost. We have already seen that when Shekhar is in jail Shashi writes to him in great distress about the marriage her mother has arranged for her, and that after his release he goes to her new home and finds her inwardly dead and lifeless.(25) In the early pages of the novel, when he is in the death cell, he reflects on this visit in one of a series of flashbacks to previous moments of his experience. He recalls that when he visited Shashi on this occasion he had an extraordinary moment of unclouded insight, such as comes only rarely in life, when there was

> an overcast sky, a lightless evening, hardly a breath of wind, without the barest movement to be seen, and suddenly a solitary lone bird falling, its wing broken in mid-flight. Then it anxiously struggled to fly again, to find its own place [*apnā sthān*].(SL Vol. 1 p. 17)

This suggests that Shashi's unhappy marriage is an unnatural state, it is not 'her own place' which is the free air of the bird in flight. In the same way when Shekhar observed his parrot high in the tree he reflected that the call to freedom is a call to 'be what you are [*vahī ho-o jo ki tum ho*]'.(SL Vol. 1 p. 61) This reflects the anthropology of the Hindu philosophical tradition where the human predicament is that we are ignorant of our true nature. Our spiritual task is therefore to discover what we essentially are beneath the layers of illusion which conceal it from us, rather than to be changed into something different. This is especially so in the currently dominant philosophy of *Advaita Vedānta* which we consider in a slightly different context below. In IS the image of flight is not so important, nor is it used so powerfully as in SL, but it is still there: when Chandramadhava is trying to engineer a trip to the hills with Rekha, with Bhuvan coming along to preserve appearances, he describes Rekha to Bhuvan as 'a free bird [*mukta vihaṅgam*]' (IS p. 55) -- a phrase which on the lips of Chandramadhava merely implies that unlike other women Rekha is free of conventional social restraints and so (he hopes) sexually available to someone like himself. He was to be quickly disillusioned about Rekha, and after her abortion, when she knows her health is permanently broken, she writes of herself to Bhuvan, 'that this wounded bird should ever fly again as it used to is impossible [*yah āhat pakṣī phir vaise hī uṛa sake, yah to asambhava*]'.(IS p. 251) The picture of the winged bird falling to the ground reminds us of the abrupt summons of the moon-gazing Shekhar's sister, telling him to come down from the roof of the boat's cabin.(26) Both images imply that freedom is ultimately elusive.

Our final example of the image of the bird in flight comes from Shekhar's time at college in Madras. After he has discovered that Raghavan has let him down over the arranged marriage he pours his anger and frustration into an editorial which he writes for the group's student magazine. He sees that all efforts at reform invariably come to grief after a promising start:

> In literature [*sāhitya*], in society [*samāj*], in art [*kalā*], in life, everywhere, there is the same encouraging beginning, the same encouraging development, and in the end the same deep ditch ! The bird of life [*prāṇoṁ kā pakṣī*] flies upward, it seems as if it will touch the roof of the sky [*ākāśa kī chat*], but all of a sudden it plunges down broken, as if struck by a thunderbolt.(SL Vol. 1 p. 223)

Except for this last instance, all the examples of this image to which we have referred are intensely individualistic, and here, where it does have a collective reference, its use appears forced and artificial. There is no hint of the bird being anything but solitary, nor is there any half-way stage between the two absolutes of flying in total freedom on the one hand, and being either confined to a cage or winged, and so unable to fly at all, on the other. We noticed a similar absolute contrast when we considered the image of height. Both the images make for an uncompromising starkness of choice: we are either totally free or totally unfree. Ajneya does not question this starkness for it appears to reflect very closely both the experience of his characters and his own view.

We move on to the third of our images: water, and experiences connected with it. From Vedic times water has played a key role in Hindu symbolism. It is the primal element, the source of all life, as the following quotation illustrates:

> In the boundless waters in the centre of the universe, on the back

> of the firmament, greater than the great,
>
> having suffused with his splendour all the lights: the Lord of beings stirs within the womb.(*Mahānārāyaṇa Upaniṣad* 1.2, translated in Panikkar [1977] p. 335)

Water is not only the source of all creation but also the final element into which all life is eventually absorbed in death. Thus the *pralaya* in *Puranic* mythology is the great flood (or fire) which overwhelms everything at the world's end, before it becomes the source of a new world in the unending cosmic cycle. In accordance with this basic imagery immersion in water can symbolise both death and renewal. This can be clearly seen in a famous story of the sage Narada [*Nārada*] who asked Vishnu to tell him the secret of his *māyā* (27): at Vishnu's command he plunged into a pool of water and emerged as a beautiful girl, Sushila [*Suśīlā*], daughter of the king of Banares. In course of time she married and had children, but her father and husband quarrelled. In a terrible battle they, along with her sons and all her relations, were killed. She had a great funeral pyre erected, applied the torch to it and then threw herself onto it. At once the fire turned into a pool of water, Sushila became Narada again and Vishnu led him out of the pool, asking him, 'Whose was this son whose death you are bewailing ?'(28) The story is thus at one level about the illusoriness of human love and affection, and indeed of human life itelf, but for our purposes the point to note is the function of water in twice effecting radical transformation. Further, in ordinary mundane discourse the endless series of rebirths which forms the context of human and other life is referred to as *saṃsār*, the flow or stream of life. Whereas in English we commonly talk of 'getting through' something, Hindus will speak of 'getting across' both the ocean of life itself and the lesser experiences of which life is made up. Thus when Shekhar, after all his questions, has finally discovered the nature of the sex act, and is just about to leave home for the first time as a student, we read that he realised that he has 'crossed the sea, he is now complete, he is free, and he is a man [*vah samudra pār kar āyā hai, ki vah sampūrṇa hai, mukta hai aur puruṣa hai*]'.(SL Vol. 1 p. 191)

Ajneya offers us nothing as dramatic as a sex change, but it is striking to see what a prominent -- and ambivalent -- role is played by water in all three novels. Any experience of 'transcendence' seems to take place near water which thus serves either as a means for lifting people to new levels of experience, or as a necessary backcloth against which that experience happens. At the same time it is threatening, for Shekhar nearly drowns when he goes for a swim (SL Vol. 1 p. 231-2), an incident which we examine in more detail below, and we think of the terrible flood which forms the setting for Selma's strange romance with Jan Akelov. This is actually compared to 'the muddy stream of the flood at the end of the world [*pralaya kī maṭmailī dhārā*]'.(TEHS p. 69) Ajneya's second novel even takes its title from water, which as we shall see, becomes within it the key symbol for the interpretation of human relationships. Water is also closely connected with a number of important experiences on which Shekhar looks back in the first volume of SL. Thus, after one of his periodic quarrels with his elders he goes for a long walk on his own. He has no idea where he is going but ends up by a waterfall where he sits and watches for a long time:

> I thought that life should be like that, shining [*śubhra*], pure [*svaccha*], filled with music, unimpeded [*aruddha*], continually awake and moving, free from the ties of family life [*gharbār ke bandanoṁ se mukta*] and always rebellious [*vidrohī*]...then slowly getting up I walked underneath it.(SL Vol. 1 p. 40)

Yet there is an ambivalence about the waterfall for when this incident is described later at its natural place in the story:

> At first he felt respect [*ādar*] for it, there was an attraction [*ākarṣaṇa*], but then a monotony [*eksvaratā*], a changelessness [*parivartanhīntā*], and so a powerlessness [*akṣamatā*] began to be apparent.(SL Vol. 1 p. 149)

The freedom 'from the ties of family life' emphasises once again the individualism of Ajneya's understanding of freedom. It also reminds us of the *saṃnyāsin* who renounces all domestic ties to live (ideally) in the solitude which only nature can afford. When his family are in Kashmir Shekhar pays a solitary visit to a ruined temple overlooking the Dal Lake which is in Srinager. There he is overwhelmed by a sense of a powerful but indescribable presence which makes him feel unclean. He takes off all his clothes and wonders what this presence is -- 'God ? nature ? beauty ? the devil ? suppressed passion ? God ? [*Īśvar* ? *prakṛti* ? *saundarya* ? *śaitān* ? *dabī vāsanā* ? *Īśvar* ?]'(SL Vol. 1 p. 101) On another occasion, when his family have moved to Patna, a city on the banks of the Ganges, he makes a raft out of the stumps of three banana trees (29) and launches out onto the river. He drifts along for hours, pretending in his day-dream that he is being taken to an imaginary island in the sunset, a land without obstacles where there is a beautfiful princess who will welcome him. He plays on this theme at some length:

> Obstacle [*bādhā*] -- it seemed to him that the life he is living is nothing but an obstacle. Today he has found an opportunity to escape from its bondage [*bandhan*], now with the help of three cut trees he is going to that beautiful country where the Ganges goes, where it joins the sea, where the golden island of the sunset is, and where the princess lives who wears clothes made of threads which have merged in the blue expanse of the sky...Shekhar will go to her and will say, 'I am Shekhar, I come from the land of bondage [*bandhanoṁ ke deśa se*]' and she will seat him by her side and will say, 'Here you are without obstacles [*abādh*] -- you will live in that palace of acacia flowers and do whatever you want'.(SL Vol. 1 p. 109)

This is an experience of total irresponsibility, almost a return to the unbroken waters of the womb, and it reminds us of the god Vishnu lying on the waters of the primeval ocean before the beginning of creation.(Monier-Williams [1899] p. 999)

Yet floating too, like all our other images, is ambivalent. In one of his moments of despair Shekhar compares himself to a an empty tin bobbing up and down on the ocean of life (SL Vol. 2 p. 114), an image which is picked up by Chandramadhava in IS. He compares himself to such an empty tin when he writes to Gaura about the absence of freedom in modern existence. He is in Europe at the time and she replies that 'Freedom is a tendency in an individual's mind [*svādhīntā...vyakti ke mānasa kī ek pravṛtti hai*]'. She claims that society cannot give us freedom since it is we who make society and 'I am training my mind for freedom [*maiṁ...svādhinta ke lie apnā man* train *kartī hūṁ*]'.(IS p. 70) He says she can only think in these terms because she lives such a sheltered life,

> but think of those whose lives are cast upon the fathomless ocean [*athāha sāgar*] like empty tins: are they free, can they train themselves ?(IS p. 70)

For Chandramadhava freedom is whatever bit of pleasure he can grasp and before long

> Europe's pessimism [*nirāśavāda*] will overshadow the whole world...To surrender or sink will be the only freedom [*svādhīntā*] that remains.(IS p. 79)

Thus floating can be an image both of freedom and of its opposite. Bhuvan does not subscribe to Chandramadhava's bleak view of the human prospect, but he still describes himself at the end of the book as a piece of flotsam cast up on the shore.(IS p. 274) This is the negative side of the basic image of this second novel, an image which is most clearly set out in a pivotal passage when Rekha has just arrived in Kashmir, and is waiting for Bhuvan. Although her family had been settled in Calcutta for several generations they originally came from Kashmir (IS p. 27) and so in a sense Rekha is returning home. She reflects to herself:

> This was Kashmir -- her ancestors' [*pūrvajoṁ kā*] Kashmir, and therefore her Kashmir in which everything was strange [*gair*] to her. The climate, the vegetation, the sky, the people -- so much so that she did not even know the names of her own relations who were scattered about all over the place, let alone their faces. Indeed most of them were not even aware of her existence. How strange, solitary and alien [*ajnabī, akelā aur gair*] a person [*vyakti*] can be when he is a stranger in his own home...But this was really a boon, for in this strangeness no-one was really alien; everyone was an island, surrounded by a flowing river. In it there were other islands too. There was no shared area defined by limits, no direct contact with anyone except through the river, the river which was the mother [*maṁ*], the upholder who carried one across and which would finally one day absorb [*samā legī*] one into her flow.(IS p. 197)

To interpret this passage we need to realise that Ajneya is not describing an English river whose islands are permanent fixtures in its unchanging course. In India, especially on the vast and sandy Gangetic Plain where there is very little rock, rivers can change course dramatically in a short period, and islands rapidly form and reform. This passage recognises symbolically the change from tradition, where people lived in close-knit face to face communities tied to one place and to its memories, to the modern world of the big city where they are mobile and uprooted, and cast much more on their individual resources and initiative. This imagery recurs throughout the book and there are hints of it too in SL. Yet in a way which is wholly characteristic of our author modernity is described in very traditional terms, for 'the river' suggests the holy mother Ganges and we have already noted that getting across the river or the ocean, or simply 'getting across' is a common Hindu metaphor for the journey of life.(30)

In 1949 Ajneya wrote a poem which he also called 'Islands in the Stream'. (Ajneya [1986] Vol. 1 p. 242) We recall that the novel was published only two years later, a fact which suggests the importance of this image to him at that time. The poem takes us further into the meaning of the image. Its gist is as follows:

> We are islands in the stream which is our mother and gives us form. We are not the stream itself, because if we flowed we would disintegrate and turn into sand, and then all we would do would be to make the water dirty and so be useless. It is not a curse to be islands, that is our fate. 'River, keep on flowing and cleansing us.' We accept the fact that the river becomes the flow of time and so destroys our works and fame. We do become sand in the end but perhaps we will reform into new individuals.

The last words give a hint of possible rebirth which is not to be found in the novel, but the whole poem demonstrates how the novel's central image is for Ajneya an important metaphor of human life. Rekha's use of this image suggests her freedom from the constraints of society, indeed she is perpetually on the move and hates the thought of being tied to a particular place.(31) Further, we saw in the last chapter how when her relationship with Bhuvan is beginning to blossom, the two of them take a boat to an island in the Gomati river. There they play at being Robinson Crusoe and Man Friday and Bhuvan builds a sandcastle, carried away by an almost boyish enthusiasm which totally absorbs him in his task. Rekha has not seen this side of his normally reserved character before. Watching him at work she reflects on her own childhood and wonders why she had never found such completeness [*sampūrṇatā*] and freedom [*mukti*] herself.(IS p. 119) Yet the freedom here is limited and it is difficult to discern any hint of a transcendent dimension to it.

There is such a hint in an incident in SL which occurs when Shekhar, now a student in Madras, makes a journey to Mahabalipuram, which is a little further down the coast. He travels by sea. It is a still moonlit light and there are fish darting about in the water -- a combination of images which -- the moonlight apart -- we have already met in the *Rāmāyaṇa*.(32) Once again he finds himself sitting on the roof of the boat's cabin, ostensibly because it is too hot to be inside, though even if it had been cool enough, we suspect he would have made his way to the roof anyway ! He is enfolded by a great sense of mystery:

> It was as if Shekhar slowly began to emerge [*nikalne lagtā hai*] from himself, began to open [*khulne lagtā hai*]. Merging [*milkar*] with this all-embracing [*vyāpta*] mysterious silence he began to be himself.(SL Vol. 1 p. 230)

For the last sentence the text actually says 'he began to be *svastha*', a word which literally means 'standing in his own place'. In other contexts it is usually translated by the English word 'healthy'. The use of this word here suggests that in this experience Shekhar is more really himself than he is in his normally restricted life. This view of the text is reinforced by the next few lines:

> The hostel boys, the college girls, the people of the city, all began to be erased [*miṭane lagte haiṁ*] from his consciousness [*cetanā*], and the wounds and hurts he had suffered from them began to be washed away like dirt in this pure [*svaccha*] moonlight. (SL Vol. 1 p. 230)

We recall the imagery applied to the unhappily married Shashi of the winged bird which tried to fly again to 'find its place'.(33) Both images suggest that the realm of freedom is the place where people are truly themselves, and in each case that realm is in nature and not in civilisation.

After he reaches Mahabalipuram Shekhar goes for a swim which takes him some distance from the shore. He has difficulty in getting back and almost drowns. He becomes unconscious and is rescued by some fishermen. Yet in spite of having put his life at risk he reflects that what has happened is right. He is now doubly prepared for the struggle of life which lies ahead of him, and the whole experience becomes for him almost one of transformation and rebirth -- he actually uses the word for this -- *punarjanma,* and we recall the myth of Narada and Sushila. We also recall his very different experience by the muddy drain in the slum area, where he remembers the baptism of Jesus -- another experience of transformation through immersion in water -- and decides to embark on his programme of helping the slum dwellers.(34)

In SL, therefore, water is closely associated with a number of important experiences all of which in different ways suggest a kind of momentary liberation from the constraints of normal life. They are all intensely individualistic and with the significant exception of the one by the open drain they all occur in the world of nature. In IS the water of the river is the all-pervasive image for interpreting the lives of its four main characters which at one level can be described as lives lived in freedom from the constraints of tradition, but it is a fragile freedom which can easily disintegrate and disappear, a point which is underlined by Ajneya's poem of the same title.

The fourth and last of our images is that of absorption into a larger whole. This is rooted in *Advaita Vedānta* philosophy and it is common to find this sort of reference in Indian writing without explicit reference to *Vedānta* whose assumptions in modern North India are all-pervasive. This school of Indian philosophy, like many of the others, traces its origins to the Upanishads where an important strand of teaching is that the innermost essence of a human being is identical with the innermost heart of the universe, or all that is outside the individual. For example the great sage *Yājñavalkya* explains to one of his pupils the nature of the 'inner controller [*ātmā-antaryāmin*]':

> He who dwelling in the earth, yet is other than the earth, whom the earth does not know, whose body the earth is, who controls the earth from within -- he is your Soul, the Inner Controller, the Immortal. (*Bṛhadāraṇyaka Upaniṣad* 3.7.3, translated in Hume [1931] p. 115)

The sentence is repeated more than twenty times, with waters, fire, atmosphere, wind, sky, the sun, and other elements being in turn substituted for 'the earth' in our quotation. In *Chāndogya Upaniṣad* 6.7.1 - 6.16.3, (translated in Hume [1931] pp. 244-50) the sage *Uddālaka Aruṇi* gives the same teaching to his son *Śvetaketu* in a somewhat different form. Here the famous sentence 'Thou art that [*tat tvam asi*]' is repeated several times. 'Thou' refers to the essential being of the student, and 'that' to the inner essence of the visible world. From these origins *Advaita Vedānta* was worked out into a coherent and complex philosophy, principally by the great *Śaṅkarācārya* (? 788 - ? 838 CE) who wrote a series of commentaries on sacred texts which he expounded according to his doctrine. Also, according to tradition he founded four monasteries in the four corners of India so that his message could actually be lived and taught by *saṃnyāsins* who were dedicated to its realisation.(Walker [1968] Vol. 2 pp. 348-52) While few people are familiar with all the intricacies of this philosophy, in a popular and simplified form its fundamental insights are widely known and correspond to a deeply-felt longing within the hearts of many Hindus. It is therefore no surprise to find that at certain points in our novels the characters long to find their true being beyond the confines of their separate identity by absorption into a mysterious larger whole where they can find freedom from all the constraints which bind them. In *Advaita Vedānta* it is not only such constraints as these but also the sense of separate individual identity itself which is conceived as an obstacle on the path to freedom. Here *Advaita* goes beyond *Sāṁkhya* for which a separate and purified identity [*kaivalya*] is itself the supreme goal. Thus towards the end of SL, when Shashī is dying, Shekhar reflects on the nature of their relationship:

> Education [*śikṣā*], civilisation [*sabhyatā*], training [*saṃskār*] (35),...raise us above ourselves, and take us beyond the boundaries of our individuality [*vyaktitva*] into the realm of a larger existence [*astitva*], of a higher, other-worldly [*aparalaukik*], universal perception [*sārvalaukik anubhūti*].
>
> But how great a knot [*gāṁtha*] in the life of the individual [*vyakti*] are rituals and education ! Because whoever is educated recognises the finer movements of a trained life [*saṃskārī jīvan*] (those movements which are deeper than mere polite [*śiṣṭa*] behaviour), they find in the great moments of life -- they suddenly find in love or some other great emotional moment -- that there is no fulness

> [*pūrṇatā*] in it, no merged identity [*tanmayatā*], no reaching of the summit. Instead there is a strange detached neutrality [*taṭasthatā*] -- a separateness even from one's own deepest emotions [*apne gahare bhavoṁse*] which makes the doer [*karttā*] into the spectator and critic of the deed -- that is to say it deprives one of the fulness of one's own selfhood [*apnepan kī sampūrṇatā*]. In our imagination [*kalpanā*] we picture a beloved whose heart beats in time with the deepest movements of our own heart, who can not only be a sharer [*sahabhāgī*] in our bodily and social existence but can share in our most inarticulate and deeply personal perceptions [*atyanta vyaktigat sūkṣma anubhūtiyoṁ meṁ*] -- of art, poetry, music, even in our pleasure and pain...but in fact we find in love [*prem*] that at no time or place can we ever merge our separate personalities into one [*apne alag vyaktitvoṁ ko ek meṁ*] or the other [*dūsare meṁ*] or each into both [*pratyek ko donoṁ meṁ*]...there is friendship [*sakhya*], there is relationship [*sambandha*], a relationship of profound inner unity [*antaraṅga abhinnatā*], but always that relationship depends on a medium [*ek mādhyam kā āśrit hai*], it depends on something outside our existence -- in some picture, thought, poem, song, movement, voice or beautiful dream which is ours, but even in being ours is not ours because we ourselves are not we, but only the educated [*śikṣā-maṇḍit*], ritualised [*saṃskārī*], civilised [*sabhya*] sloughed off snake skin of the basic and eternal 'we' [*maulik aur ātyantik 'ham'*].(SL Vol. 2 pp. 225-6)

The 'knot in the life' in the first line of this quotation reminds us of the 'knot in the heart' of which the Upanishads sometimes speak.(36) In a characteristically Vedantic fashion Shekhar is claiming that even the greatest emotional moments in life fail to satisfy because there is at their heart a 'separateness'. This separateness means that there is neither 'merged identity' nor 'reaching of the summit'. (We note that here the imagery of height is combined with that of absorption into a larger whole.) The longing for the experience of unity of which the Upanishads speak is at the heart of *Advaita Vedānta*, whose characteristic tones are clearly discernible here. For this reason we have found this passage harder to translate into English than any other quoted in this book. This reflects the fact that the language and assumptions of *Advaita Vedānta* cannot easily be fitted into a Christian context (37) and that the English language has been shaped by a different set of (largely Christian) presuppositions. The last sentence of the quotation points again to the fact that according to *Advaita* our true identity is not to be found in the external particularities of education, civilisation and the training imparted by ritual, but within our deepest selves, 'the basic and eternal "we"'.

Shekhar has similar though less developed thoughts elsewhere. For example as a child he finds himself accidentally locked in a museum after it has closed one evening. In the quiet before he is discovered and released he remains seated in the silence unconcerned about whether he will have to stay there all night, what he will have to eat and whether his father is looking for him. When he says to himself

> that in him there is a part [*aṁś*] of universal peace [*viśva-śānti*], of the world soul [*viśva-ātmā*], then does he lie and deceive himself ?(Vol. 1 p. 71)

Here 'world-soul' is a totally inadequate translation of *viśvā-ātmā* which refers to the one underlying eternal reality with which, according to *Advaita Vedānta*, our inmost being is ultimately to be identified. There is a hint of the same thought when Shekhar is floating down the Ganges on his banana-stem raft:

> There filled his being the unhampered vastness of the sky, the free atmosphere. He was himself unhampered [*abādh*], vast [*viśāla*], free [*mukta*], and reality [*yathārthatā*] was a long way behind him. (SL Vol. 1 p. 109)

When he is in Madras he sits on the beach one evening by the light of the full moon with Kumar [*Kumār*], the fellow-student who befriended him only to deceive him later. At this point Shekhar has not yet discovered Kumar's real character and intentions, and says to him:

> Nothing seems real today, everything is a dream [*svapna*] but how sweet seems the dream of which I am now a part [*aṅga*].(SL Vol. 1 p. 201)

In IS Rekha expresses something of this same mood in a letter to Bhuvan, though she writes from a rather different perspective. She is pondering on the fact that women often locate events by referring them to family births or marriages -- 'It happened in the year so-and-so's child was born':

> How people place the whole world [*jagat*] round the little

> happenings of their own insignificant life, how the whole truth of the vast universe [*virāṭ*] becomes dependent on their own private truth ! But why is that private truth small ? However small it may be it is still my window onto the boundless universe [*virāṭ asīma*]: firstly it is my window and secondly it encloses the universe for me -- it is the frame of the universe. But as I reflected I realised that it was a mistake to look through a window, any window, for to do so was to separate oneself from the universe and to look at it as something outside myself. I ought to merge [*laya*] myself in it...I should come out of the house, out of the cage of my own experience [*anubhūti ke piñjare*] and surrender myself to the boundless universe, and become one with it.(IS p. 252)

We are not far removed here from Shekhar and his parrot, though Rekha writes in more abstract fashion. Bhuvan says the same thing more briefly elsewhere: writing to Rekha he says he is thinking of going to the sea, for 'after surrendering oneself before the infinite [*viśāla*], sufferings [*kleśa*] seem to cease, or at any rate lose their sting'.(IS p. 264) This reminds us of Shekhar's experience beside the sea at Madras, sitting with Kumar. At the very end of the novel Bhuvan reflects:

> How huge is life, so wide, so deep, so full of movement; in it there are tiny individual units [*vyakti kī ye choṭī-choṭī ikaiyāṁ*] which have no existence [*astitva*], no meaning [*artha*] apart from the flow, and yet they are complete [*sampūrṇa*] and autonomous [*svāyatta*], unique [*advitīya*] and self-sufficient [*svataḥ-pramāṇa*], because in the last analysis the individual person is disciplined only by himself, responsible only to himself; heaven [*svarga*] and hell [*narak*], sin [*pāp*] and merit [*puṇya*], reward and punishment, peace and satisfaction -- all these if outside the individual are mere conventions; they are real only if they arise from within. (IS p. 335)

Here is the clearest statement we have yet seen of Ajneya's doctrine of individualism. Yet in spite of the rejection of tradition explicitly made in the last few lines, in the early part of the quotation there are echoes, if unconscious, of the world of *Advaita Vedānta*, for in this teaching too the individual is simply a manifestation of the one Brahman. To believe in one's own separate existence is false.

We turn finally to the theme of freedom in TEHS which as we said earlier, in this and other respects stands somewhat apart from the other two novels. We have already drawn attention to

Ajneya's debate with Sartre in this novel, and to various remarks in TEHS which are opposed to Sartre's view of freedom.(38) At the end of the book, by committing suicide Yoke does exercise freedom of choice for the first time in her life -- she chooses when to die: 'I have chosen freedom [*maiṁ ne svatantratā ko cun liyā*].'(TEHS p. 109) There may be a hint here of Indian tradition, for it is believed that the true *yogin* can choose the moment of his own death. Those hints are much more obvious in the serenity which Selma consistently displays in the face of her own impending death. We considered this in the last chapter when we discussed the theme of forgiveness: Selma's perpetual willingness to forgive the bitter and angry Yoke was one mark of that serenity. Another was the inner radiance reflected in her skin, which, we suggested, may be unconsciously based on the Indian ideal which is especially found in the *yogin*.(39) That ideal is made much more explicit in some of Yoke's reflections when she contrasts Selma to herself:

> Selma too lives only in time [*kāla*] just like the rest of us, but it seems as if she lives not in any one time, but in all time. It's as if there time is not a single stream. It's as if there is no before and after [*āge-piche*], but everything is simultaneous [*sab ek sāth hai*]. Everything is simultaneous and so there is no history [*itihāsa*]. So there is memory [*smṛti*] and together with it there is freedom from reciprocity [*parasparatā*] -- all is momentary [*sabhī kuch kṣaṇa hai*].(TEHS p. 22)

In a key passage later on Yoke repeats these thoughts more succinctly:

> Selma has no history [*itihāsa*], she only has memory [*smṛti*]. And Selma herself is not history, she is memory, pure [*śuddha*] memory. She lives here and somewhere else at the same time. She lives in today and yesterday and in all days at the same time. And for this reason she is neither separate [*alag*] nor alone [*akelī*].

Yoke then goes on to describe herself as the antithesis of Selma:

> And as for me, I am living here and now in this very moment [*kṣaṇa*]-- in me there is no memory. I ought to be free [*mukta*] but I am consumed [*kṣayagrasta*] by history [*itihāsa*] and I am alone [*akelī*]. It is Selma who has to die and die she will, but I am the one who is actually dying -- and I am alone.(TEHS p. 61)

At every point the two are opposites: Selma neither is nor has history, but is pure memory. Yoke is consumed by history and has no memory. Selma is not alone, but Yoke is. And paradoxically Yoke sees that she is the one who is really dying. At the heart of this contrast lies Yoke's wistful comment, 'I ought to be free' which implies that it is Selma who is really free. Selma's freedom lies beyond history and so beyond time -- a theme we shall explore more fully in the next chapter. At this stage we point out how close Selma's inner freedom is to the freedom from constraints to which we have seen Ajneya's characters aspire in the first two novels. The Indian roots of this freedom are somewhat obscured in TEHS which is not only given a setting in Scandanavia, but takes place during the Christmas season to which there are frequent references.(40) Indeed at one level Selma seems to be portrayed as a Christian, for Yoke overhears her singing a Christmas carol (TEHS p. 30) and Selma refers to her own trust in God.(TEHS p. 39) The important references to forgiveness which we considered in the last chapter also make most sense in a Christian context. Thus although Ajneya claims that in this novel he is contrasting a western with an eastern attitude to impending death (41) we can also discern a blending of certain elements of Hinduism and Christianity in the way which we have already observed him doing elsewhere, with the possible addition of Buddhist influence in Selma's compassion.(42)

A glance at one of his essays helps us to see how he could regard such a blending as possible. He says that unlike Christianity and Islam, 'Indian' religion requires no faith in certain key points [*nukta*] the rejection of which makes one into an 'infidel'or 'kafir', and makes it possible for faith [*āsthā*] to be in danger. 'In Indian religion there is no such claim [*Bhāratīya dharma meṁ aisī koī śarta nahīṁ hai*]'.(Vatsyayan [1983] p. 356) In the original this last sentence is printed in bold type. In the same passage he claims that in contrast to Islam and Christianity, in 'Indian' religion 'human life is based on certain fundamental values [*mānava jīvan kuch buniyādī mūlyoṁ par ādhārita hai*]'. (Vatsyayan [1983] p. 356) This gives us the context in which to interpret Chaturvedi's remark, to which we referred earlier, that Ajneya's visits to a Zen monastery in Japan and to a Christian one in France enabled him to recover his 'faith' *āsthā*. We pointed out that these two experiences did not appear to have created in

Ajneya any felt need to choose between Buddhism and Christianity.(43) Yet there is surely an implicit choice in his argument about values, for if values are 'fundamental' they are based on a 'foundation' and is not this a kind of 'fixed point' ?

At earlier points in this book we have pointed to a gradually emerging area of agreement which we share with Ajneya. This consensus included the pursuit of integrity and human dignity, a pursuit which involved pain and suffering.(44) Ajneya's characters rejected traditional norms of conduct, particularly in the area of ritual purity. Life was now stripped of the transcendental *framework* within which it had traditionally been interpreted(45), yet at the same time we have on several occasions noticed hints of a transcendent *dimension* (46), hints which are most explicit in the character and demeanour of Selma which we have just examined. We have also observed, particularly in SL, the outlines of Ajneya's human ideal: 'completeness' and 'victory' were seen in the person who takes someone else's place as Shekhar -- deeply influenced by the words of Shashi -- took the sentry's place in the pouring rain.(47) Both Shekhar and Ajneya himself see the roots of such substitutionary action in the self-offering of Christ.(48) But in the terms of our previous paragraph that self-offering appears to be not a 'particular point' in which we must have faith and to which we must give our assent, but rather a (the ?) supreme example of a 'fundamental value'. The significance of such action can be enlarged when it is seen as akin to sacrifice, especially to the sacrifice sometimes made by women within the Hindu tradition, and more particularly in our novels by Shashi and Rekha.(49) But according to Ajneya sacrifice must be offered for a worthy object and here Rekha, by his own admission, fails to measure up to the ideal because her sacrifice -- her abortion -- is offered for an unworthy cause.(50)

At all these points we find ourselves, from our Christian perspective, if not in actual agreement with Ajneya, at least in an area where meeting and conversation are possible. That area can be described as the world of everyday human relationships, a world which can readily be interpreted within the terms of the argument which we set out in the Introduction. We we claimed there that our modified version of Lindbeck's cultural-linguistic hypothesis provided a useful model for the interpretation of religions: language, symbols and community make us what we are and enable us to have experiences which can then be interpreted within their context.(51) Lindbeck's priorities can be summed up in Fergus Kerr's rhetorical question about the later Wittgenstein which we also quoted in the Introduction (52) and now repeat:

> Why do we retreat from our world, why do we withdraw from the body in the hope that more direct illumination about our minds and about the gods is to be found by gaining access to something other than what we say and do ?(Kerr [1986] p. 147)

'What we say and do' imply and depend on the cultural-linguistic context for whose priority we have argued. However, in contrast to the previous two chapters, most of the evidence we have considered in this one suggests that Ajneya and his characters believe that we must withdraw from the world of our everyday experience in order to find true freedom. In our study of this theme we have seen that both words and images are commonly used in the novels, as they are in that part of the Hindu tradition which Ajneya knew best, to point people in a direction away from society. The four words for freedom which we studied all have this thrust inherent in their meaning: we saw that *mukti* means release from that which binds and restricts -- which includes society -- while *svādhīna, svatantra* and *svacchanda* all begin with the same prefix which means 'one's own' which implies the separate self for whose existence relationship is not essential. Here Ajneya seems implicitly to disagree with the anthropology of relationship for which, with the support of McFadyen, we argued in the Introduction.(53) The image of height works in the same way: to make this point we have only to recall the quasi-mythical isolation of Bhuvan and Rekha 'on the roof of the world', and Shekhar in his fourth storey room where he reflects on the fact that he is an isolated unit, far above the very society about which he feels moved to write and which he longs to change. The bird in flight is also an image of solitariness. Shekhar's parrot, in escaping from his hand and flying off into a tree, becomes a symbol of his own longing to escape from the constraints of the adult world in order to be his true self. Rekha and even more markedly Shashi have, as 'winged birds', fallen from their 'own place' of freedom -- Rekha by the ruin of her health as a result of the abortion, and Shashi by being married against her will to the wholly odious Rameshvar, and then rejected by him.

Shekhar's experiences in or near water are all of a piece with this evidence. When he takes off his clothes above the Dal Lake, sits with Kumar by the sea at Madras, goes on a long walk to a waterfall, or lies on the roof of a boat's cabin, first in Kashmir, and later on during his sea journey to Mahabalipuram, he too enjoys quasi-mystical moments of 'transcendence' in which he is removed from society. In all of these examples freedom is to be found only in the world of nature, and normally by stripping away the superficial veneer of 'civilisation' which hides a person from their real naked self. Here we saw echoes of the ultimate solitude or *kaivalya* which *Sāṁkhya* posits as the goal of spiritual endeavour. The experience of or longing for absorption into a larger whole, which several characters display, points in the same direction but goes further, for here separate identity itself is an obstacle on the path of true freedom, and we saw in this echoes of *Advaita Vedānta*. All of this evidence therefore points us away from our own hypothesis and towards an ideal of the self which has more in common with the ideal of the solitary Cartesian monad to which we referred in the Introduction, pointing out that we found difficulty in accepting it.(54) This view of what it means to be human has resonances with Ajneya's description of his search for the appropriate setting for his last novel. We recall that he wanted his characters to be stripped of particularity and to be examples of 'naked human existence'.(55) In the next chapter we explore further the contrast we have discussed in the preceding paragraphs, but in the different context of the themes of time, narrative and death. We end this chapter by pointing out that this is not a straight contrast between Christianity and Hinduism. Much Christian theology has functioned and continues to function according to the Cartesian ideal, so much so that, as we noted earlier, Lindbeck gives it a separate title: the 'experiential-expressive model'.(56) This notion actually stands the cultural-linguistic hypothesis on its head by claiming that individuals first have experiences and then put them into words. If this is so then it follows that language, symbols and culture are of secondary importance, for it is possible for people to have the same experience and then express it in different cultural and symbolic forms. These forms can then have only relative significance. This stance underlies, for example, the theology of John Hick (57) and his followers. On the other hand we have seen that Namvar Singh, Devesh Thakur, and Om Prabhakar, among others, have criticised Ajneya's individualism from their own perspectives -- Marxist in the case of the first and possibly the second, and Hindu in the case of the third. They all take Ajneya to task for withdrawing his characters from society.This implies an anthropology more akin to the one for which we ourselves have argued.

NOTES

1. See above, p. 108.
2. See above, p. 91.
3. For a summary of Sartre's thought, see Roberts [1957] pp. 195-226.
4. These and the other figures given in subsequent paragraphs need to be set in the context of the total number of words in each novel. These are approximately: SL, 212,000; IS, 144,500; and TEHS, 30,250.
5. For a summary of this philosophy, see above, pp. 111-3.
6. Shortly after India became independent in 1947 the nominal form of the first word was chosen for the name of a now defunct political party -- the Svatantrata Party.
7. Because snakes are dangerous and destructive of human and other life.
8. This word normally means 'socialist', but here it obviously has a larger sense which we have translated as 'related to society'.
9. See for example, Namvar Singh [1978] pp. 46-54.
10. The Hindi literary critic Nemichand Jain asks whether Ajneya created the character of Chandramadhava 'solely to vent his spleen on Communists' [*Communistoṁ ke prati apnā roṣ prakaṭ karne ke lie hī*]. More generally he says that it is a real weakness of Ajneya as a novelist that he creates his characters in entirely black or white terms.(Jain [1989] p. 30)
11. This first sentence of the quotation is in the English translation of this novel (Ajneya [1980] p. 196), but not in the Hindi original. Possibly it was inadvertently omitted from the Hindi for the text hardly makes sense without it.
12. See above, pp. 94-5.
13. See above, p. 97.
14. For an account of this aspect of *Puranic* geography, see Upadhyaya [1965] p. 323.
15. There is a similar example in Kalidasa's *Meghadūtam*, where the poet is telling the rain cloud of a river which it will pass on its way North. The river is compared to a beautiful and scantily-clad woman:

    Her dark-blue waters like a garment
    slipping off the sloping banks of her hips,

still cling to the reed-branches
as if lightly held up by one hand:
drawing it away as you bend over her, my friend,
will it not be hard for you to depart ? (*Meghadūtam* 43, translated in Chandra Rajan [1989] p. 147)

16. See above, pp. 88-9.
17. See above, p. 97.
18. See above, p. 112-3.
19. See above, p. 46.
20. The two images are brought together in the opening lines of Cardinal Newman's famous hymn:
    Praise to the holiest in the height,
    And in the depth be praise.
21. We recall the famous incident described by the Venerable Bede when the missionary Paulinus came to the court of the king of Northumbria. One of the king's courtiers described human life as being like a bird which flies into a hall, stops for a moment by the open fireside, and then flies out again into the darkness.(Shirley-Price tr [1955] pp. 124-5)
22. Kalidasa, estimates of whose dates vary from about 350 to 600 CE, was the most famous of Sanskrit dramatists and court poets.
23. In *Advaita Vedānta* those who attain final liberation in this life are called *jīvan-mukta*. Other schools of thought maintain that final liberation is only possible after death. Some of them, such as the various schools of Vaishnavism, believe in the 'descents' [*avatāra*] of God to earth in human or other forms. *Jīvan-mukta* and *avatāra* thus serve as symbols of potential liberation, in this life or the next, for those who have not yet attained it. For a valuable discussion of this subject see Dubey, 'The Concept of Soul in Hinduism', in Religion and Society (CISRS Bangalore Dec 1972) Vol. xix No 4 pp. 16-32.
    The word *haṃsa* really means goose, but by 'poetic licence' it often means swan.(McGregor [1993] p. 1053)
24. See above, p. 91.
25. See above, p. 122.
26. See above, pp. 154-5.
27. *māyā* literally means trick, illusion, or fraud (Monier-Williams [1899] p. 811), and so here refers to the wrong because illusory view of reality with which Vishnu has deceived Narada, but from which he now frees him at Narada's own request.
28. This myth is conveniently retold in Campbell ed [1962] pp. 27-31.
29. The trunks of banana trees are made of a soft fibrous substance which can be cut very easily with any sharp metal tool.
30. See above, p. 161.
31. On her first train journey with Bhuvan she remarks that she seems to spend most of her time travelling and compares herself to 'the Tree of Knowledge -- with roots upwards -- my roots wander about lost in the sky [*jñāna ke taru...-- ūrdhva-mūla -- merī jareṁ ākāśa meṁ khoyī phirtī haiṁ*]'.(IS p. 32) Rekha is perhaps confusing her symbols, for 'the Tree of Knowledge' is biblical (Genesis 2.17), while the tree with its roots in the sky is found in the Upanishads, *eg Kaṭha Upaniṣad* 6.1 (translated in Hume [1931] p. 358), and in *Bhagavadgītā* 15.1-3.(translated in Zaehner ed [1978] pp. 309-10)

Rekha is aware of the symbols to be found in her scriptures but is either unaware of or uninterested in their significance. She simply makes use of them to describe her own attitude and feelings. A little later in this same conversation she remarks that in a moving train she experiences a sense of freedom [*svacchandatā*], while if staying in the same place she would only be a misfit.(IS pp. 32-3)

32. See above, pp. 94-5.
33. See above, p. 159.
34. See above, pp. 92-3.
35. *saṃskār* which we have rendered here as 'training' is difficult to translate into English. Its basic meaning is 'putting together, forming well, making perfect', and so also 'adornment, purification, cleansing'. It can be used of food, animals, plants, language, or of the body and its attire. It can mean, as it does here, 'forming the mind, training, education'. It is the word used to refer to the sixteen domestic rituals which members of the three highest castes have to undergo as rites of passage, and from it is derived the word *saṃskṛta* -- Sanskrit -- which thus means 'purified' or 'well put together according to the rules'.(Monier-Williams [1899] p. 1120)
36. *eg* in *Chāndogya Upaniṣad* 7.26.2.(translated in Hume [1931] p. 262)
37. In the mediaeval period Meister Eckhart came near to *Advaita Vedānta* in his thinking. The following passage is remarkably close to it:

    > I pray to God that he may make me free of 'God', for my real being is above God if we take 'God' to be the beginning of created things. For in the same being of God where God is above being and above distinction, there I myself was, there I willed myself and committed myself to create this man. Therefore I am the cause of myself in the order of my being, which is eternal, and not in the order of my becoming which is temporal.(Sermon 52, translated in Colledge and McGinn eds [1981] p. 202)

    For a modern attempt to do justice to the essential insights of *Advaita Vedānta* from the perspective of Christian theology, see Abhishiktananda [1974 and 1976].
38. See above, pp. 148-9.
39. See above, pp. 126-7 and 133-4.
40. For example, Selma remarks that there will be plenty of snow for Christmas (p. 10), Yoke's diary covers the period from 15th December till 14th January (pp. 15 and 59), and there is a reference to Santa Claus.(p. 23)
41. See above, p. 4-5.
42. Macve refers to Buddhist influence on some of his later poetry as well.(Macve [1992] p. 39)
43. See above, p. 44.
44. See above, p. 87.
45. See above, pp. 75-7.
46. For example, see above, pp. 77-8 and 126-7.
47. See above, pp. 120-1.
48. See above, p. 122.
49. See above, pp. 122-3 and 127-8.
50. See Chapter Four, note 58.
51. See above, pp. 8-11.
52. See above, pp. 11-12.

53. See above pp. 12-13.
54. See above, p. 11.
55. See above, pp. 46-7.
56. He includes Lonergan and Rahner in a modified version of this category.(Lindbeck [1984] p. 24)
57. For example:

> It is thus possible to consider the hypothesis that the great religions are all, at their experiential roots, in contact with the same ultimate divine reality, but that their differing experiences of that reality, interacting over the centuries with the different thought forms of different cultures, have led to increasing differentiation and contrasting elaboration -- so that Hinduism, for example, is a very different phenomenon from Christianity, and very different ways of conceiving and experiencing the divine occur within them.(Hick ed [1974] p. 151)

Here 'the divine' is evidently the one underlying reality which is experienced and interpreted in different ways.

6

TIME AND NARRATIVE

We begin this chapter by recapitulating the main points of our argument so far: we begin with Chapter Three where we saw how in his novels Ajneya reshaped the transcendental and social parameters within which, according to his Hindu inheritance, human life is perceived as being lived. His claim that this life is all we have opened up new possibilities for the interpretation of suffering: on the one hand it provoked a sense of outrage at 'God' who permitted it (1) and at the 'sub-contractors of religion' who justified it with spurious and hypocritical arguments.(2) On the other hand instead of being seen in terms of punishment for offences committed in this or some past life, it could now be seen as that which could purify the vision of individuals.(3) We saw in Chapter Four how this purification took place, particularly in the case of Madansingh, and more especially in Shashi, Rekha and Selma, who are the central female characters respectively of our three novels.(4) The evidence we discussed in these two chapters enabled us to discern an area of gradually emerging consensus with our author. This was not based on a direct conversation between a Christian theologian and a Hindu novelist: it arose out of a much more complex relationship. (5) We saw that Ajneya was fiercely critical of many elements in his Hindu inheritance, and at certain key points in his novels showed a willingness to use Christian themes. This was particularly evident in Shekhar's moment of reflection on Christ's baptism by the open drain (6), in his later reflection on the significance of substitutionary atonement when he took the place of the sentry (7), and reached its climax in the forgiving attitude consistently shown by Selma to Yoke.(8) In other words we are not only

Ajneya's 'dialogue partner' but also the privileged listener to a dialogue which is already happening within the novels.

In Chapter Five we saw that freedom was a goal to which all Ajneya's characters aspired, but that their pursuit of it invariably took them away from other people and from culture, and into the world of nature, for it was only here that any glimpse of true freedom, and any kind of transcendent experience, was possible.(9) An examination of the vocabulary and images for this pursuit showed us that here Ajneya's roots were to be found within the very Brahminical Hinduism which in other ways he so totally rejected. As in other contexts where the evidence pointed us in a similar direction (10), we suggest that this too was an area of assumption which he had not brought to the level of conscious reflection. The pursuit of a solitary freedom in the world of nature is consistent with Ajneya's comments on the choice of a setting for TEHS, where he tells us that he wanted the characters to be stripped of all cultural particularity and so made into examples of 'naked human existence'.(11)

In Chapter Five too we were not simply engaged in a direct conversation with Ajneya. We have already argued that the fact that he published novels at all was an act of 'testimony' in the sense described by Paul Ricouer (12), a testimony which by the very fact of its being made implicitly invited a response. The flood of critical writing which Ajneya's novels continue to evoke (13) is an important part of that response. We observed that some of his critics find fault with him for his romantic and anti-social individualism -- though without tracing its roots to his Brahminical inheritance in the way in which we have done.(14) We therefore agree with these critics but want to press the point they make further than they do themselves. Further, Ajneya's emphasis on the importance of the isolated individual as the source of values also stands in contrast to our own view for which we argued in the Introduction. There we suggested, following McFadyen and others, that relationship rather than isolation should lie at the heart of a Christian anthropology. Such relationship implies a shared language and a shared symbolic universe, which create a common world of discourse within which the experiences belonging to that world become possible.(15) We saw that such a view is somewhat different from the idea of the detached Cartesian monad, the isolated individual as the one who has experiences which are then clothed in linguistic and symbolic form, though this latter view is implicit in much Christian theology.(16) Patently Ajneya's view has more in common with this position than it does with our own. In questioning him therefore we are implicitly questioning some of our fellow-Christian theologians as well. The complexity of this conversation serves to underline our claim that the novel offers a richer field for inter-religious conversation than do purely religious texts, with which the patterns of conversation are more simple and direct.(17)

In the present chapter we examine the themes of time and narrative -- both of which terms will require elucidation. This discussion will serve to highlight the areas of disagreement which we have just described. We shall also see towards the end of the chapter that Ajneya's views contain an implicit questioning of, and point towards a potential enriching and enlarging of, our own Christian perspective. We begin our discussion with an important statement by Paul Ricoeur:

> [W]hat is ultimately at stake in the case of the structural identity of the narrative function as well as in that of the truth claim of every narrative work, is the temporal character of human experience. The world unfolded by every narrative work is always a temporal world...time becomes human time to the extent that it is organised after the manner of a narrative; narrative, in turn, is meaningful to the extent that it portrays the features of temporal experience.(Ricoeur [1984] Vol. 1 p. 3)

A novel is patently a 'narrative work' in the sense that Ricoeur describes.(18) If that be so, and if we accept his argument, then it follows that for Ajneya, as indeed for any novelist, such a positive estimate of both narrative and the temporal process is necessarily implicit in the fact that he wrote novels at all. Yet against this we must set two facts: first, he published only three novels, the last of them twenty-six years before his death. Why did he write or at least publish only three, and what made him stop? Second, across the three novels taken as a single 'canon' (19) we have noted a progressive withdrawal from society and its concerns.(20) We shall have to ask in this chapter whether this withdrawal also includes giving a diminishing significance to the temporal process. As we have already seen, that withdrawal is most extreme and deliberate in TEHS. It is also in this final novel that we find most reflection by the characters on the nature and significance of time, though such reflection is not absent from SL and IS. Ajneya wrote about this subject outside his novels and we shall see that his views there largely co-incide with what his characters say within them. Further, the nature and significance of time was a subject of much speculation and debate in the Hindu tradition of philosophy-theology and we must therefore attempt to locate Ajneya's views within the range of possibilities which this material affords.

Before moving on to that agenda some further preliminary comments are necessary. Time is a theme which has attracted a vast range of discussion not only in Hinduism but in Christianity as well, and the two traditions have often been somewhat crudely contrasted in their attitudes towards it. Put baldly and simplisticly the debate has gone like this: Christianity is a faith rooted in historical events and therefore committed to giving a high value to the temporal process. Unlike Marxism, it does not assert that human life is limited to and so ultimately to be interpreted within that process alone. Christians claim that time is ultimately redeemed and taken up into eternity, for historic events -- and so the temporal process in which they take place -- cannot be deprived of significance without cutting the nerve of Christianity. Hindus by contrast believe that in the ultimate experience time can and indeed must be finally transcended. This means that historical events are finally discarded and so can have no ultimate significance.

That oversimplified view of the contrast has been challenged (21), and to set it in the context of our novels is to give it an added depth and complexity. Nonetheless our own view is that the temporal process is indeed of ultimate significance for Christians in that it must finally be taken up into eternity, but we shall want to expound and defend that view in a much more nuanced and less confrontational fashion than has happened in the debate which we have just described. In this chapter, therefore, we shall be examining three issues: first, how far do our novels give, or at least leave open the possibility of giving, a positive evaluation to time? And in so far as they do not, do they compel us to revise our own view in the light of any alternative which they propose? The second issue is narrative. Theoretical interest in narrative, as we have already pointed out, is only recent (22), but is already both wide-ranging and complex. In Chapter Two we examined the question of what kind of narratives our novels are.(23) Our second task in the present chapter will be to expand the description we gave there and also to ask what kind of 'sub-narratives' the novels contain, and the significance of these for human identity and anthropology. Third, we shall briefly link this discussion of narrative to our previous examination of the question of time, relating this to our continuing debate with the novels about human nature and destiny.

We begin our discussion of time by outlining the three possible attitudes to the temporal process which are to be found within that part of the Hindu tradition with which we know Ajneya to have been familiar, bearing in mind his own *caveat* that he was a writer and not a philosopher.(24) We start with the view of *Advaita Vedānta* (25): here the temporal process has a qualified reality in the world of sense perception, but is of no ultimate significance because that world is of secondary importance compared to the non-temporal world of ultimate consciousness.(Balslev [1983] pp. 69-72) In the context of this school of thought, therefore, we can indeed tell stories but they can only belong to the secondary and in the last analysis inferior world of sense-perception and so at best serve as illustrations for what we believe to be true on other and higher grounds. Thus while a Shekhar could certainly tell a story to make sense of his life within the parameters of this philosophy, it would be difficult for the writing of it to have the kind of urgency which Shekhar himself attaches to it (26), for to look for ultimate significance in time and events, as Shekhar does, is precisely to miss the point of *Advaita Vedānta.* On the other hand Selma seems to have reached something akin to the kind of ultimate experience which this philosophy posits as the final goal of human endeavour. Her own personal story, contained in the flashback in the middle of the novel, can be read as an account of how she began that journey. She is not, like Shekhar, driven by the desperate attempt to find meaning within time. Instead, having transcended time, she is serenely looking back over her past experience which she uses as an illustration to encourage Yoke, who says of herself, 'I ought to be free but I am consumed by history'.(27) Thus the contrast between the stories of Shekhar and Selma, while not absolute, is certainly significant.

The second of the classic Hindu options is to be found in *Sāṁkhya* philosophy, which we have already had occasion to discuss in some detail.(28) In contrast to *Advaita Vedānta* this school of thought gives ontological status to multiplicity and change in the principle of *prakṛti*, and so maintains the reality of past, present and future.(Balslev [1983] pp. 44-8) This view therefore seems in principle to give the temporal process a higher status than does *Advaita Vedānta*, though insofar as the second ontological principle -- *puruṣa* -- is pure consciousness and non-temporal it seems to work in the opposite direction. As we have already seen the final aim of *prakṛti*'s dance is the liberation of *puruṣa*, a liberation which includes deliverance from time. So here too it seems that narrative can only have a limited and secondary status which is ultimately transcended in the liberation of *puruṣa*. It is perhaps not mere co-incidence that *Sāṁkhya* notions are pervasive in the *Purāṇas* and Epics and that the many stories which are to be found in these works are given secondary status in the Hindu tradition. They are not unsubstitutable -- saying that which can be said in no other way. Rather do Hindus interpret them as illustrating truths which are already known from other sources.(29) In the terms of our novels they support Selma rather than Shekhar. This is made clear in the following quotation from a work on the *Purāṇas* by a contemporary Hindu scholar:

> The conclusion is that we should never pay attention to the outward part [*bahiraṅga*] of the *Purāṇas*. Their inner part [*antaraṅga*], that is their inwardly described truths [*antaḥ varṇit tathya*], through being in conformity with the Vedas, definitely come within the scope of authenticity [*pramāṇa koṭi*], and that being so we ought to entertain no doubts about the truth of their external part.(Upadhyaya [1965] p. 3)

In other words the function of the *Puranic* narratives is to illustrate and act as additional confirmation for truths which are already to be found in the Vedas, not to provide truths which are essentially new. Upadhyaya's statement makes it easy to understand why the *Purāṇas* and the two great Epics (the *Mahābhārata* and the *Rāmāyaṇa*) are placed in the lesser scriptural category of *smṛti* rather than in the primary one of *śruti*.

Ajneya in his separate essays, and his characters in the novels, all agree in giving supreme value to the present moment [*kṣaṇa*], and in doing so they stand closer to the school of *Yoga* (Balslev [1983] pp. 48-53), which is the third main Hindu option, than to any other. *Yoga* too puts great weight on the significance of the present moment and 'designates all ideas about sequence or objective temporal series as nothing but a conceptual construction'.(Balslev [1983] p. 51) As we shall see shortly, Ajneya agrees with *Yoga* in insisting that the moment is the point at which the temporal process can be transcended in the experience of individuals. This stress on momentariness also suggests Buddhist influence.(Balslev [1983] p. 80)

His first essay on time appeared in a Volume entitled *Āla-vāla* which was published in 1971, ten years after TEHS.(30) The ideas contained in this essay are developed and expanded but not essentially changed in two subsequent books. The first of these is a series of lectures which were delivered in English and entitled A Sense of Time: An Exploration of Time in Theory, Experience and Art.(31) In a later volume, entitled *Saṃvatsar* (*Epoch*) (32), these lectures are reproduced in Hindi translation and are preceded by four additional essays. The interpretations of time in the first essay of *Āla-vāla* and in TEHS are identical. In the essay Ajneya takes the analogy of an Indian drum called the *ḍamarū*, the shape of which is important for his argument. The drum is not a musical instrument but is used by touring entertainers to draw attention to their presence. Its shape is in the form of two inverted cones of which the apices meet in the middle. The cones are hollow and their bases consist of circles of stretched leather. The drum, which is very light and only about eighteen inches from end to end, is grasped by the hand at the middle and thinnest point, where the two apices meet. It has two strings attached to it, each of which has a small weight on its end. As the drummer vigorously twists his wrist from side to side so the weights repeatedly strike the leather bases at the two ends of the drum.

Ajneya likens this drum to our experience of time: human consciousness is represented by its centre which represents present time. Consciousness projects the past backwards and the future forwards from itself. Past and future correspond to the drum's two cones. In making the present moment the focal point of his argument Ajneya is at one with *Yoga*, but he goes further than *Yoga* itself by linking this view to the *Purāṇas*. He points out that in these latter texts the flow of time is conceived as a perpetually repeated cycle of four successive ages of diminishing length, starting from the golden age which is the longest, and ending with the present *kali yuga* which is the shortest of all.(33) Ajneya explains this progressive cycle by saying that the ages are a projection from consciousness. They get longer the further they are away (in past or future) from the consciousness which imagines them, just as the circumferences of the two cone-shaped halves of the drum increase in size the further they are away from the centre. Apart from the obvious links with *Yoga* Ajneya is also in accord at one important point with both *Sāṁkhya* and *Advaita Vedānta*. He agrees with both of these schools in putting a transformed human consciousness, rather than action in the empirical world, at the centre of his anthropology. At the heart of his argument in this essay, therefore, is the further claim that an individual can experience a moment of the living present which is 'beyond memory and desire [*smṛti aur ākāṅksā se pare*]':

> and then he becomes a person [*vyakti*] with no shadow -- he will have such a pure time consciousness [*śuddha kāla cetanā*] that he will become free from time [*kāla-mukta*].(Vatsyayan [1971] p. 103)

This claim that time can be transcended in experience is clarified and re-inforced when we see how it makes Ajneya take issue with T S ELiot (and therefore with Paul Ricoeur's statement which we quoted above). Eliot wrote in Four Quartets:

> But only in Time can the moment in the rose-garden.
> The moment in the draughty church at smokefall.
> Be remembered, involved in past and future.
> Only through Time is Time conquered.(Eliot [1944] p. 10)

On these lines Ajneya comments:

> It is clear that when he...talks of 'the remembered moment [*smaraṇa kie gaye kṣaṇa*]' then his whole argument is flawed [*dūṣit*], because memory is bound to time [*kāla*] -- to past time. If the conquest [*vijaya*] of time is possible then it is not through memory, it is only possible by means of a conscious existence [*ātmacetana asti*] in the eternal present [*atyanta varttmāna*].(Vatsyayan [1971] pp. 104-5)

The last sentence of that quotation sums up the positive side of Ajneya's philosophy of time, a view which is profusely illustrated by what some of the characters actually say in our three novels.

In the two books which we mentioned above he also suggests that the West is caught up in a kind of historical consciousness which leaves no room for the dimension of eternity (34), a view which we can see epitomised in the words and in the character of Yoke in TEHS. Yet we have already pointed out that Yoke embodies the Existentialist philosophy of Sartre (35), a philosophy which we agree with Ajneya in rejecting. It seems that Ajneya's understanding of western historical consciousness was too limited.(36) It is fascinating if unfortunately fruitless to speculate on how an encounter with the writings of Paul Ricoeur might have led him to modify his views. We note also the centrality of 'consciousness [*cetanā*]' in his argument and the word 'conquest [*vijaya*]'. These are both important words in the tradition which often speaks of the individual's conquest of passion, of the senses, as well as of time itself.(37) So here again our author's thinking reveals its traditional origins.

The essence of Ajneya's view of time as momentariness is most clearly articulated in IS where it is embodied in the person of Rekha. She often says that she has no faith in the future, only in the present from which all else, including the future, continuously unfolds. Thus early in her acquaintance with Bhuvan she says to him:

> All destinations [*maṁjileṁ*] become false and there is no road left. I truthfully [*sacmuc*] don't want to arrive anywhere -- I don't even want to want. For me even the stream of time [*kāla kā pravāha*] is not a stream, it is only the effect of joining [*yogaphal*] moment [*kṣaṇa*] on moment on moment. Just like 'humanity' [*mānavatā*], the 'stream of time' too is for me nothing more than a concept [*yukti-satya*]; the reality [*vāstviktā*] is only that of the moment. The moment is eternal [*sanātan*].(IS p. 36)

Chandramadhava recognises that this is at the heart of Rekha's view of life: 'Rekha talks of offering [*samarpit*] (*sc* herself) to the moment. The moment alone is supreme [*virāṭ*].'(IS p. 44) Characteristically he views her words with scepticism:

> But does she really believe this? Whenever an opportunity has come to surrender herself [*ātma-samarpaṇa*] to the moment, hasn't she refused it?(IS p. 44)

By which he really means that she has not made herself sexually available to him. Her attitude to time is bound up with her negative view of civilisation, for as she says:

> The life of civilisation [*sabhya-jīvan*] is like a vast crowded waiting room -- and restaurants and suchlike places are there to pass the time [*vakta*] in -- a means of filling an empty space [*rikta*]. But what do we wait for? Emptiness [*rikta*] between what and what? Nobody knows.(IS pp. 107-8)(44)

We have already noted several times that it is the world of nature which is important and real to Rekha and indeed to Ajneya's other characters apart from the likes of Chandramadhava: civilisation, especially the civilisation of the big city, is the place where all human values are destroyed.(38)

After the traumatic memories which are brought to the surface again by her night time visit with Bhuvan to the Jantar Mantar Rekha says: 'I live from moment to moment, so nothing leaves its print on me. It's as if I am born again every moment.'(IS p. 115) After Bhuvan's refusal of her first offer of herself to him in sex he reflects on the significance of what she has said about time:

> There is no stream of time, there is [only] moment [*kṣaṇa*] on moment on moment...the moment is eternal...little oases...separate moments...islands in the stream. To deny the successiveness of time [*kāla-paramparā*] is actually to deny the chain of cause and effect [*kārya-kāraṇa paramparā*], only in that way is it possible to remain so indifferent to consequences [*pariṇāmoṁ ke prati itanī upekṣā*] -- that is a kind of freedom from responsibility [*anuttardāyī*]. But so what? To whom else am I reponsible? Can I be responsible to myself alone? And if I am not responsible to myself then I will accept the consequences -- that I am responsible for my irresponsibility.(IS p. 138)

So Bhuvan links Rekha's view of time to his own (and Ajneya's) view of the moral independence of the individual. Yet Rekha's philosophy of the moment, though repeatedly articulated in her words, is belied by what she actually does. This is apparent in two ways: first, we saw in Chapter Four that at the heart of Ajneya's vision of human significance in these novels is the claim that suffering purifies the heart of the individual, a purification which conveys insight into the future. Rekha has such insight and we have already noted that it is particularly apparent when she sings. She becomes aware of the blossoming of her and Bhuvan's mutual love long before he does and even more important, she foresees the coming of Gaura into his life and so to speak hands him over to her in her first attempt to give Gaura the ring which her own mother had once given to her.(39) How can Rekha believe in the importance of and actually practise this kind of insight and yet at the same time claim to have no belief in the future? There is an inconsistency here, but it is one which may be less stark than it appears to be at first sight. Rekha's insight into the future is quasi-supernatural, that is, it cannot be traced to any source either in the course of events or in her natural human endowments. In the *Yoga Sūtras* of Patanjali, the basic and classic text of *Yoga* philosophy (40), the *yogin* attains to supernatural powers which include insight into the moment of his own death, if this is to happen by accident (*Yoga Sūtras* 3.22), and more generally, 'mastery over the senses' which according to Patanjali

> results in a mindlike swiftness of bodily movements; in the ability to move freely from the origins to the terminations of things irrespective of time, space and circumstances.(*Yoga Sūtras* 3.48, translated in Deshpande [1978] p. 133)(41)

Since we have already found that Ajneya's own philosophy of momentariness is closer to *Yoga* (and Buddhism) than to any other school, and that it is the same as Rekha's, it could also be right to interpret her strange gift of insight into the future in terms of this philosophy. We re-iterate that we are not suggesting a conscious and deliberate link in the mind of Ajneya. What we do propose is simply that given his upbringing and background it is by no means impossible that *Yoga* may have unconsciously shaped what he wrote about Rekha at this point. We also note that the *yogin*'s mastery over time and circumstance as described by Patanjali is remarkably close in a literary context to the omniscience of the author of the traditional realist novel.(42) Thus Rekha's gift sits uneasily with Ajneya's 'stream of consciousness' technique.

Rekha's inconsistency is apparent in a second way: at the level of ordinary behaviour, and not only of quasi-supernatural insight, she takes a keen interest in Bhuvan's future, to the extent of actually urging him to marry Gaura towards the end of the book.(IS pp. 319-20) There are other and rather different hints of such an interest earlier in the book when she writes to Bhuvan to tell him she is pregnant by him. She says of their unborn child: 'That is my confidence [*āsthā*] in the future and you have given it to me.'(IS p. 199) A little later she writes to Bhuvan exposing her internal conflict. She wants him to be completely free and to make no claims on him, and yet she asks: 'Can our future become one -- is there any possibility of this?'(IS p. 251) Later she writes to him that since the divorce from Hemendra the latter's lawyer has written her a sympathetic letter saying that:

> He hopes I won't go on nursing old wounds but will create [a new] future [*bhaviṣya kā nirmāṇa*] -- he has faith in my future and asks me to let him know when anything important [*mahatvapūrṇa*] happens in my life.(IS p. 271)

She asks Bhuvan how she should answer this letter. Should she just laugh, or should she write and tell the lawyer that his suggestion has come too late, because for her 'everything important has already happened'?(IS p. 271) So here we find no philosophy of the present moment but a sense of dashed hopes for the future, hopes which however tenuous had still been real. We also saw in Chapter Four how a sense of continuing meaning for her own life was vitally important for her and that this depended on Bhuvan not holding the abortion against her.(43) We must therefore say of Rekha that her life belies her theories, or to use more abstract language: in the figure of Rekha an implicit belief in the significance of the temporal process finally triumphs over her explicit philosophy of the timeless moment.

Rekha's verbally expressed ideal of momentariness is curiously void of content when we compare it with Ajneya's high claims in his Āla-vāla essay for the possibility of transcending the time process in the eternal present. She and others who know her seem content simply to state her view somewhat baldly without further explanation. The content is supplied towards the end of the book in Gaura's reflections, which we have already quoted at length (44), on a letter written to her by Bhuvan. What Gaura says is very close to what Ajneya writes about the possibility of transcending the present moment in his Āla-vāla essay. This possibility reaches its climax in the figure of Selma, whom Yoke describes in a series of passages which we have already quoted (45), and one of which we repeat:

> Selma too lives only in time [*kāla*] just like the rest of us, but it

> seems as if she lives not in any one time, but in all time. It's as if there time is not a single stream. It's as if there is no before and after [*āge-pīche*], but everything is simultaneous [*sab ek sāth hai*]. Everything is simultaneous and so there is no history [*itihāsa*]. So there is memory [*smṛti*] and together with it there is freedom from reciprocity [*parasparatā*] -- all is momentary [*sabhī kuch kṣaṇa hui*].(TEHS p. 22)

At the heart of the contrast which Yoke makes between Selma and 'the rest of us' lie two issues: the true meaning of freedom which we discussed in the previous chapter, and the significance of the temporal process which is our present concern. Selma's view of this latter theme is set out in an extended meditation on the nature of time which is to be found in the long flashback in the middle of the novel. It is not clear from the context whether this passage should be read as Selma's or Ajneya's own, but that hardly matters. What it does is bring this theme to a climax. Selma -- if we attribute the passage to her -- has been reflecting on the ways in which time can be measured. There are several of these and their relative value is to be assessed in terms of their proximity to our actual experience:

> One is by the clock, which is perhaps the most flawed [*ghaṭiyā*] method because it has the least connection with experience [*anubhava*]. A second way is by the sequence of day and night, sunrise and sunset, light and darkness, and by the hunger and thirst, the waking and sleeping by which we are connected to these phenomena. Since this is a way of measuring not mechanical [*yantra ke*] but experiential [*anubhava ke*] time, it corresponds more closely to reality [*kuch adhik saccā aur yathārtha*].
>
> Then there is yet another way: the way of measuring time by counting the currents in the swirling water, and then counting one's own recurring breaths [*bahatī huī sāṁsoṁ ko*] according to that rhythm. This is a way even more deeply rooted in experience because it brings the experience of time [*samaya*] closer to the experience of life [*jīvan*]. And what is the borderline between time and being free from time [*samaya aur samaya-mukta*], between time and timelessness [*kāla aur kāla-nirpekṣa*], between the evanescent and the eternal [*anitya aur sanātan*], other than our breathing and our awareness of life [*jīvan-bodha*] in the consciousness [*cetanā*] of breathing? It is not the case that such awareness of life is found only in breathing, for drawing breath is an instinctive act. It is only when breathing is obstructed that such awareness occurs for

> it is then that our mind [*citta*] recognises how intensely we cling to life.(TEHS pp. 71-2)

The really significant point here is Selma's reference to breathing in the final paragraph, for control of the breath is the key to the *yogin*'s transcendence of the human condition, a condition which is normally bound by the constraints of time. Here we turn once more to the *Yoga Sūtras* of Patanjali. After describing the correct bodily posture Patanjali writes of breath control:

> While established in *āsana* (the correct bodily posture), the break in continuance of incoming and outgoing breath is called *prāṇāyāma*. It is a stillness consequent on a break in the continuity which comes at the end of the incoming and outgoing breath. It is found to have measurable length in space and time-duration; and it becomes prolonged and subtle...Thereby the veils which cover self-illumination are removed.(*Yoga Sūtras* 2.49-50 and 52, translated in Deshpande [1978] p. 103)

In the first paragraph of the long passage from TEHS which we have just quoted Selma rejected the way of measuring time by the clock because it is farthest removed from our experience. But this is the only kind of time which Yoke can understand and it holds her in thrall:

> A hazy light -- a petrified [*ṭhiṭhakā huā*] detached life. It is as if the clock alone makes life move on, as if a tiny machine whose key is in our hand, has taken the place of God [*Īśvar*]. And we do not even have the power to stop winding this machine, to let the clock stop, to rebel against the machine which has usurped the place of God and declare ourselves free [*svatantra*].(TEHS p. 16)

Thus for Yoke time affords no moments which can be the source of insight and of vision, instead the whole process is one of deadliness, it is 'petrified'. Finally,

> Yoke did not know when Selma died. There was no way of knowing. Perhaps Selma herself did not know -- because her death did not occur at any one point [*bindu*] in time.(TEHS p. 94)

Yoke seems to epitomise Ajneya's view of the western attitude to time, but the stark and uncompromising way in which she is contrasted to Selma means that he has made her into a caricature. There is no space within her outlook for the positive understanding of the temporal process to which we alluded earlier in this chapter. Because she is, in her own words, 'consumed by history'

(46), she cannot imagine a new future for herself. All she manages to do in the end is to choose to die in the presence of a good man, Jagannathan.(47)

So if the figure of Rekha in IS represents the triumph of narrative over philosophy, the figure of Yoke in TEHS represents the reverse. But are we reading too much into the negative view of history which she articulates? Can the evidence we have adduced from her words actually bear the weight of our argument? On its own perhaps it cannot, but it receives powerful if indirect endorsement from the book in which Ajneya describes his visit to Europe in 1955. During his stay in the monastery in France he was allowed as a guest to converse for an hour each day with one of the monks, and he seems to have put this opportunity to good use. He asked the monk assigned to him why Christians insist on the uniqueness and historicity of Jesus. Does this not destroy Christianity's universal and cosmic claims? And does not the West's insistence on historical consciousness inhibit an understanding of the universal, for it binds people to time, to fear and to desire? These words can almost be read as a description of Yoke's attitude. Finally he asks his interlocutor: if the effects of the Cross are universal does not this undermine the claim to historicity?(Vatsyayan [1955] pp. 64-5) One senses that here Ajneya is struggling with a set of ideas which he finds strange and uncongenial. He cannot see how the particularities of history can be compatible with cosmic and universal claims. He does not tell us what the monk said in reply to his questions, but our own response would have been that the Christian claim is that in the Resurrection of Christ the historical events of his life and death are not left behind but taken up into eternity and so made universal and cosmic in their scope. We note also that Ajneya does not appear to separate 'western' from 'Christian' in his questions. In the light of this conversation, tantalisingly brief though its record is, it seems that the figure of Yoke can readily be fitted into the larger context of his thought. This would appear to substantiate our claim that she does indeed represent his understanding of the western attitude to time and history.

We shall return to the subject of time towards the end of this chapter, but at this point we must leave it in order to consider our second main theme: narrative. In Chapter Two we quoted at length from a book by a Hindu literary critic, N Varshaneya.

He readily agreed that there are many stories to be found within the Hindu tradition, in the *Purāṇas* and Epics, as well as in the Upanishads and elsewhere. Yet he refused to accept the claim made by some of his fellow literary critics that the roots of the Indian novel are to be found in these stories. This case, he argued, cannot be granted, for the novel is a western import.(48) We also referred to Ajneya's own crucial comment that it is no longer possible to write an epic poem and that the modern epic is the novel.(49) With this we link his important remarks on the emergence of personality as being a key issue with which modern Hindi novelists, often to their embarrassment, have found themselves compelled to engage.(50)

While the case for 'the novelty of the novel' is thus incontrovertible, it does not follow that the break with past forms of narrative is absolute, indeed several examples of the use of the traditional material to which Varshaneya referred can be found in SL and IS. For instance Shekhar's father decides that the whole family will go on a pilgrimage to the temple of the goddess *Khira Bhavānī* (51) in Srinagar. As part of their preparation he and his wife gather their children together every day after the evening meal in order to tell them traditional stories. Characteristically Shekhar is not enthusiastic about this exercise:

> The stories were only those which in India are told to children -- stories of the gods [*devatāoṁ ki kahāniyāṁ*], tales from the *Purāṇas* [*purāṇa-gāthāeṁ*], stories to which a moral purpose [*naitik uddesya*] or tail-piece was always added. Little illustrations of the greatness of God, long lectures to establish the importance of truth [*satya*]...Sometimes these stories were entertaining, but when it came to demonstrating their 'moral purpose' Shekhar got bored. (SL Vol. 1 p. 89)

It was on this pilgrimage that Shekhar dramatically announced to his family, 'There is no God ! [*Īśvar nahīṁ hai* !]'(SL Vol. 1 p. 91) For this he earned a beating from his father though his brothers told him in secret that they agreed with him. He did not always take quite such a jaundiced view of his inheritance as the above quotation might lead us to suppose. Later on we read that he was much impressed by a drama called *Satya Hariścandra* (SL Vol. 1 p. 114-5)(52), and the night before Ramaji was executed Shekhar told him stories, 'some from the *Purāṇas*, some from foreign literature and a few of events in his own life'.(SL Vol. 2 p. 93)

Since in IS the characters have at the conscious level moved much further away from their Hindu roots than have their counterparts in SL it is not surprising that in the former work we find only one reference to traditional stories, though that one is significant. It comes just after Rekha has first offered to make love to Bhuvan, an offer which he refuses. Later Bhuvan asks himself whether he was right to refuse and instinctively turns to the *Purāṇas*:

> A woman [*strī*] never used to ask [*māṅgtī*]: and when she did ask...A rejected [*pratyākhyātā*] woman never forgave [*kṣamā kiyā*] the man. She always cursed [*śāp diya*] him and there is nothing in the *Purāṇas* to say that the curse is inappropriate [*anucit*]. On the contrary it was clearly stated somewhere that if a woman demanded [*strī māṅge*] (*sc* sex), the man had no right to say 'no'.(IS p. 137)

So Bhuvan, who on the surface is a sophisticated and secular modern man, turns at a moment of stress and uncertainty to the traditional stories which he has apparently left behind.

We now turn to consider the other kinds of narrative which are to be found within the novels. They have different functions all of which raise important questions for the nature and significance of human identity. For the sake of analysis we divide them into five groups, though such division is inevitably somewhat arbitrary. Our first type is the most comprehensive: we will simply call it 'Narrative' with a capital 'N'. The particular kind of narrative structure of all three novels, and indeed the fact that they are novels at all and not some other literary form, is in itself significant. In Chapter Two we located them within the developing tradition of the modern Hindi novel as 'psychological' in that Ajneya is more interested in the inner workings of his characters' minds than he is in what happens to them or in what they do in the outer world.(53) We must now develop what we said in that chapter in more detail.

SL begins with Shekhar in the condemned cell. So overwhelmed is he by his emotions in the face of death that he cannot organise his thoughts and so looks back on his early life in a series of disconnected cameos. He presents us with a series of remembered incidents which are out of chronological order, and he compares himself to someone who is trying to rethread a broken string of pearls.(SL Vol. 1 p. 22) At the end of the novel, when he is describing the events leading up to Shashi's death, he is again overwhelmed by his emotions. He says that the internal and external events are so inextricably confused in his mind that he cannot distinguish what actually happened from what he thought about it.(SL Vol. 2 p. 245) He recalls the unexpected arrival of the injured Shashi on the threshold of his fourth storey room after she had been thrown out of her home by Rameshvar.(54) He goes on to say that her experience has become so profoundly his own that he has become her. Yet he cannot remember how this happened or how it was that he heard her whole story. He then reflects in more general terms:

> They say that events which are experienced with very intense emotion [*tīvra anubhūti*] are indelibly fixed on the scroll of consciousness [*cetanā*] like a line drawn on stone, and that their memory [*smaraṇa*] is a memory of the whole picture, not a memory of this or that line [*rekhā*] or shape [*ākṛti*]. That is to say, when those events come into the memory, they come in an inescapably fixed form in which the pen has no free will to create memory but is compelled to follow [*bādhya anugatiktā*] the event.(SL Vol. 2 p. 185)

He then says that consciousness tries to forget memories born of intense pain and buries them under so many layers of self-deception that their outline vanishes and they disappear from memory altogether. Here the pressure of interior life clearly takes precedence over outward events.(55)

In the opening pages of IS chronology is also fractured, though in a rather different way, and the emotion is less intense. Having said goodbye to Rekha, Bhuvan has just got on to a train at Lucknow station and is thinking about the pressure of her hand on his elbow as she saw him off. He thinks to himself that she was almost trying to hold him back rather than let him go.(IS p. 11) We are then taken back to his first meeting with her a few days earlier and to their meetings in the intervening period. Only on page 36 do we find ourselves back with Bhuvan on the train at the point where the novel began. Like SL this novel belongs in the psychological school, but there is a difference: instead of the whole novel being written from within the 'stream of consciousness' of a single individual, different sections of it describe the same events through the minds of different characters.

In TEHS the first part of the novel consists of Yoke's thoughts which are often taken from her diary, so chronological sequence is maintained apart from the extended flashback when Selma is describing her past experience of being marooned on the bridge many years previously. Nonetheless, what Yoke mainly records are her own thoughts about the situation in which she has inadvertently found herself. Actual events are few and of minimal significance.

In all three novels the effect of this deliberate break with chronological order, and in IS and TEHS the effect of the use of letters, notebooks and diaries, is twofold: first, it turns the reader's attention away from asking the question: what happens next? Instead we are directed to what is going on in the minds and hearts of the characters, to their inner lives. Second, we do not read the book as a chronologically consecutive story which is related by a detached and omniscient author who controls events and who has direct access to the minds of all the characters at once. Instead our position is much more humble and so more genuine: we relive the story as it is reshaped and reinterpreted in the mind of its central character (or characters in the case of IS and TEHS). Thus as we have already indicated, in technical literary terms these are 'stream of consciousness' novels, and this fact also enables us to locate them in the canon of the twentieth century European novel.(56) Moreover, by putting such weight on the individual consciousness and its development Ajneya is himself taking part in that struggle for personality to which he drew attention as one of the hallmarks of modern Hindi novels, and to which we have just referred.(57) Can we argue that all cultures have to make this modern journey and that their novelists are among their most important pathfinders?

The second kind of narrative consists of small segments within the Narrative which serve to 'place' a character who is thus identified not so much by virtue of having a recognised place within a social structure but through being described in terms of a personal story which is different from anyone else's. We will call these 'narratives of identity'. To claim that they actually define identity would be to overstate the case, but they do provide a kind of external identification, and construct a framework within which identity will eventually be elaborated. Thus at the beginning of IS when Bhuvan asks Chandramadhava who Rekha is, Chandramadhava responds not in terms of her caste and family but by telling part of her story: some people say that she had been in love with someone whom she could not marry, was broken-hearted [*marmāhata*] as a result and so had meekly accepted the man (Hemendra) eventually chosen by her parents. Others said that her husband's 'habits were rotten from the start [*ādateṁ śuru se kharāb thīṁ*]' and that he was 'indifferent [*udāsīn*]' towards his wife. Whatever the truth, Chandramadhava says, she is now separated from her husband and he is living with another woman in Malaya.(IS p. 27)

Another example of the narrative of identity reaches further back in time: when we first hear of Gaura we are told of how Bhuvan had known her many years before when she was a little girl in pigtails. Later, when she was preparing for her matriculation examination, he became her home tutor. This connection blossomed into a more equal relationship as she grew to maturity. We learn of her intellectual brilliance and of her interest in the arts.(IS pp. 61-2) In this way we begin to learn who Rekha and Gaura are by reading key parts of their personal history.

A slightly different example which we can place within the same category is the story of Rama-ji in SL.(58) This is a complete short story within the novel. We recall that Shekhar meets Rama-ji in jail. He is under sentence of death because he murdered his brother's wife and her lover when he discovered they were having an affair in his brother's absence. His importance lies in the fact that he lives entirely within the parameters of traditional assumptions, where one of a man's duties is to protect the honour of his family. What Rama-ji has done is what many others like him would have done in similar circumstances. His unquestioning acceptance of traditional values gives him an inner security which Shekar does not enjoy. (SL Vol. 2 pp. 90-3)(59) Here the narrative does provide the total identification of a character and not just a framework for it which will be filled out later, for the significance of Rama-ji lies precisely in the fact that he is not a unique individual with a unique story, but the 'everyman' of North Indian village culture. His story is thus typical of many other such stories, indeed another novel, Śatrañja ke Mohare (Pieces in a Game of Chess) by Amrit Lal Nagar, refers to a very similar incident: one of the characters says that he killed his own wife and her lover.(Nagar [1957] p. 12) The difference in the way in which Rama-ji is identified on the one hand, and Rekha and Gaura on the other is thus real though not absolute. As we shall see below, we can place the three of them at different points on the same spectrum.

The third kind of narrative is much more powerful and emotionally charged: its purpose is not to introduce or describe a new character to the reader but to describe the re-creation of one whom we already know. We will therefore call this category 'narratives of renewal'. What happens in them is that someone relives a painful experience from their own past in the presence of a sympathetic listener and in doing so finds a kind of healing or 'redemption'. This sets them free from the burden of the past and opens up a more hopeful future. This is particularly important in IS where it happens twice: on the first occasion, which we have already looked at in the context of suffering (60), Bhuvan gently raises with Rekha the subject of her failed marriage to Hemendra. She says to Bhuvan:

> They say, don't they, that if you tell a good dream you lessen the possibility (*sc* of its coming true). In the same way if you tell a bad dream you lighten its weight [*bojha*]. When I talk about my own problem [*bāt*], or make up my mind to do so, that is one layer of its shadow less. I think only by talking about it again and again can one talk oneṣelf out of it -- become free [*mukta*] of it. But actually deciding to talk about it is very difficult.(IS p. 108)

We recall that the next evening the two of them are strolling in the grounds of the Jantar Mantar in Delhi and climb to the top of the observatory when Rekha suddenly and unaccountably asks to leave. A short while later she actually tells Bhuvan the story of her marriage. She explains that Hemendra had told her that it was on this very spot that he had sworn eternal fealty to a boy. For our present purposes the point is that having told Bhuvan the story she is free of her burden:

> I said, didn't I, that if I tell my bad dream I shall be free [*mukta*] of it? Up till now I couldn't bear to talk about it and that was its power [*tākat*].(IS p. 117)

On the second occasion Bhuvan gets rid of his own mental burden in the same way: after Rekha's abortion he has withdrawn into himself and gone with a scientific expedition to

Java.(IS p. 267) From there after a six months' silence (IS p. 272) he at last writes a long letter to Gaura in which he says:

> Already there is an old burden [*bojha*] on my shoulders, the burden of a living curse [*sajīva śāp*], like the Old Man of the Sea on Sindbad's shoulders, which takes him helplessly who knows where. For several months I have known that my life is flowing in some new unknown and unimagined direction, and perhaps towards some tragedy...
>
> It seems to me that I have stood by and watched precious things being destroyed [*naṣṭa hote*], I have watched them dying [*marte*] and watched alone, and therefore I am dying with them myself; if I could somehow emerge from that loneliness [*akelepan*] and talk about what I have seen, then I could perhaps be saved from that death [*mṛtyu*] as well.(IS p. 273)

The curse which inhibits or confines a person until it is removed is a familiar theme of traditional narrative. Thus according to the *Rāmacaritamānasa* of Tulsi Das the erring *Ahalyā* is cursed and turned to stone by her husband, and only resumes her normal form when the divine Rama passes by and touches the stone with his foot.(*Rāmacaritamānasa* C 208-Ch 22, translated in Hill [1952] p. 97) Bhuvan will have had some such incident in mind as he wrote to Gaura of the 'living curse'. Eventually he returns to India and manages to confess to her both his love for Rekha and the abortion of their unborn child. Gaura listens to his story without condemning him and so he too finds healing and new life through having told and relived the painful experience.(IS pp. 291-300)

Similarly Shashi eventually manages to tell Shekhar the story of her wretched marriage to Rameshvar (SL Vol. 2 p. 169), emphasising that the act of marrying him at all was a sacrifice which she made willingly and open-eyed. There is nothing which directly suggests that she finds release and healing in telling her story, yet the fact that she felt she had to do so suggests that she realises that Shekhar needs to know and accept this part of her experience if he is to share her life now. Her telling of the story and his acceptance of it open up the possibility of, and provide the moral justification for, their new life together. This justification cannot be made within the context of the old social structures, where as we have already seen (61), a wife was expected to stay with her husband no matter how badly he might treat her. What Ajneya implicitly proposes here is a new morality based on common human values: a woman as unjustly treated as Shashi had been, and turned out of the house by her husband as well, surely had the right to appeal to a protector, especially a protector who was a relation, and who would live with her in a purely platonic relationship. Selma's story of what happened on the bridge in the flood in TEHS (TEHS pp. 64-91) belongs with both our second and third types of narrative. The story tells us who Selma is by relating part of her past history and so is a 'narrative of identity', but that history is also told in order to remove a burden, not from Selma's own heart but from Yoke's, and so we can also call it a 'narrative of renewal'. Selma seems to hope that by telling the story of her own deliverance from an attitude of hostility towards everyone she will be able to deliver Yoke from her similar failings and so open up new possibilities of life for her.(TEHS p. 62) In other words all these stories are told in order to achieve something beyond themselves. Those who tell them hope that the results of doing so will effect change and bring benefit either to themselves or to their listeners. We can also link them with what Bhuvan said about pain potentially having value for the personality of the sufferer.(62) The sub-narratives in this category are stages on the journey to the purification of vision. Because in Bhuvan's account such value is only possible when traditional interpretations of suffering have been rejected we can claim that these narratives are further removed from tradition than were some of the 'narratives of identity'.

A fourth kind of narrative is to be found in the second part of SL. We will call it a 'narrative of purpose' for the key to it is Shekhar's need for an aim after his release from jail, for without this his life becomes meaningless. We have already seen that at this point of the story he makes frequent use of the word *uddeśya* which means 'capable of being described' and so 'goal' or 'aim'.(63) An important turning point comes when Shashi visits him in his fourth storey room which she finds with great difficulty. None of the other residents in the large building even know his name, so withdrawn has he become.(SL Vol. 2 pp. 125-6) Shashi's husband Rameshvar has been sarcastic about his literary efforts and this has made him lose heart.(SL Vol. 2 p. 119, 121 and 125) He spends four or five days sitting disconsolately in his room unable to put pen to paper. He says to Shashi:

> If I finish writing (*sc* the book) then it won't get printed. If it does get printed then people will make a fool [*bevakūf*] of me. Even in being made a fool of there can be some satisfaction but to what end?

To this Shashi replies:

> Shekhar, is there not satisfaction [*tṛpti*] in suffering a measure of pain for the sake of one's purpose [*uddeśya*]? I think there is very great satisfaction in it.(SL Vol. 2 p. 126)

He says that his ideal of revolution needs to be embodied in a symbol if his purpose is to find shape and direction. She then asks if he could write for her as that symbol. He says that he could and from then on shows her everything he writes. He needs her support because he has taken on himself an enormous psychological burden. As a 'total and ideal revolutionary [*ek sampūrṇa aur ādarśa vidrohī*]' (SL Vol. 1 p. 29) he has set himself against the whole of society. We have seen that he has refused to opt into that society by finding a normal job and getting married (SL Vol. 1 p. 219) and indeed when his father pleads with him to marry he replies:

> I have chosen a mission for my life, so why should I now deliberately put an obstacle in its path?(SL Vol. 2 p. 141)

The fact that he actually uses the English word 'mission' seems significant and may point to the fact that he is very much aware at this point of his break from his own tradition. His very being now depends on him having such a mission or aim for this alone can provide him with the foundation for a meaningful life, the life which he is retrospectively describing in the Narrative. That necessity is implicit in his conversation with Shashi from which we have just quoted. It is emphasised in a negative way not long afterwards when he is reduced to despair at the cynical rejection of his book by a series of publishers, for if his very being now depends on his writing, then nothing can be worse than to have that writing rejected. It is this that leads him to make his half-hearted attempt at suicide.(SL Vol. 2 p. 68) Immediately after this attempt he returns to his room, and then breaks down and weeps in Shashi's arms:

> His defeated heart [*mana*] knew that before him there was no road

> [*gati*]...no aim [*anuddeśya*], no aim, at bottom he has no aim.(SL Vol. 2 p. 166)

In other words he not only needs the story of his past, to which we turn in a moment, he must also have before him the prospect of a future in which that story can be continued. An aim which had the prospect of being fulfilled would enable him imaginatively to project himself into the future, and without such a prospect he is lost. The importance of the future in this context becomes clearer if we set beside this incident one from from the novel to which we referred above, Śatrañja ke Mohare by Amrit Lal Nagar. This novel is set in the turbulent years of the mid-nineteenth century when the British were in the process of annexing the kingdom of Avadha (or Oudh) in the Gangetic Plain. A Hindu rebel of the *kṣatriya* or warrior caste is taken prisoner by his Muslim enemy who is a local ruler. The Muslim says to his prisoner: 'So you want to be a king then? [*to āp rajā bananā cāhate haiṁ? kyoṁ*?]' At his order seven outcastes [*bhaṅgī-camār*] throw the Hindu pretender to the ground and urinate on his head in a deliberate parody of the ceremony in which a Hindu king was anointed with the water of seven rivers. For a Hindu living in the traditional world of ritual purity it would be impossible to imagine a more total or more extreme act of defilement. The *kṣatriya* is tortured and released a few days later, but that very evening he commits suicide 'because his *dharma* has been destroyed [*apnā dharma naṣṭa ho jane ke kāraṇa*]'.(Nagar [1957]pp. 143, 147)

In contrast to Shekhar, what this man has lost is not a meaningful purpose to follow within the temporal process, but his proper status within the caste structure where alone he can find his identity. When that status has been destroyed, then like Shekhar though for totally different reasons, he has literally nothing left. Thus Shekhar and the *kṣatriya* are as far apart in terms of their identity as it is possible to be. We can therefore regard them as the two opposite poles of the spectrum to which we have already referred (64) and which we shall fill out in more detail at the end of the chapter, but at this point we return to 'narratives of purpose' and the need for a realistic future hope. We find this in IS as well as in SL, though what is at stake is not now an aim to be pursued but the continuing into the future of a relationship between two people, namely Rekha and Bhuvan. We have already considered this in the context of purification of vision in Chapter Four.(65) Some time after her abortion Rekha receives a letter from Bhuvan. At first reading she thinks he is holding her guilty because of the abortion. She writes back to him:

> If this accusation [*abhiyoga*] stands there can be no liberation, neither for me nor for you...I used to think that the great pain of all that happened, and of my own brokenness, would bear some fruit in our characters -- in yours more than in mine...Now all that hope will be illusory; the suffering will be a meaningless tragedy [*ek arthahīn* tragedy], because in it will be accusation and its meaninglessness will drag us both down into a bottomless pit. For me this hardly matters because I have already sunk to the bottom -- but you, Bhuvan, you ! You are the centre of all my hopes [*āśāoṁ kā kendra*], do not let all my deepest suffering [*vyathā*] go for nothing in this way ! (IS p. 268)

On re-reading Bhuvan's letter she realises that she was mistaken. It was full of remorse, not of accusation, and so at once she writes again:

> Perhaps you did not blame [*doṣ diyā*] me. In your letter there is only remorse [*paritāp*] which I thought was accusation [*abhiyoga*];... and so the wound I suffered begins to heal -- I take back my anger [*ākrośa*] and ask for forgiveness [*kṣamā*].(IS p. 268)

If Rekha's life is to have any kind of continuing meaning -- she does not write of an aim as Shekhar had done -- then she must be assured that Bhuvan does not accuse her. Her future identity now depends on him and on his attitude towards her, though she does not actually write of the future here, and indeed, as we have already seen, explicitly (and inconsistently) rejects any belief in it.

Our fifth type of narrative we call the 'narrative of the victim'. Such narratives are often closely connected with impending death. We must first enlarge on this subject in order to put this category into its proper context. We recall that it is the imminence of his execution which forces Shekhar to construct the narrative of his life in the first place. Indeed death is a major pre-occupation of all three novels. The young Shekhar asks adults direct and uninhibited questions about death which reduce them to a fearful and embarrassed silence.(SL Vol. 1 pp. 83-5 and 88) Several times his own recklessness brings him near to death -- when his brothers go swimming and he plunges into the deep water with them even though he cannot swim himself (SL Vol. 1 p. 81), when he nearly drowns at Mahabalipuram(SL Vol. 1 pp. 231-2), and when he nearly commits suicide.(SL Vol. 2 p. 164) When he is in jail he asks to be put on death row, ostensibly for the solitude (SL Vol. 2 p. 81), but beneath the surface we can detect a fascination with death which may even be described as morbid. Further, an extraordinarily large number of the people with whom he manages to establish some kind of relationship end up by dying. When he is in jail Rama-ji is executed (SL Vol. 2 p. 94), and the old Madansingh sickens and dies.(SL Vol. 2 pp. 95-7) Several of his female friends die -- Pratibha Lal suddenly and without explanation (SL Vol. 1 p. 100)(66), Shanti of tuberculosis (SL Vol. 1 p. 185-9)(67), and of course above all Shashi, who dies at the very end of the book. Shekhar is thus perpetually surrounded by death. He also feels a need to talk about it and ask questions. In doing this, and in sometimes almost deliberately putting his own life at risk he is breaking a taboo. Yet he justifies this when he reflects to himself:

> Perhaps knowledge of death and desire of life are one thing. One often hears it said that only he who knows how to die knows how to live. One does not hear it said that life is most precious to him who knows how to die. But that too is a fixed truth [*dhruva satya*]. People think that those who love life are afraid of death, but that is entirely wrong. Those who fear death cannot love life because in life they can never have a moment's peace [*śānti*].(SL Vol. 1 p. 128)

In IS too Rekha breaks a taboo in having her abortion.(68) After it has happened the theme of death assumes a large prominence in the book. She writes to Bhuvan:

> In Srinagar I went through death without actually dying [*markar bhī nahīṁ marī*]. But since then I have experienced several half deaths [*adhūrī mṛtyu*]. The doctor has just told me that I must have another operation, or else I will just melt into death. It does not seem that death will bring anything new. But even so I don't want to die with lingering dragging steps.(IS p. 272)

This mood of all-pervading death is shared by Bhuvan himself in the letter he wrote to Gaura from which we quoted above.(69) We have already pointed out that Ajneya says he wrote TEHS because he wanted to examine what happened when someone was face to face with death (70), and that this pre-occupation was shared by the Existentialism which he was criticising on other grounds.(71)

For Ajneya this pre-occupation was not new for it has its roots in Brahminical Hinduism. For example, in the *Bhāgavata Purāṇa* which is a very well-known devotional text, a certain King Parikshit [*Parīkṣit*] is hunting in the jungle. He arrives at a forest *āśrama* (72) hot and thirsty from the chase. He asks a drink of a sage whom he sees sitting there deep in meditation. So profoundly is the sage absorbed that he does not hear the king speaking. The king however suspects that the sage may not be really meditating at all but only pretending. He picks up a dead snake with the tip of his bow and drapes it round the neck of the offending sage who continues his meditation undisturbed (thus demonstrating that he was not pretending after all). Any direct contact with death is defiling and so when the sage's son hears what has happened he is mortally offended at the grievous insult done to his father. He promptly curses the king to die exactly a week later. The king has by now returned to his palace but he gets news of the curse. Deeply penitent for what he has done he goes to the bank of the Ganges, renounces all worldly pleasures and asks some other sages to tell him how a man should conduct himself when he knows that death is imminent.(*Bhāgavata Purāṇa* 18.24-19.24)(73) The rest of the *Purāṇa* consists of discourses addressed to the king in this extreme situation.

Thus when Ajneya's pre-occupation with death is set within the context of his inheritance it cannot be dismissed as a personal, and morbid, aberration. Nor is this all, his challenging of taboos about death can also claim a kind of support from the tradition. In the *Kaṭha Upaniṣad* the young Nachiketas [*Naciketas*] is handed over to death (who is personified as the god Yama [*Yama*]) by his father. When he arrives at Yama's abode Yama is absent and only returns after three days. He is sorry to find that his young visitor has not been accorded the hospitality due to a Brahmin and so to make amends for this lapse asks him to choose any three boons he likes. Nachiketas does so and all goes well until he chooses the third, which is to know whether or not a man exists after death. Yama tries to steer him away from this question but Nachiketas persists and eventually is given his answer.(*Kaṭha Upaniṣad passim*, translated in Hume [1931] pp. 341-61).(74)

We are now in a position to set our 'narratives of the victim' in context: Shekhar faces execution, Rekha has deliberately had her child aborted, and Selma faces death from cancer. We can describe all these characters as in different ways victims of death, but there are other characters to whom the word victim can be applied: their stories are not yet written but need to be. Thus when Shekhar is having one of his bouts of despair and says he has nothing to write about, Shashi characteristically rebukes him:

> I cannot agree that there is no material [*sāmagrī*] for you to write about. You haven't forgotten it, you are refusing to look at it. Is there nothing to write about Baba Madansingh? Did you get nothing from Mohasin which in future could be given to others? Is Rama-ji not worth writing about?(SL Vol. 2 p. 217)

These three men were all victims in that they were fellow-prisoners of Shekhar when he was in jail, and two of them had died. After making her suggestion Shashi appears to contradict herself and tells Shekhar to forget everyone else and write his own 'personal truth [*apnā nijī satya*]'. Shekhar laughingly replies: 'Then I should write your story -- [your] personal truth.' Shashi did not smile at this, but said, even more seriously:

> Yes, when I too have become such a truth, pure truth which you can look at with detachment, then write my story -- and it won't be such a bad story Shekhar !(SL Vol. 2 p. 218)

Though she has not been in jail Shashi too is a victim, for it is the wound inflicted on her by Rameshvar from which she eventually dies.

There is an important theological significance in the fact that she urges Shekhar to write these stories: if the story of the victim is told then its meaning no longer rests with the oppressor's account of events. Though the events when they happened were not in the control of the victim their meaning now is. This means that these unwritten 'narratives of the victim' belong to a *genre* not far from that of the passion story of Christ. The four

Evangelists also tell their story in such a way that the meaning of events is now vested in the victim. Pilate, the soldiers, the religious leaders and everyone else are made part of the story of Christ. It is his story and not theirs. This is not to suggest that either Ajneya or his characters are crypto-Christians. We can distance ourselves from such a suggestion by making another comparison. Two survivors of Auschwitz, Eli Wiesel in Night (75), and Primo Levi in If This Is A Man (76), both felt moved to tell their own stories. Both of them wrote as atheists, yet both felt that their stories had to be told. Shekhar too is an atheist who feels bound to tell his story, and here our category of 'narrative of the victim' overlaps with our first category of Narrative. If to compare him with Holocaust survivors is at one level wholly inappropriate, at another it is instructive, for it opens up another dimension to our study: we have seen that for Ajneya intense suffering can lead to the purification and intensification of vision, a process which leads the sufferer in the direction of 'transcendence'. Here suffering leads to something else: it impels the sufferers, or the sufferers' friends, to tell their story and in doing so to wrest the meaning of what was done to them from the hands of the oppressors.

Because death is universal a figure such as King Parikshit has functioned as a role model for countless Hindu people. What he actually does is not important, what matters is that he puts himself in the posture of a learner and a listener at the feet of wise men who tell him what his attitude in the face of death should be. Can some of the characters of our novels be seen as providing role models in their own very different context? That possibility would seem to follow from our earlier suggestion, that one of the functions of the novel as a literary form is precisely to provide a means of interpreting life for those whom traditional ways can no longer satisfy.(77) This begins to happen when readers can see their own lives and the questions which they face embodied in the characters of the novel. It is in this way that a good novel constructs a new world of the imagination and in doing so opens up new possibilities for living. It is with some such intention as this in mind that at the end of the Introduction to SL Ajneya says to his readers:

> And, who knows, in the contemporary world when I and you are all composite [*saṃśliṣṭa*] characters then you may find somewhere

even within yourself a Shekhar.(SL Vol. 1 p. 12)(78)

So too, the story of Bhuvan and Rekha is one that spoke to many who had emerged from what were perceived as the inhibiting constraints of tradition and who were looking for new patterns and possibilities in the relationships between women and men.

We are now in a position to elaborate on the spectrum of characterisation to which we referred above: at one end are Amrit Lal Nagar's *kṣatriya* and Rama-ji whose identity is defined by and confined within the traditional structure of caste where the key values were ritual purity and personal (and family) honour. Such characters can figure within a modern novel but they belong essentially to the world to whose disappearance the coming of the novel testifies. 'Narratives of identity' -- in which we included the story of Rama-ji -- also include stories of people such as Rekha and Gaura who are to be identified at least in part by personal stories which others do not share. This points to the fact that they are on the way to becoming individual personalities. 'Narratives of renewal' mark out individuals rather more strongly, for a person who has been through a process of healing and renewal, by retelling a painful experience in the presence of a sympathetic listener, has moved further along to the road of becoming a whole and integrated person. Their story is not just a matter of external identification, it has become much more deeply part of what they are. This process was even more marked in our fourth category: 'narratives of purpose'. Shekhar's very being depended on him having a purpose (his writing) for which he could work, and which afforded a realistic prospect of achievement. Without this he was literally lost -- in the same way as Amrit Lal Nagar's *kṣatriya* though for wholly different reasons. The same was true in a rather different way for Rekha who needed not so much a continuing purpose as the assurance of a continuing relationship with Bhuvan.

Thus within these three categories of narrative we can discern an increasing emphasis on the growth and independent responsibility of the individual. We might call this 'the journey from type to personhood'. All these narratives imply and depend on the positive evaluation of the temporal process to which we referred at the beginning of this chapter. 'Narratives of the victim' are of people who have made this journey and whose purpose has ended in failure or in unremembered death. This was true of Madansingh and of Shashi who urged Shekhar to tell these stories. Shekhar's own story belongs within this category as well as being a 'Narrative'. The 'narrative of the victim', like 'the Narrative' itself, is an act of public testimony, an act of witness to the world. The victim's story must not be lost, and its meaning must be wrested from the grasp of the oppressor. That meaning depends on but cannot be contained within its own temporal process: something more is needed. We have already noted that this brings Ajneya close to the Passion narratives of the Gospels. Can we go a step further and claim that the very incompleteness of these narratives within their own parameters points to what Christians believe is the final retrieval of all our stories -- Resurrection?

Yet against this we must set that transcendence of the present moment which we saw to be the heart of Ajneya's philosophy of time. Pushed to its extreme form as it is in TEHS this appears to deny the ultimate value of all narratives, for over them stand Yoke's words as a kind of epitaph: 'I ought to be free but I am consumed by history'. We have already suggested that this gives a much too restricted view of western attitudes to history. It is belied by all that we have written of Ajneya's use of narrative. At the same time the philosophy of the transcendence of the present moment cannot be dismissed. Here indeed is Ajneya's -- and much of traditional Hindu thought's -- most important challenge to our own view. It reminds us that the temporal process alone cannot deliver final human significance. Can it be seen as that which indeed points to the possibility of history's being transcended but on the further side of death? To that question we return in our final chapter.

NOTES

1. See above, pp. 114-5.
2. See above, p. 75.
3. See above, pp. 116-7.
4. See above, pp. 117-8, 128-30 and 136-8.
5. See above, pp. 6-7.
6. See above, pp. 92-3.

7. See above, pp. 119-23.
8. See above, pp. 133-4.
9. See above, pp. 175-7.
10. See above, pp. 94-5.
11. See above, pp. 96-7.
12. See above, p. 14.
13. See above, p. 2.
14. See above, pp. 152-3.
15. See above, pp. 8-9.
16. See above, p. 11.
17. See above, p. 7.
18. Ricoeur's argument clearly does not relate to myths, such as the one related on p. 161, where the story is extended over several 'births' and implicitly denies the significance of the temporal process as a source of meaning.
19. See above, pp. 42 and 54.
20. See above, pp. 41-2.
21. See Hooker [1989] pp. 55-89, and Rayan 'Indian Theology and the Problem of History', in Taylor ed [1976] pp. 167-93.
22. For some of the literature, see Chapter Two, note 5.
23. See above, pp. 61-7.
24. See above, p. 32.
25. For the basic elements of this school of thought, see above, pp. 167-8.
26. This sense of urgency is apparent in the very first word of the novel: 'Hanging [*phāṁsī*]', and is continued throughout the two opening pages.(SL Vol. 1 pp. 15-6)
27. We have already quoted this important sentence as a part of the longer passage which forms its context: see above, p. 172.
28. See above, pp. 112-3.
29. Modern scholars challenge this traditional view and claim that the myths by no means always agree with the philosophy. See, for example, O'Flaherty tr [1975] pp. 13-4. See also Chapter Four, note 30.
30. '*Kāla kā ḍamarū-nāda*' (Time's Drum-Beat), in Vatsyayan [1971] pp. 97-110. The word *āla-vāla* literally means 'a basin for water round the root of a tree'.(Monier-Williams [1899] p. 153) Nearly the whole of India's annual rainfall comes in the three-month monsoon period. In order to nourish young saplings during the remaining nine rainless months of the year, an earthen basin is hollowed out around them -- shaped like a wheel with the sapling in the middle -- and into this water is regularly poured. On the dust cover of the book in question it is explained that the volume contains a number of essays which Ajneya maintains are essential for understanding literature. Literature is compared to a tree and the essays to the water it needs for nourishment.
31. Vatsyayan [1981].
32. Vatsyayan [1989]. The word *saṃvatsar* can also mean 'year', but 'epoch' is probably the more appropriate translation here.
33. The theory of the four *yugas* is conveniently set out in Walker [1968] Vol. 1 pp. 6-8.
34. But how did history come to such a pass in the modern, that is, the Western world?...

    History destroyed eternity. The vast and astonishing patterns of change in human history, the wonderful new dimensions opening up before man in *this* world, obscured the dimensions of eternity and led to its decline and gradual collapse.(Vatsyayan [1981] pp. 10-1)

35. See above, p. 148.
36. That criticism is echoed from a different perspective from our own by the novelist Anita Desai, who in a review of Ajneya's A Sense of Time comments:

> Sanskrit drama recognised the power of invocation (*sc* of the gods) and Vatsyayan quotes from it but betrays an unfortunate parochialism by ignoring the fact that Greek dramatists employed the same device which rather obscures the dividing line he draws so sharply between eastern and western cultures...claiming that whereas eastern literature captures Eternity, western literature makes do with mere Time.(Hindustan Times, Magazine Section, page iv, columns 1-8, 31st January 1982)

37. Monier-Williams [1899] p. 420 lists no fewer than twelve compounds containing the prefix *jita-* and which mean, for example, 'one who has conquered' anger, lust, his senses, the desire for food. Consciousness [*cetanā*] is a central concept in the main schools of philosophy.
38. For example, see above, pp. 95-6.
39. See above, p. 135.
40. Patanjali, who may have lived at any time between 200 BCE and 500 CE, is traditionally believed to have been the compiler of the *Yoga Sūtras* which bring together a wide variety of earlier theory and practice into a single coherent system which is the starting point for all subsequent development of *Yoga*.(Walker [1968] Vol. 2 pp. 195-6).
41. The writer of this book helped Deshpande with the English text of his book and with the translation of the *sūtras* into English.
42. See above, p. 65. We also note again the theme of mastery or conquest over the limitations of the human condition. See above, note 37.
43. See above, pp. 132.
44. See above, p. 77.
45. See above, p. 172.
46. For the passage of which this phrase forms a part, see above, p. 172.
47. We have already pointed out that this man's name is the one explicitly Indian reference in the book. For Ajneya's own comments on his significance, see above, pp. 45-6 and 83-4.
48. See above, pp. 61-2.
49. See above, p. 30.
50. See above, p. 58.
51. This is the name of a temple in Srinagar dedicated to *Bhavānī* which is one of the many names given to the great mother goddess in Hinduism.
52. *Hariścandra* is a famous king of Hindu myth who was renowned as a defender of the oppressed. In one story, reduced to destitution by the sage *Viśvāmitra*, he eventually 'conquered heaven by his good works' but refused to go there unless he could take his faithful subjects with him.(Dowson [1968] pp. 118-9). It is not surprising that Shekhar was attracted by such a character as this.
53. See above, pp. 64-7.
54 See above, pp. 89 and 155.

55. Possibly this is traceable to the influence of Freud on Ajneya.
56. See above, pp. 65-7.
57. See above, p. 196.
58. We have already discussed this story: see above, pp. 124-5.
59. See above, pp. 124-5.
60. See above, p. 130.
61. See above, p. 80.
62. See above, p. 116.
63. See above, Chapter 4, note 40.
64. See above, p. 201.
65. See above, pp. 130-3.
66. She is the small daughter of a doctor who apes western ways to the point of caricature. Shekhar first meets her on one of his solitary walks. He is invited to her home for a very western 'dinner'.(SL Vol. 1 pp. 96-100)
67. She is a teen-age girl who is already dying of tuberculosis when Shekhar first meets her. She knows she has not got long to live and asks him to come and sit with her regularly, which he does.(SL Vol. 1 pp. 185-8)
68. See above, pp. 130-1.
69. See above, p. 202.
70. See above, p. 44.
71. See above, p. 148.
72. Here this word means 'the sanctuary of a hermit', but it can also mean 'one of the (four) stages of life'.
73. For the Sanskrit original of this story, with Hindi translation, see Poddar [1940] Vol. 1 pp. 134-40.
74. We have already referred to this Upanishad in another context. See above, Chapter Four, note 27.
75. This book was first published in French in 1958. It is available in English translation.(Wiesel [1981])
76. This book was first published in Italian in 1958. It is available in English translation.(Levi [1987])
77. See above, pp. 55-9.
78. Ajneya has just claimed that Shekhar himself is a 'composite [*saṃśliṣṭa*]' character.

7

CONCLUSION

In the preceding chapters we have tried to show that Ajneya's three novels are worthy of serious study by Christian theologians. This is not because they are particularly great novels but because they have enabled us to focus on particular themes in a distinctive and original way. We began our study of them by setting Ajneya in his own social, political and religious context. He was born into a rapidly changing society, which in his youth was struggling for independence from Britain, and in his mature years experiencing a measure of disillusionment after this independence had been achieved. Religious change was also part of this context and we saw how he rejected some and modified other elements of the Brahminical Hinduism in which he was nurtured. He rejected any kind of imposed sacredness in terms of heaven, hell, and rebirth as traditionally understood. He also rejected traditional understandings of ritual purity and the social divisiveness which they entailed. This rejection enabled him to give a high status to women, and to oppose any kind of discrimination on the grounds of caste. He was equally hostile, though on rather different grounds, to the materialistic culture he saw emerging in India's big cities. He saw this as eroding all spiritual values and ethical principles.

In SL and IS in particular we see his characters struggling to become persons in the sense which he himself described in the essay he wrote in English in 1959.(1) The nature of this struggle became particularly clear when in the last chapter we set it within the framework of the different kinds of narrative which the novels both are and contain. Narratives of identity, of renewal, and of purpose can be placed on an ascending scale of developing self-conscious personhood. We pointed out that this opened up a possibility of conversation with Christians for whom also personhood and personal relationship is a central concern (2), and we shall have more to say about it below.

We referred several times to Ajneya's struggle as the creation of a new anthropology--though this term should not be taken to indicate a coherent and consistent philosophical position. Ajneya the novelist, like Ajneya the poet, was a creative artist and not a philosopher. His characters search for integrity and honesty in personal relationships, a search which can sometimes involve them in suffering. At certain points Ajneya drew on Christianity to interpret this suffering. His rejection of the traditional framework within which human life was understood enabled him to give a positive value to suffering as leading to a purification of vision. This was especially manifested in Shashi, Rekha and Selma. Here was a real re-interpretation of *Yoga* which teaches that such purification lies beyond rather than within suffering, and on the whole confines the renewed vision to men. It was not only *Yoga* which was re-interpreted in this way. The *sūtras* written on the wall of his prison cell by the wise old Madansingh enabled Shekhar to class him with the Rishis, the seers and prophets of ancient Vedic tradition.

At all these points we find ourselves agreeing with or at least sympathetic towards the case our author makes. Yet in the last two chapters we looked at evidence which pointed in a rather different direction. In their pursuit of freedom his characters are engaged in an individualistic search which takes them away from society and community and into solitude, and away from culture and into nature. We agree with Indian critics of the novels that there are real weaknesses here. This withdrawal deepens in intensity across the novels and we have suggested that it could be a contemporary manifestation of a traditional pattern in Hindu life, a pattern which M M Thomas sees reflected and transposed in the lives of several of India's public figures of modern times.(3) It reaches a climax in TEHS. It is hardly surprising that the author of this work published no more novels for the last twenty five years of his life. The withdrawal finds a parallel and a support in Ajneya's view of time. Novels, we argued in the last chapter, presuppose a positive evaluation of the temporal process in the terms suggested by Paul Ricoeur.(4)

When that process is seen instead as a prison which inhibits growth and insight, as it does in the character and words of Yoke, then it is difficult to see how more novels can be written. So too when time is interpreted solely within the parameters of the individual consciousness, as Rekha's philosophy of the present moment implies, and when time itself is transcended, as it appears to be by Selma, then there is an inevitable devaluing of narrative in so far as this depends on a positive evaluation of time. This too makes uncongenial soil for the growth of the novel.

A further point, which is not unrelated to the ones we have just considered, is to be found in the fact that the life of the metropolis is dismissed as 'civilisation' [*sabhyatā*]. We have seen that this word always has bad connotations for our author. This is especially clear in one of his best known poems:

> Snake ! you were not civilised [*sabhya*]--
> You never even learnt to live in the city.
> Can I ask you just one thing--(will you answer me?)
> How then did you learn to bite?--where did you find your poison?(Ajneya [1986] Vol. 1 p. 269)

Ajneya wrote this poem in Delhi in 1954, three years after the publication of IS. So the life of the big city is to be rejected, there is no sense in the novels that it can be embraced and transformed. Shekhar and Bhuvan, Rekha and possibly Selma have either left it or want to leave it in order to find their real identity elsewhere. Also, there is in all three novels a notable absence: we find in them no small communities within which Ajneya's characters can find identity and support, and which can command their loyalty and enable them to grow with the help of others. In a Christian context we might call such a community 'church', though it need not take such an explicitly religious form. Thus Shekhar first belongs to his family which he totally rejects. He joins a small circle of outcaste friends when he is in college in Madras, but is disillusioned by their lack of support for his schemes. This is epitomised by Raghavan's tame submission to an arranged marriage. His one experience of genuine community seems to be in jail, but this only embraces Madansingh, Mohasin and perhaps Rama-ji, and comes to an end when he is released. Towards the end of the novel he and Shashi fall in with the revolutionaries who provide them with accomodation but even here there is no feeling that Shekhar really belongs to the group, and its members remain shadowy and unreal. The sense of isolation is more marked still in IS where all the characters are solitary individuals with the possible exception of Gaura who still maintains close links with her family even though she rejects her father's choice of a marriage partner. In TEHS isolation reaches its most extreme possible form. This means Shekhar, Bhuvan and Rekha, and finally Yoke are all fragile and solitary individuals who lack any kind of social supports. None of them finally succeeds in carrying the load which solitary personhood imposes upon them.

However, in their very different ways Shashi and Selma do succeed: their sufferings are transformed, they experience a kind of re-interpreted *yogic* vision. It is this which offers perhaps the greatest challenge in these novels to our own Christian vision. What is the nature of this challenge? We argued in the Introduction for the priority of language, symbol, community and relationship as the framework within which religions can best be interpreted and as the basis for our own anthropology which we can sum up in the single sentence: 'I relate therefore I am'. In other words I need 'the other' fully to be myself. I can neither be nor become a fully human being if I remain an isolated Cartesian monad. Yet in spite of the mutual inter-dependence of Shekhar and Shashi, of Bhuvan and Rekha, which in some measure exemplify our ideal, in the final analysis Ajneya seems to reject it: his own ideal is of the solitary individual as the source of insight and of moral values. We recall that in IS Bhuvan sees the choice of a marriage partner as an essentially private and personal choice. But more than this, in TEHS, society, history and inter-personal involvement seem to represent the world in which Yoke is trapped, and from which Selma in her solitary vision has found deliverance. The pursuit of 'naked human existence' (5) in Ajneya's search for the setting of this final novel is also evidence for the rejection of society and we have shown that while his individualism has provoked criticism from his fellow Hindus it has deep roots within the tradition within which he was nurtured. If Ajneya was a single idiosyncratic writer he could be dismissed at this point, but Ajneya as representing an ancient tradition can be seen as providing a focal point at which we can engage with that tradition in an original way. Perhaps we could say that our own position is always in constant danger of being trapped within its own parameters and needs to be corrected by the *yogic* vision, and vice versa. At the end of the last chapter we suggested that *yogic* vision can for Christians point for the transcending--or should we say 'transforming' of history on the far side of death. If heaven is seen not as the realm of static enjoyment but of endless growth, that might point to a possible reconciliation of the two perspectives. We can see a hint of such a possibility in some words of Gregory of Nyssa:

> Contemplation of God's face consists in journeying toward God ceaselessly, in moving forward constantly in the endless following of the Word.(6)

Do these words point to a way in which Hindu and Christian traditions could be open to one another in a mutual critique and purification? We might also argue that each needs and to a degree must depend on the other for this purpose.

Such mutuality is only possible if neither tradition is fixed and enclosed: each needs to be capable of embracing and adapting for its own purposes elements from the other. We have already seen Ajneya do this to considerable effect in writing novels at all, and in his use of the principle of substitutionary or repesentative atonement. But there is more to this process of mutual learning. We have several times in our argument pointed out that where Ajneya is conservative he seems not to have brought certain key elements of his own tradition to the level of consciousness. This was true of sacred geography in IS, of the possible patterns of *Sāṁkhya* philosophy in the behaviour of Rekha and of Shashi who 'set their menfolk free', and most of all in the progressive withdrawal from society and its concerns which we have repeatedly noticed in the three novels read as a single 'canon'. The process of bringing largely unconscious areas of thought to the level of consciousness is one which within the dialogue we can encourage in one another. We would claim that it is as an outsider to Brahminical Hinduism that we are able to do this for the readers of an Ajneya. They could perform exactly the same task for us in bringing our own unconscious Christian assumptions into the open. Mary Douglas expresses a similar idea in rather different terms:

> The first Copernican revolution, the discovery that only man's subjective viewpoint made the sun seem to revolve round the

> earth, is continually renewed. In our own culture mathematics first and later logic, now history, now language and now thought processes themselves and even knowledge of the self and of society, are fields of knowledge progressively freed from the subjective limitations of the mind. To the extent to which sociology, anthropology and psychology are possible in it, our own type of culture needs to be distinguished from others which lack this self-awareness and conscious reaching for objectivity.(Douglas [1970] p. 96)

While agreeing with Douglas' basic point we would claim that her distinction is too sharp. There are degrees of the self-awareness which she describes, it is not just something which individuals or cultures have or do not have. Thus in our novels the picture is varied. In SL Rama-ji does not have it at all. He knows what his values are but he does not know that he knows them. Shekhar is making the painful journey to becoming self-aware. It is one of the strengths of this novel that it shows that that journey *is* painful. Shekhar can stand apart from the society which has nurtured him and be critical of it. He can even buy a copy of the Laws of Manu in order to criticise it on the basis of another scale of values. He can write a book about his criticism. This may not be sociology or anthropology in the strictly academic sense of the terms, but the self-awareness of many a Shekhar is necessary, as Douglas insists, for these disciplines to exist at all. Nor is this all. What Douglas describes as 'our own type of culture' is one in which people can now read and write novels. In this modern culture we can look back, perhaps with nostalgia to the old world in which, in the words of Fuentes, 'we all understood every-thing'.(7)

In that world the epic was possible but not the novel. Here is the context for the new kind of Hindu-Christian dialogue for which we have argued throughout this book. From the Rama-jis of Hinduism--and they are many--I can learn much, but I cannot have dialogue with them. That can only happen with people who are sufficiently detached from their inheritance to know that they know. Such knowledge also makes it possible to recognise that they belong to a plural world. Similarly Christians who have never stepped outside the parameters of their own mental world cannot practise dialogue, they can only make assertions. True dialogue follows on the loss of innocence which is the price that always has to be paid for growth in self-awareness. Shekhar affords a moving illustration of the cost of such growth. When 'I know that I know' then I can be open to the other person and the mutual enlarging of one another's horizons to which we have referred can take place. Each remains committed to the truth as they perceive it, but it is a commitment which demands and includes openness in the way we have described.

I conclude this chapter and the book with a change of style which I deliberately mark with a shift from the formal academic 'we' to the more personal 'I': this book is the fruit of five years academic work but behind it lie thirty years of study of the Hindu tradition, in India and also in Britain. The foundation of this was the learning of both the Hindi and Sanskrit languages. Without this foundation it would not have been possible to write the book at all. During these years I have met many Hindus whom I am now honoured to count as my friends. I have had them in my mind as I have written. At the same time I struggle with the large questions for Christian theology with which the encounter with other faiths now confronts all Christians, and which are the more urgent and pressing when they are raised in the context of the kind of study and friendship which I have described. How can that encounter be enriching and fruitful rather than barren and destructive?

First, it lays upon some Christians the inescapable task of studying other faiths in depth, of trying, so far as possible, to understand them from within. Only on that basis is the mutual openness and critique for which I have argued possible. That does not entail, as some influential voices would urge, that we have to abandon some of our deepest convictions in order to make the meeting possible. Instead the meeting demands of us a deeper study and appropriation of those convictions. Here the person of the other tradition has the indispensable role of enabling that study and appropriation by helping us to bring our hidden assumptions into the open, for all our speech and all our faith depend on much that we perforce leave unsaid and of which we are often scarcely aware. We place our convictions openly 'on the table' in the way of testimony. In this way, Ajneya, we have argued, has 'testified' to his own powerful convictions by publishing these novels (among his many other works). Such testimony by its very nature invites a response. This book is both a response to Ajneya's testimony, and itself a testimony which invites its own response in turn. If we take seriously George Steiner's claim that an implicit faith in God underlies all our use of language (8) then this conversation can be seen as part of our struggle to discover who God is and therefore who we are in our plural world which desperately needs models by which different communities can live together fruitfully rather than destructively. The advantages of setting such a conversation in the context of novels I have, I hope, sufficiently demonstrated in these pages. Not least these and other novels bring together religious and secular concerns, a linkage which is surely essential if the dialogue is not to be an escapist flight into a religious ghetto. As for the question of where truth finally lies, I believe that Christians have to live by faith. This means that in testimony my own faith must be continually put at risk: it is a 'Risking Christ for Christ's Sake'--to quote the happy title of a book by M M Thomas.(9) In other words, we all have to risk the dialogue.

NOTES

1. See above, p. 58.
2. See above, pp. 58-9.
3. See above, p. 42.
4. See above, p. 183.
5. See above, p. 46.
6. The Life of Moses (PG, 44.1025), quoted in Panikkar [no date] p. 144.
7. See above, p. 68.
8. See above, pp. 16-7.
9. For publication details, see the Bibliography.

APPENDIX

A SUMMARY OF THE CONTENTS OF THE NOVELS

As we explain more fully in the body of the book, especially in Chapter Two, Ajneya's novels are 'psychological' in that they are more concerned with what is going on in the minds of their characters than with what they do or with what happens to them in the outer world. We therefore look at events through the medium of their thoughts and reactions. This places the novels in the 'stream of consciousness' school. For this reason none of them is a straight chronological narrative directly related by the author, for the characters do not consider events in a direct chronological sequence. However it is necessary for us as readers to have in each case a grasp of the main outline of that sequence in order to understand the novel.

The three novels vary considerably in length: SL contains some 212,000 words, IS about 144,500, while TEHS is much the shortest, with only about 30,250. This difference is reflected in the amount of space which we devote to the synopsis of each work. Further, the number and significance of events diminishes across the novels. Much more happens in SL than in the other two and this means we devote a disproportionately large amount of space to it.

1. *Shekhar: A Life*

The book begins melodramatically, with the word 'Execution [*Phāṁsī*]'. A young man, Shekhar, is sitting in the condemned cell and since he finds himself face to face with imminent death, he is driven to make sense of his short life. In the early pages we are given a series of disconnected and disordered cameos in which we get glimpses of various things which have happened to him. Most of these are more fully described later in the work. The narrative proper begins with his birth at an archaeological site near Patna. (His father is an archaeologist.) His family move from Patna to Kashmir. On a solitary walk in the jungle he encounters a little girl who describes herself in English fashion as 'Miss Pratibha Lal'. He is invited to dinner at her very westernised home but cannot cope with the English table manners which are expected of him. From Kashmir the family move to Ootacamund in the Nilgiri Hills of South India. During this first part of the book we read of his early education, his rebelliousness against all authority, his endless questions about taboo subjects such as sex and death, and his rejection of belief in God. At Ootacamund he has an adolescent love affair with Sharada, the daughter of the family's nearest neighbours. When this comes to an abrupt and painful end with the unannounced departure of Sharada's family he spends a little time in the company of Shanti, a young girl who is dying of TB and who asks him to sit with her. After her death he is sent to college in Madras where he is placed in a Brahmin hostel. He does not know any of the other students and is 'befriended' by one of them, called Kumar. They go to the cinema and wander along the beach in the moonlight together. Kumar tells Shekhar a hard luck story and the latter, who is innocent to the point of naivete, lends him some money which is not returned. The friendship ends and Shekhar becomes aware of the appalling attitudes of the other Brahmins in the hostel towards students of lower caste. Eventually he moves out of this hostel -- the Brahmin students are angry because he does not observe the rules of caste behaviour -- and joins the outcaste hostel. He talks with these students about how society can be changed. One of them is a young man called Raghavan. Shekhar attempts to start a school for slum children in an impoverished area of the city, and a discussion society for his fellow students which he calls The Antigonum Club. During holiday time he explores the South on his own and nearly drowns when he swims in the sea off Mahabalipuram, a short distance south of Madras.

The novel is in two volumes and at the beginning of the second Shekhar leaves Madras and goes to Lahore where he enrols in another college to begin the next stage of his education. Here he is appalled not by traditional caste attitudes as he had been in the South, but by the effete and morally corrupt aping of western ways of which the epitome is a young woman lecturer called Manika, who has recently returned from Oxford. While he is in Lahore Shekhar renews his links with the family of Shashi, who is probably his cousin, though their precise relationship is left, perhaps deliberately, unclear. She is to have a profound effect on his life. He had first met her when she and her mother visited his family when the two of them were small children. Shashi's family live in Lahore, and just after his return from a strange journey to the Himalayas in a search for absolute beauty, he hears that her father has died and so visits her home. Shortly afterwards, along with other students he becomes a volunteer officer at a Congress Party session which takes place in a camp set up for the purpose. He is unimpressed by the lack of dedication and discipline among his fellow volunteers and among the Congress officials who are responsible for running the camp. He takes the place of a sentry who is doing his third successive stint in the pouring rain because his two replacements have failed to turn up. The camp has been infiltrated by under cover CID agents (employed by the British rulers of India in whose eyes Congress was a suspect organisation) and he is wrongly arrested for an offence committed against one of these men by someone else. He finds himself in jail where he is to spend ten months. During this period, which was to be a turning point in his life, he met three other prisoners who had a profound influence on him. These were Madansingh, Rama-ji and Mohasin. Shashi came to visit him several times. She also wrote to him in great distress about the marriage her widowed mother had arranged for her. This caused great emotional turmoil in the heart of Shekhar who of course could do nothing about it.

When he emerged from jail he struggled to rebuild his life and eventually saw that he must write to further the cause of social revolution. He tries to get his early efforts into print but either the publishers turn them down outright or else they try to impose impossible terms on Shekhar. He falls in with a self-styled social reformer called Amolak Rai, but his claims prove empty and all he and his friends really want from Shekhar is for him to marry one of their own (Brahmin) daughters. Shashi, by now married against her will, is the only person who affords the increasingly lonely Shekhar any comfort or encouragement. His progress as a writer was far from smooth and at one point he was driven to such despair that he made a half-serious attempt at suicide. He confessed this to Shashi who stayed with him for the whole of the following night in order to make sure that he did not try again, but when she went home next morning she was literally thrown out of her home by her brutal and jealous husband who put the worst possible interpretation on her absence. From then on she and Shekhar lived together, but did not have sex. Shekhar tried in vain to get his writing published and eventually fell in with a young revolutionary who offered to help him. The young man asked him to produce some simple revolutionary literature and said he would help with accommodation should this prove necessary. So in this way Shekhar was almost accidentally drawn into the revolutionary movement. When it became too dangerous to go on living in Lahore the couple moved to Delhi, to accommodation provided by the revolutionaries. Here Shashi's health went into a terminal decline which was caused by the injury she sustained when her husband threw her out of the house. Shekhar was approached by a group of the revolutionaries who were planning to release one of their comrades from jail. He was entrusted with the care of some firearms. This made Shashi very uneasy on moral grounds. Her unease was increased when Shekhar returned very late from a preliminary expedition with one of the group to test the weapons. Shortly after this expedition she died. Here the second volume of the novel ends with Shashi's death, and we return to Shekhar in his condemned cell. A projected third volume was never published, though Ajneya always maintained that he had written it. For this reason the story remains incomplete in several respects: in the series of disconnected flashbacks with which the novel opens we read of the corpse of someone killed by an explosion lying by the side of a river. There is no further reference to this in the main part of the novel, nor do we discover how Shekhar came to be arrested a second time and condemned to death.

2. *Islands in the Stream*

In this novel, instead of viewing events through the mind of one character as in SL, we see them through the minds, and sometimes through the letters, of each of the four main characters. Two of these are men: Bhuvan and Chandramadhava, and two are women: Rekha and Gaura. The book is essentially about the relationships between these four.

The actual story is simple: Bhuvan is in Lucknow, visiting his old friend Chandramadhava, who is a journalist with a crude and superficial attitude to life. He embodies the 'animalism' or 'mere survivalism' of which we saw Ajneya to be so critical in our Introduction. Chandramadhava introduces Bhuvan to a young woman called Rekha to whom he is immediately attracted. He learns from Chandramadhava that she is married but separated from her husband. She has held a succession of jobs, from at least one of which, unbeknown to her, Chandramadhava has engineered her dismissal. He tries to arrange for Rekha to accompany him on a journey to the hills proposing to her that Bhuvan should come with them as a chaperone, but he overplays his hand when in the gardens of the Residency at Lucknow he declares his love to Rekha in terms which embarrass and indeed repel her. After this she wants nothing more to do with him and goes to the hills with Bhuvan. They first go to Sat Tal, near Naini Tal and there their relationship blossoms to the extent that Rekha offers herself to Bhuvan in sex, an offer which Bhuvan, who is deeply moved, refuses. Some time after this Bhuvan goes on a scientific expedition to Kashmir and Rekha meets him there on her own initiative. They finally have sex together by a mountain lake in Kashmir and as a result Rekha becomes pregnant.

In the meantime her husband Hemendra is trying to arrange a divorce. He is told by a lawyer that the only grounds on which he can do this are change of religion. He is further told that he has no case against Rekha and indeed that it is she who is the injured party because he is living with another woman in Malaya. However, Chandramadhava hears that Rekha is pregnant though he does not know by whom. He passes this information on to Hemendra who writes to her. We are not explicitly told of the contents of this letter, but the important point is that having received it Rekha realises that Hemendra now knows of her condition. She is therefore afraid that Bhuvan will become implicated in the divorce case and in order to prevent this she has an abortion which nearly kills her. Bhuvan arrives, finds her very sick, and gets her to hospital in the nick of time. Too late, she hears that the divorce had already gone through before Hemendra wrote and so Bhuvan would not have been implicated anyway. Bhuvan proposes marriage but she refuses, partly because she does not want to control his future, and partly because she feels his offer was made because of her pregnancy and so merely in order to satisfy what she believes is now an obsolete social convention.

The fourth character of the novel is Gaura whom we first meet when she is an adolescent student of Bhuvan. She goes to Bangalore to study music, having refused the marriage her parents wanted to arrange for her. She is cultured and intelligent and as she grows to maturity so does her relationship with Bhuvan who at the very end of the book proposes marriage to her. He does this with the blessing of Rekha who had in fact foreseen before either Bhuvan or Gaura realised it that this would happen. Rekha marries a kindly doctor, Dr Rama Chandra, who operated on her after her abortion, while Chandramadhava becomes a Communist and marries a film star.

Such are the bare bones of this story, which, like SL, is more important for what goes on in the minds of its characters and for the shifting patterns of their relationships than for what they actually do in the public realm.

3. *To Each His Stranger*

An old woman, Selma, and a much younger one, Yoke (pronounced 'Yōkay'), find themselves imprisoned together in a mountain hut under an avalanche of snow. Selma had deliberately planned to stay in the hut for the winter rather than accompany her family to the grasslands below the snowline for she knew she was dying of cancer and wanted to die alone. Yoke is there involuntarily, having taken shelter in the hut during a storm while she was on a skiing holiday. Selma is possessed of an unearthly serenity in the face of her impending death. Yoke's philosophy is one of unrelenting hostility towards others and the older woman's untroubled attitude eventually drives Yoke to make a half-hearted attempt to strangle her.

Selma forgives Yoke for this and tells her a story from a period in her own life when she too felt a similar hostility towards others: Selma along with two men was marooned on a bridge by a flood. The bridge was a large one and all three stranded people had their own shops on it. Selma refused to help the other two by letting them have food or water without payment and as a result one of the two men drank water from the flood which killed him. Even after this she still maintains her hostility towards the other man, whose name is Jan Akelov. But this is only for a time and eventually she marries him, though by the time she is in the mountain hut with Yoke she is a widow. Presumably she hopes that by telling of her own conversion from hostility towards others to acceptance of them she will enable Yoke to make the same change. Eventually Selma dies and shortly afterwards a rescue party arrives and Yoke is saved. In the final part of the novel Yoke is a prostitute somewhere in Nazi-occupied Europe. She is queuing for food along with others when suddenly she stubs out her cigarette in a piece of cheese bought by one of the other customers whose name turns out to be Jagannathan. She runs off and he chases her. When he has caught up with her she takes a poison pill, saying just before she dies that she has achieved her aim of dying in the presence of a good man. In addition to the story there is much reflection by Yoke (who keeps a diary) on the significance of time and of death. Selma in her serenity is above time and in Ajneya's view stands for the eastern attitude, while Yoke, who in her own words is 'consumed by history', is the prisoner of time and stands for what in Ajneya's view was the western attitude.

BIBLIOGRAPHY

Note: A date in square brackets indicates when a book was first published. A date without brackets indicates the edition used in this book. Where this differs from the original because it is a new edition, this is stated, as for example in the first book listed below.

A. *Books in English*

Abhishiktananda, Hindu-Christian Meeting Point, [first French edition 1965], revised English edition 1976, Delhi, ISPCK.

Abhishiktananda, Saccidananda: a Christian Approach to Advaitic Experience, 1974, Delhi, ISPCK.

Abrams M H, A Glossary of Literary Terms, [1957], fifth edition 1988, Fort Worth, Chicago and London, Holt, Rinehart and Winston, Inc.

*Agyeya and Nathan L (trs), Signs and Silence: Selections of Agyeya's poetry translated into English with an Introduction by Agyeya, 1976, Delhi, Simant Publications.

Ajneya, Islands in the Stream, 1980, New Delhi, Vikas Publishing House. (This is a translation of Ajneya's second novel, *Nadī ke Dvīpa*.

Ajneya and Das M, Preparing the Ground, 1984, New Delhi, Abhinav Publications. (This is a translation (incomplete) of Ajneya's *Antara* which was first published in Hindi in 1975.)

Ajneya and Roadarmel G C (trs), To Each His Stranger, 1967 Delhi, Hind Pocket Books (P) Ltd. (This is a translation of Ajneya's third novel, *Apne Apne Ajnabī*.)

Alter R, The Art of Biblical Narrative, 1981, London, George Allen and Unwin.

Antoine R, Rama and the Bards, 1975, Calcutta, Writers' Workshop.

Ayrookuzhiel A M A, The Sacred in Popular Hinduism, 1983, Madras, Christian Literature Society.

Balslev A N, A Study of Time in Indian Philosophy, 1983, Wiesbaden, Otto Harrassowitz.

Barnes M, Religions in Conversation: Christian Identity and Religious Pluralism, 1989, London, SPCK.

Barton J, Reading the Old Testament: Method in Biblical Study, 1984, London, Darton, Longman and Todd.

Basham A L (ed), A Cultural History of India, 1975, Delhi, Bombay, Calcutta, Madras, Oxford University Press.

Berger P, The Heretical Imperative, 1980, London, Collins.

Bethge E (ed), Bonhoeffer's Letters and Papers from Prison, 1953, London, SCM Press.

Béteille A, Society and Politics in India: Essays in a Comparative Perspective, 1992, Delhi, Bombay, Calcutta, Madras, Oxford University Press.

Bloom H (ed), The Selected Poetry and Prose of Shelley, 1966, New York, The New American Library.

Bowker J, The Sense of God: Sociological, Anthropological and Psychological Approaches to the Origin of the Sense of God, 1973, Oxford, Clarendon Press.

Brockington J L, The Sacred Thread: Hinduism in its Continuity and Diversity, 1981, Edinburgh, The University Press.

Brown J M, Modern India: the Origins of an Asian Democracy, 1985, Oxford, Oxford University Press.

Bühler G (tr), The Laws of Manu, translated with extracts from seven commentaries, Sacred Books of the East Vol. xxv, 1886, Oxford, Clarendon Press.

Campbell J (ed), Zimmer H, Myths and Symbols in Indian Art and Civilisation, [1946], 1962, New York, Harper Torchbooks, The Bollingen Library.

Carstairs G M, The Twice-Born, 1957, London, Hogarth Press.

Chatman S, Story and Discourse, 1978, Ithaca and London, Cornell University Press.

Chidester D, Word and Light: Seeing, Hearing and Religious Discourse, 1992, Urbana and Chicago, University of Illinois Press.

Colledge E and McGinn B (trs), Meister Eckhart: the Essential Sermons, Commentaries, Treatises, and Defense, 1981, London, SPCK.

Coward H, Lipner J J, and Young K K, Hindu Ethics: Purity, Abortion, and Euthanasia, 1989, New York, State University of New York Press.

Daiches D, The Novel and the Modern World, 1960, London and Chicago, Phoenix Books, University of Chicago Press.

Daniel N, Islam and the West: the Making of an Image, 1960, Edinburgh, The University Press.

Danielou A, The Myths and Gods of India, [first published as Hindu Polytheism, 1964, New York, Bollingen Foundation], 1991, Rochester, Vermont, Inner Traditions International.

D'Costa G, Theology and Religious Pluralism, 1986, Oxford, Blackwells.

D'Costa G (ed), Christian Uniqueness Reconsidered: the Myth of a Pluralistic Theology of Religions, 1990, New York, Orbis Books, Maryknoll.

Derrett J D M, The Death of a Marriage Law: Epitaph for the Rishis, 1978, New Delhi, Vikas.

Deshpande P Y, The Authentic Yoga, 1978, London, Rider and Company.

Doctrine Commission of the Church of England, Believing in the Church: the Corporate Nature of Faith, 1981, London, SPCK.

Doniger W and Smith B K (trs), The Laws of Manu, 1991, London, New Delhi, Penguin Books.

Douglas M, Purity and Danger: an Analysis of Concepts of Pollution and Taboo, [1966], 1970, Harmondsworth, Penguin Books.

Dowson J, A Classical Dictionary of Hindu Mythology and Religion, Geography, History and Literature, [?] eleventh edition, 1968, London, Routledge and Kegan Paul Ltd.

Dumont L, Homo Hierarchicus, 1972, London, Paladin.

Eagleton T, Literary Theory: an Introduction, 1983, Oxford, Blackwell.

Edwardes M, Bound to Exile: the Victorians in India, 1969, London, Sidgwick and Jackson.

Eliade M, Patterns in Comparative Religion, 1958, London and New York, Sheed and Ward.

Eliot T S, Four Quartets, 1944, London, Faber and Faber.

Eliot T S, Selected Essays, [1932], third revised and enlarged edition, 1951, London, Faber and Faber.

Forrester D B, Caste and Christianity: Attitudes and Policies on Caste of Anglo-Saxon Protestant Missions in India, 1980, London and Dublin, Curzon Press Ltd, and Atlantic Highlands, New Jersey, Humanities Press Inc.

Frei H W, The Eclipse of Biblical Narrative, 1974, New Haven and London, Yale University Press.

Fuller C J, The Camphor Flame: Popular Hinduism and Society in India, 1992, New Delhi, Viking, Penguin Books India (P) Ltd.

Gaeffke P, Hindi Literature in the Twentieth Century, 1978, Wiesbaden, Otto Harrassowitz.

Gandhi M K, An Autobiography: the Story of My Experiments with Truth, [1949], 1966, London, Jonathan Cape.

Gosling D, Science and Religion in India, 1976, Madras, Christian Literature Society.

Griffith T H, The Ramayan of Valmiki Translated into English Verse, [?], third edition 1963, Varanasi, Chowkhamba Sanskrit Series Office.

Griffiths B, Return to the Centre, 1978, London, Collins.

Griffiths B, The Marriage of East and West, 1982, London, Collins.

Hauerwas S and Jones L G (eds), Why Narrative ? Readings in Narrative Theology, 1989, Grand Rapids, Michigan, William B Eerdmans Publishing Company.

Hazra R C, Studies in the Puranic Records on Hindu Rites and Customs, [1940], second edition 1975, Delhi, Patna, Varanasi, Motilal Banarsidass.

Hick J H, God and the Universe of Faiths, 1973, London, MacMillan.

Hick J H (ed), Truth and Dialogue, 1974, London, Sheldon Press.

Hick J H and Knitter P (eds), The Myth of Christian Uniqueness, 1988, London, SCM Press.

Hill W D P, The Holy Lake of the Acts of Rama: a Translation of Tulasi Das's Ramacaritamanasa, 1952, Bombay, Calcutta, Delhi, Madras, Oxford University Press.

Hiriyanna M, The Essentials of Indian Philosophy, 1949, London, George Allen and Unwin Ltd.

Hooker R H, Themes in Hinduism and Christianity: a Comparative Study, 1989, Frankfurt, Verlag Peter Lang GmbH.

Hume R E (tr), The Thirteen Principal Upanishads, [1877], second edition revised, 1931, Oxford, Oxford University Press.

Hutton J H, Caste in India [1946], fourth edition 1963, Bombay, Delhi, Calcutta, Madras, Oxford University Press.

Jaini P S, The Jaina Path of Purification, 1979, Delhi, Varanasi, Patna, Motilal Banarsidass.

Jenkins D E, The Glory of Man, 1967, London, SCM Press.

Keith A B, A History of Sanskrit Literature, [1920], 1966, London, Oxford University Press.

Kerr F, Theology after Wittgenstein, [1986], 1988, Oxford, Blackwell.

Klostermaier K K, A Survey of Hinduism, [1989], first Indian edition 1990, New Delhi, Munshiram Manoharlal.

Knitter P, No Other Name ? 1985, London, SCM Press.

Larson G J, Classical Samkhya: an Interpretation of Its History and Meaning, [1969], second revised edition 1979, Delhi, Varanasi, Patna, Motilal Banarsidass.

Leslie J (ed), Roles and Rituals for Hindu Women, 1991, London, Pinter Publishers.

Leslie J, The Perfect Wife: The Orthodox Hindu Woman according to the *Strīdharmapaddhati* of Tryambakayajvan, 1989, Delhi, Oxford University Press.

Levi P, If This is a Man [first published in Italian 1958]; The Truce [first published in Italian 1963], 1987, London, Abacus.

Lindbeck G A, The Nature of Doctrine: Religion and Theology in a Postliberal Age, 1984, London, SPCK.

Lipner JJ, Hindus: their Religious Beliefs and Practices, 1994, London and New York, Routledge.

Lipner J J, The Face of Truth: a Study of Meaning and Metaphysics in the Vedantic Theology of Ramanuja, 1986, London, MacMillan.

McConnell F (ed), The Bible and the Narrative Tradition, 1986, New York and Oxford, Oxford University Press.

McFadyen A I, The Call to Intersubjectivity: a Christian Theory of the Individual in Social Relationships, 1987, unpublished Ph.D. thesis, University of Birmingham, Birmingham.

McFadyen A I, The Call to Personhood: a Christian Theory of the Individual in Social Relationships, 1990, Cambridge, Cambridge University Press. (This is a revised version of the above.)

McGregor R S (ed), The Oxford Hindi-English Dictionary, 1993, Oxford and Delhi, Oxford University Press.

Mohan K, Militant Nationalism in Punjab 1919-1935, 1985, New Delhi, Manohar.

Monier-Williams, Sir M, Sanskrit-English Dictionary, 1899, Oxford, Oxford University Press.

Moore A C, Iconography of Religions: an Introduction, 1977, London, SCM Press.

Niebuhr H R, The Meaning of Revelation, 1941, New York, MacMillan.

O'Flaherty W D (ed), Hindu Myths, 1975, Harmondsworth, Penguin Books.

O'Flaherty W D, The Origins of Evil in Hindu Mythology, [1976], 1980, Berkeley, Los Angeles, London, University of California Press.

Pandey R B, Hindu Samskaras: Socio-Religious Study of the Hindu Sacraments, [1949] second revised edition 1969, Delhi, Varanasi, Patna, Motilal Banarsidass.

Panikkar R, Myth, Faith and Hermeneutic: Cross-Cultural Studies, 1979, New York, Ramsey, Toronto, Paulist Press.

Panikkar R, The Silence of God: the Answer of the Buddha, no date, New York, Orbis Books, Maryknoll.

Panikkar R, The Vedic Experience, *Mantramañjarī*, An Anthology of the Vedas for Modern Man and Contemporary Celebration, 1977, London, Darton, Longman and Todd.

Pargiter F E, Ancient Indian Historical Tradition, [1922], 1972, Delhi, Varanasi, Patna, Motilal Banarsidass.

Radhakrishnan S, The Hindu View of Life, [1927], 1960, London, Unwin Books.

Rajan C (tr), Kalidasa, the Loom of Time: a Selection of His Plays and Poems, 1989, New Delhi, Penguin Books (India) Ltd.

Riches J, Jesus and the Transformation of Judaism, 1980, London, Darton, Longman. and Todd.

Ricoeur P, Essays on Biblical Interpretation, 1981, London, SPCK.

Ricoeur P, Time and Narrative, Volume 1, [first published in French as *Temps et Récit*, 1983, Editions du Seuil], 1984, Chicago and London, University of Chicago Press.

Roberts D E, Existentialism and Religious Belief, 1957, New York, Oxford University Press Inc.

Rowland B, The Art and Architecture of India: Buddhist, Hindu, Jain, [1953], third revised edition 1967, Harmondsworth, Baltimore, Victoria, Penguin Books.

Samartha S J, Dialogue Between Men of Living Faiths, 1971, Geneva, WCC.

Sarma D S, The Renaissance of Hinduism, 1944, Benares, Benares Hindu University.

Scholes R and Kellogg R, The Nature of Narrative, 1966, New York, Oxford University Press.

Shirley-Price L (tr), Bede: a History of the English Church and People, 1955, Harmondsworth, Penguin Books.

Smart N and Thakur S (eds), Ethical and Political Dilemmas of Modern India, 1993, London, St Martin's Press.

Smith W C, The Meaning and End of Religion, [1962], second edition 1978, London, SPCK.

Smith W C, Towards a World Theology, 1980, London, MacMillan.

Steiner G, Real Presences, 1989, London and Boston, Faber and Faber.

Taylor R W (ed), Society and Religion: Essays in Honour of M M Thomas, 1976, Madras, Christian Literature Society.

Thomas M M, Risking Christ for Christ's Sake: towards an Ecumenical Theology of Pluralism, 1987, Geneva, WCC Publications.

Thomas M M, The Christian Response to the Asian Revolution, [1966], 1967, Lucknow, Lucknow Publishing House.

Thomas M M, The Acknowledged Christ of the Indian Renaissance, 1970, Madras, Christian Literature Society.

Tillich P, Systematic Theology, Volume One, 1953, London, Nisbet.

Tracy D, The Analogical Imagination: Christian Theology and the Culture of Pluralism, 1981, London, SCM Press.

Vatsyayan S H, A Sense of Time: an Experience of Time in Theory, Experience, and Art, 1981, Delhi, Oxford University Press (India).

Vatsyayan S H and Das M M (trs), Preparing the Ground, 1984, New Delhi, Abhinava Publications. This is a translation (incomplete) of Ajneya's *Antarā* which was first published in Hindi in 1975.

Walker B, Hindu World: An Encyclopedic Survey of Hinduism, two volumes, 1968, London, George Allen and Unwin.

Whaling F, The Rise of the Religious Significance of Rama, 1980, Delhi, Varanasi, Patna, Motilal Banarsidass.

Wiesel E, Night, [first published in French 1958], 1981, Harmondsworth, Penguin Books.

Zaehner R C (tr and ed), Hindu Scriptures, [1966], 1978, London, Melbourne and Toronto, J M Dent and Sons.

* Ajneya's name is occasionally anglicised in this fashion.

B. *Articles in English.*

Bowker J, 'Religions as Systems', in Doctrine Commission 1981.

Carman J B, 'Inter-Faith Dialogue and Academic Study of Religion', in Samartha 1971.

Desai A, Review of (Vatsyayan's) Ajneya's 'A Sense of Time: an Experience of Time in Theory, Experience, and Art, in Hindustan Times, Magazine Section, page iv, columns 1-8, 31st January 1982.

Dubey S P, 'The Concept of Soul in Hinduism', in Religion and Society, Vol. xix No 4 (December 1972) pp. 16-32, Bangalore, Christian Institute for the Study of Religion and Society.

Ford D, '"The Best Apologetics is Good Systematics:" A Proposal about the Place of Narrative in Christian Systematic Theology', in Anglican Theological Review, LXVII, 3 (July 1985): pp. 232-54, reprinted in Hauerwas and Jones (eds) 1989, as 'System, Story, Performance: a Proposal about the Role of Narrative in Christian Systematic Theology'.

Fuentes C, 'I would give my life for a man who thinks he is looking for truth...but I would gladly kill a man who thinks he has found the truth', in The Guardian Weekly, 5th March 1989 pp. 8-9.

Geertz C, 'Religion as a Cultural System', in Banton 1965.

Heeger G A, 'The Growth of the Congress Movement in Punjab 1920-40', in Journal of Asian Studies Vol. 32 no 1, November 1972.

Kripalani K, 'Modern Literature', in Basham 1975.

Lipner J J, 'Women and Salvation in Hinduism: Paradoxes of Ambivalence', in Smart and Thakur (eds) 1993.

MacIntyre A, 'Epistemological Crises, Narrative, and Philosophy of Science', in Monist 60, 4 (October 1977), reprinted in Hauerwas and Jones (eds) 1989.

Niebuhr H R, 'The Story of Our Life', in Niebuhr 1941, reprinted in Hauerwas and Jones (eds) 1989.

Ricoeur P, 'The Hermeneutics of Testimony', in Ricoeur 1981.

Ryan S, 'Indian Theology and the Problem of History', in Taylor (ed) 1976.

Trivedi H, 'Eliot in Hindi: Modes of Reception', in Indian Literature, No 133, Sept.-Oct. 1989, pp. 140-53.

Vatsyayan S H, 'Hindi Literature', in Contemporary Indian Literature: a Symposium, [1957] second edition, revised and enlarged, 1959, New Delhi, Sahitya Akademi. (This Symposium has no named editor, it is therefore not listed in Section A of this Bibliography.)

C. *Books in Hindi and Sanskrit.*

Note 1: The Devanagri script, in which both Sanskrit and Hindi are normally written, has no upper case letters, but for ease of reference in this Bibliography we use them in the transliteration of the initial letters of the titles of books and of the names of authors.

Note 2: As already explained (Introduction, note 5), Hindi has a single word which is used to translate the English words 'impression' and 'edition'. This means that it is often very difficult to tell which English word is meant by the Hindi. Also when a new edition of a Hindi or Sanskrit book is published in India, previous publication details are not always included. Because of these two limitations this section of the Bibliography is not always as accurate as the writer would have wished.

Ajneya, *Apne Apne Ajnabī*, 1961, Delhi, Bharatiya Jnanapith.

Ajneya, *Nadī ke Dvīpa*, 1951, Saraswati Press, Allahabad, Varanasi, Delhi.

Ajneya, *Śhekhar: Ek Jīvanī*, Vol. 1, 1941, Allahabad and Delhi, Saraswati Press.

Ajneya, *Śhekhar: Ek Jīvanī*, Vol. 2, 1944, Allahabad and Delhi, Saraswati Press.

Ajneya, *Sadānīrā*, two volumes, (containing the complete poems) 1986, Delhi, National Publishing House.

Ajneya, *Sampūrṇa Kahāniyāṁ*, (The Complete Stories) 1989, Delhi, Rajpal and Sons.

Chaturvedi R, *Ajñeya aur Ādhunik Racanā kī Samasyā*, 1968, New Delhi, Bharatiya Jnanapitha Prakashan.

Dvivedi H P, *Vāṇabhaṭṭa kī Atmakathā*, [1946], 1976, Delhi, Patna, Rajkamal Prakashan.

Gaura J P, *Gauṛapādabhāṣyasahita Sāṁkhyakārikā*, 1975, Varanasi, Chowkhamba Vidyabhavan.

Goyandaka J, *Bhāratīya Saṃskṛti tathā Śāstroṁmeṁ Nārī-Dharma*, [1967], fifth impression/edition 1980, Gorakhpur, Gita Press.

Gupta M, *Krāntikārī Āndolan kā Vaicārik Itihāsa*, 1980, Delhi?

Jain N, *Adhūre Sākṣātkār: svatantratā ke bād pramukha upanyāsoṁ kā sarvāṅgīn vivecan*, [1966], 1989, New Delhi, Vani Prakashan.

Lele M, Maheshvari R K, and Gunjan G (eds), *Ajñeya: apne bāre meṁ*, 1993, New Delhi, Akashvani Prakashan.

Macve P, *'Ajñeya'*, 1991, Delhi, Rajpal and Sons.

Mishra V, *Ajñeya: Paricaya evaṁ Pratinidhi Kavitāeṁ*, [1963], revised edition 1990, Delhi, Rajpal and Sons.

Nagar A, *Mānas ka Haṃsa*, 1975, Delhi, Rajpal and Sons.

Nagar A, *Śatrañja ke Mohare*, [1957], 1987, New Delhi, Bharatiya Jnanapith Prakashan.

Poddar H P (tr), *Śrīmadbhāgavat-Mahāpurāṇa*, (two volumes, with Hindi translation), 1940, Gorakhpur, Gita Press.

Patel B, *Ajñeya: Ek Adhyayan*, 1983, Ahmadabad, Gujarat University.

Prabhakar O, *Ajñeya kā Kathā Sāhitya*, 1966, Delhi, National Publishing House.

Prem Chand, *Godān*, 1936, Allahabad, Saraswati Press.

Rangra R, *Hindī Sāhityakāroṁ se Sākṣātkār*, 1991, New Delhi, Kitabghar.

Ray G, *Ajneya aur Unke Upanyāsa*, 1975, Delhi, MacMillan Co. of India.

Ray R, *Śikhar se Sāgar tak*, 1986, New Delhi, National Publishing House.

Ramnarayandatta (tr), *Śrīmadvālmīkīya Rāmāyaṇa* (two volumes, with Hindi translation), 1959, Gorakhpur, Gita Press.

Shukla R, *Hindī Sāhitya kā Itihāsa*, [1911], revised and enlarged edition 1940, Kashi, Nagri Pracharini Sabha.

Singh N V, *Itihāsa aur Ālocanā*, [1957], third edition 1978, New Delhi, Rajkamal Prakashan.

Thakur D, *Nadī ke Dvīpa kī Racanā Prakriyā*, 1975, Delhi, Vani Prakashan.

Tripathi R S (ed), *Vedāntasār of Srī Sadānanda*, edited with the Bhavabodhini Sanskrit and Hindi Commentaries, 1975, Varanasi, Chowkhamba Vidyabhavan.

Upadhyaya B, *Purāṇa-Vimarśa: Authentic Solution of the Critical Problems of Purāṇas* (sic), 1965, Varanasi, Chowkhamba Vidyabhavan.

Varshneya N, *Hindī-Upanyāsa Uplabdhiyāṁ*, 1970, Delhi, Radhakrishna Prakashan

Vatsyayan S H, *Ādhunik Hindī Sāhitya*, 1976, Delhi, Rajpal and Sons.

Vatsyayan S H, *Āla-vāla*, 1971, Delhi, Rajkamal Prakashan.
Vatsyayan S H, *Are Yāyāvar, Rehegā Yād ?* 1953, Banaras, Saraswati Press.
Vatsyayan S H, *Ātmanepad*, 1960, Bharatiya Jnanapith, Kashi.
Vatsyayan S H, *Ātmaparak*, 1983, New Delhi, National Publishing House. (This book is a re-issue in one volume of two books previously published separately: *Ātmanepad*, for which see above, and *Likhi Kāgad Kore*, 1973.
Vatsyayan S H, *Ek Būnda Sahasā Uchalī*, [1960], 1988, Delhi, Bharatiya Jnanapitha Prakashan.
Vatsyayan S H, *Saṃvatsar*, 1989, New Delhi, National Publishing House.
Vatsyayan S H, *Triśaṅku*, 1945, Banaras, Saraswati Press.
Yashpal, *Deśdrohī*, [1943], 1967, Delhi, Anupam Pocket Books.

D. *Article in Hindi.*

Rangra R, '*Apne Apne Ajnabī -- lekhak kī dṛṣṭi meṁ*'—, in *Jñanodaya*, July 1969, reprinted in Rangra 1991.

GLOSSARY

Note: As explained in Chapter One, note 2 (p. 48), where a Hindi or Sanskrit word is used in the main text its meaning is given either at that point or as a footnote. If such a word is used more than once, and if it is important for the argument of the book, its meaning is also given in this Glossary.

Advaita Vedānta — the philosophy which postulates the identity of the Supreme Spirit or *Brahman*, which is held to be the one reality which underlies all phenomena, and the innermost being or *ātman* of a person. This unity is held to be the one source of all reality. To realise it experientially by disciplined meditation is the final goal of all spiritual endeavour. Such meditation must have as its foundation a moral life based on ethical principles.

āhuti — the act of offering oblations with fire to the deities.

Ajñeya — as an adjective 'unknowable' and so as a noun 'the unknowable one'; the pen-name of *S H Vātsyāyan*.

ānanda — bliss.

anubhava — experience.

āśrama — a stage of life of which there are normally held to be four; also, the forest dwelling of a hermit.

āsthā — confidence, faith, hope, usually in a transcendent dimension to life, though without necessarily implying a specific object of faith, such as God.

astitva — existence.

ātaṅkvādī	one who uses violence to pursue political objectives, a terrorist.
ātman	the innermost being or 'soul' of a person.
bhakti	loving devotion to a god conceived in personal terms.
Brahman	the Supreme Spirit.
Brāhmaṇ	a member of the highest of the four *varṇas* or caste-orders, a priest.
Bhagavadgītā	part of the *Mahābhārata* but often printed and read as a separate, and very important scripture.
darśan	vision, any school of philosophy-theology, point of view.
dharma	'that which is established', law, custom. There is a universal *dharma* which applies to all people. This bans such offences as murder, theft and adultery, but there are also separate *dharmas* which apply to each caste. In modern Hindi *dharma* is also used for the English word 'religion' in the sense of *eg* the Muslim or Christian religion.
divya-dṛṣṭi	supernatural insight attained by the *yogin*.
draṣṭā	one who sees, who has vision or insight. This is a much stronger word than any English translation can suggest. It is derived from *darśan*. What the true *draṣṭā* sees is ultimate reality.
dṛṣṭi	the act of seeing, in the above sense.
duḥkha	suffering, pain.
(dukha	alternative Hindi spelling of the above.)
dvandva	pair of opposites, such as heat and cold, pleasure and pain, wealth and poverty.
Gītā	shortened form of the word *Bhagavadgītā*.
guru	teacher of a branch of traditional learning, such as Sanskrit grammar or philosophy; spiritual guide or preceptor.
homa	a Vedic sacrificial offering of parched grains which are thrown into a fire.
Īsāmasīh	Jesus Christ.
Īsāī	Christian.

janma birth.

jāti an endogamous social group or caste. See also *varṇa*.

jīvan life.

jñāna experiential knowledge of ultimate reality; often also knowledge in a lesser and more general sense.

kāla time; also death.

Kālidāsa the most famous of Sanskrit dramatists and poets.

kali yuga the last and most degenerate of the four ages in the recurring cosmic cycle.

karma an action: the fruits of good and bad actions are believed by many Hindus to determine an individual's lot in this and subsequent lives, or 'births'.

kārya-kāraṇa paramparā the chain of cause and effect. Much of Sanskrit philosophy is built around the various forms of this relationship.

kathā story.

kṣaṇa a single moment.

Mahābhārata one of the two great Epics, a vast and composite work which has as its core the story of a struggle between two related families.

Manusmṛti The Laws of Manu, the legal code which is the foundation of the Brahminical social order.

maraṇa death.

Meru the mythical Himalayan mountain believed to be at the centre of the world, and a place of paradisal purity.

mṛtyu death.

mukti release or 'salvation' in an ultimate sense, but often used in a more general and secular sense to mean freedom (from something).

narak hell.

paṇḍit a *Brāhman* teacher, usually of one of the traditional Sanskrit subjects, and so by extension, learned man.

pāp — sin.

paralok — the other or next world.

paramātmā — supreme soul or spirit, synonymous with Brahman.

prajñā — experiential knowledge of ultimate reality.

prakṛti — nature, in the sense of belonging to the natural world; also in *Sāṁkhya* philosophy, one of the two ultimate principles to which all reality is reduced: this includes both the material order and human consciousness.

prakṛt — natural, belonging to the world of nature.

pratinidhik śodha — substitutionary atonement.

punarjanma — rebirth.

puṇya — merit.

Purāṇas — traditionally held to be eighteen in number, these are vast collections of Hindu myths and other ancient material.

puruṣa — in *Sāṁkhya* philosophy, one of the two ultimate principles to which all reality is reduced. *Puruṣa* is pure spirit. In more general usage it means 'a man' or 'a human being'.

Rāma — the divine hero of the *Rāmāyaṇa*, one of the two great Epics

Rāmacaritamānasa — The Holy Lake of the Acts of Rama, the popular Hindi version, composed by *Tulsī Das*, of the Sanskrit *Rāmāyaṇa* attributed to *Vālmīki*.

Rāmāyaṇa — 'the going forth of Rama', one of the two great Hindu Epics.

Rāmānuja (or *Rāmānujācārya*) one of the most important philosopher-theologians of the Hindu tradition.

Ṛg Veda — the most ancient and authoritative of the Hindu scriptures.

ṛṣi — primeval sage or seer.

śakti — power, often in Hindu thought associated with the female principle of deity.

sabhya — civilised. (Always used by Ajneya in a pejorative sense.)

Sāṁkhya — one of the six main schools of Hindu philosophy, it reduces all reality to two basic principles: *prakṛti* and *puruṣa*.

saṃnyāsin — renouncer, someone who has given up home and family in order to embark on the fourth and final stage of life.

sampūrṇa — filled, complete.

saṃskaraṇa — edition or impression of a book.

saṃvedanā — sympathy; the act of perceiving or feeling; communication, making known.

Śaṅkara (or *Śaṅkarācārya*) — probably India's greatest philosopher-theologian, he founded the school of *Advaita Vedānta*.

śāstras — sacred texts, usually of a legal nature.

Sītā — the docile and faithful wife of *Rāma* who serves as a role model for Hindu wives.

Śiva — one of the two main gods worshipped by Hindus today usually in the form of the erect phallus as a symbol of creative energy. The River Ganges is believed to descend from heaven to earth by way of *Śiva*'s long matted hair.

smṛti — 'what is remembered', the secondary category of Hindu scripture which includes the Epics and *Purāṇas*.

śruti — 'what is heard', the primary category of Hindu scripture which embraces the Vedas and Upanisads.

śuddhi — purification.

śūdra — the fourth of the four *varṇas*, the caste of manual labourers.

sukha — this worldly pleasure.

sūtras — a collection of aphorisms, of which different collections are the foundation documents of most Hindu schools of thought; thus the *sūtras* of *Pāṇini* are the basis of traditional Sanskrit grammar.

svacchanda — free, independent.

svādhīna — free, independent.

svatantra — free, independent.

tapasyā	the practice of austerity and ascetic disciplines in order to obtain spiritual power.
Tulsī Dās	the best known devotional poet of North India, who in the sixteenth century translated and adapted the *Rāmāyaṇa*, thus making it available to ordinary people in their own language.
tyāga	renunciation.
uddeśya	aim, purpose, goal.
upanyāsa	a/the novel.
Urdū	the language of culture and administration under the Mughal Empire (c 1526-1740 CE). Before 1947 it was still widely used as a civic language in India.
Upaniṣads	an important collection of ancient texts which are the seed-bed for much subsequent philosophising about human nature and destiny.
Vaitaraṇī	the polluted river of the underworld which is the binary opposite of the pure and celestial Ganges.
Vālmīki	a mythical poet who is held to be the author of the *Rāmāyaṇa*.
varṇa	colour, one of the four castes as defined in traditional texts. See also *jāti*.
varṇāśramadharma	a combination of three words, *varṇa-āśrama-dharma*, meaning the rule or pattern of the four castes and of the four stages of life. As a comprehensive term it describes the Brahminical social order.
varaṇa	choice.
vedanā	pain, suffering; feeling, sensation.
Viṣṇu	one of the two main gods worshipped today by Hindus, usually in the form of one of his *avatāras* or 'descents' to earth. The River Ganges is believed to flow from heaven to earth by way of his toe.
viśvāsa	faith.
vivek	the capacity to discriminate between that which pertains to ultimate reality and that

	which does not, also used to mean 'discrimination' in a wider sense.
yoga	a very ancient method of concentration and contemplation whose methods include correct bodily posture and control of the breath.
yogin	a practitioner of *yoga*.
yuga	age, aeon. There are four of these in the constantly recurring cosmic cycle.

INDEX